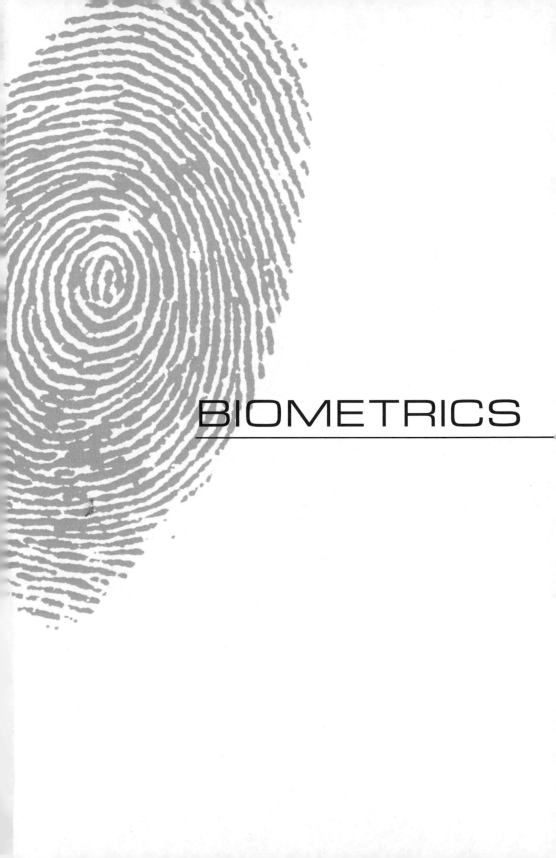

BIOMETRICS

edited by
ELIZA YINGZI DU

BIOMETRICS

FROM FICTION
TO PRACTICE

PAN STANFORD PUBLISHING

Published by

Pan Stanford Publishing Pte. Ltd.
Penthouse Level, Suntec Tower 3
8 Temasek Boulevard
Singapore 038988

Email: editorial@panstanford.com
Web: www.panstanford.com

British Library Cataloguing-in-Publication Data
A catalogue record for this book is available from the British Library.

Biometrics: From Fiction to Practice

ISBN 978-981-4310-88-8 (Hardcover)
ISBN 978-981-4364-13-3 (eBook)

Printed in the USA

Contents

Preface

Biometrics has been popularly featured in movies and on TV as a cool access control and human identification method. In real life, how does biometrics work? Is it really capable of the amazing features that popular culture depicts?

The goal of this book is to introduce readers to basic concepts, classic approaches, and the newest design, development, and applications of biometrics. Moreover, it also provides a glimpse of future designs and research directions in biometrics. In addition, it also discusses some latest concerns and issues in this area. The text not only focuses on the technologies but also covers design, development, and applications. It is suitable for a wide range of readers: people who would like to know about the latest developments in the human identification area, college students and researchers who would like to study more about biometrics, and professionals in the biometrics area who would like to dive more into specific topic areas. To fulfill this goal, professional terms are explained in plain English so that even people with high school education can understand. At the same time, we provide a lot of technical insights into the newest designs and developments in the biometrics area. Some concepts and designs discussed in this book are so new that readers may not be able to see such commercial systems in the market for the next 10 to 20 years. In addition, we list some related publications and references for readers who would like to learn more beyond this book.

The 14 chapters in this book are written by 27 contributing authorities from Canada, Korea, Italy, Thailand, United Kingdom, and the United States, and they provide a wealth of international knowledge. The book covers four important parts of biometrics:

- **Part I. Basic concepts, classic approaches, and newest designs in biometrics:** fingerprint recognition (Chapter 2), face recognition (Chapter 3), iris recognition (Chapter 4), speaker recognition (chapter 5), palmprint recognition (Chapter 6), and multimodal biometrics (Chapter 7)
- **Part II. Classic approaches and newest designs in biometric technologies and systems:** biometrics-based smart ID cards (Chapter 8) and smart clothes for biometrics (Chapter 9)
- **Part III. Challenges and concerns in biometrics:** spoofs and vulnerability of biometrics (Chapter 10) and accessibility, usability, and legal challenges in biometrics (Chapter 11)
- **Part IV. Latest designs and the future of biometric systems to address the challenges and concerns in biometrics:** cancelable biometrics (Chapter 12), continuous biometric verification (Chapter 13), and future trends in biometrics (Chapter 14)

These chapters provide an easy-to-understand yet in-depth treatment of biometrics, and this book is an excellent source to consult and study before embarking on biometric study, research, projects, or applications.

I greatly appreciate Stanford Chong's support that made this book possible. I would like to thank all authors and Sarabjeet Garcha's editorial staff who put this book together. I wish to acknowledge my students Matt Blair, Zhi Zhou, and Kai Yang for their help. My deepest gratitude goes to my family for their encouragement and support. Last but not least, thank you for reading this book.

Eliza Yingzi Du, PhD
Winter 2012

Chapter 1

An Introduction to Biometrics

Eliza Yingzi Du

Department of Electrical and Computer Engineering,
Purdue School of Engineering and Technology,
Indiana University-Purdue University at Indianapolis,
Indianapolis, IN 46202, USA
yidu@iupui.edu

In this chapter, the basic concepts and definitions in biometrics are introduced.

1.1 What is Biometrics?

Biometric systems use a person's physiological, behavioral, and psychological characteristics to perform human identification. It identifies a person by who he is (such as his face patterns, fingerprints, voice, etc.), not what he has (username, password, key, plastic card, etc.) [1—3]. Compared to the traditional identification and verification methods, biometrics is more convenient for users, reduces fraud, and is more secure [4]. It is becoming an important ally of security, intelligence, law enforcement, and e-commerce [5–7]. It has been popularly featured in Hollywood movies (Fig. 1.1) for access control and human identification.

Biometrics: From Fiction to Practice
Edited by Eliza Yingzi Du
Copyright © 2013 Pan Stanford Publishing Pte. Ltd.
ISBN 978-981-4310-88-8 (Hardcover), 978-981-4364-13-3 (eBook)
www.panstanford.com

Figure 1.1. Biometrics has been featured in many Hollywood movies.

In real life, how biometrics works? The biometrics characteristics could be anything unique and stable that is intrinsic to a person, which include fingerprint [8, 9], face [10, 11], voice [12, 13], iris [14, 15], palm [16, 17], gait [18, 19], etc. [3, 20]. In general, biometrics characteristics can be categorized into three groups: physiological, behavioral, and psychological characteristics (Table 1.1).

A comparison of these three kinds of biometrics is shown in Table 1.2. The physiological characteristics based biometric systems are often used for access control and border security. Behavior-based biometric systems are often used for remote authentication or used with other biometrics for authentication/identification. The psychological-based biometric systems are still in early stage of design and development. Currently, the accuracy is pretty low and the signals are often unstable over the time. But psychological-based biometric systems can potentially be used for spoof protection or can be used in highly secured applications to ensure the user is alive and willingly perform biometric authentication.

Table 1.1.   List of biometrics characteristics

Physiological	Behavioral	Psychological
Face	Voice	Brain function
Fingerprint	Signature/handwriting	Cognitive-based biometrics system
Iris	Keystroke dynamics	
Palm	Gait	
Ear	Heart beat	
Vein	Breath pattern	
Footprint	EEG	
Retina	ECG	
DNA		

Table 1.2.   Comparison between different types of biometric characteristics

Type	Stability	Accuracy	Signal acquisition	Applications
Physiological characteristics	Relatively stable	Accurate	Easy	Widely applicable to all three functions of biometrics
Behavior characteristics	Not very stable	Somewhat accurate	Easy	Mostly used for authentication, or combined with other biometrics for authentication/identification
Psychological characteristics	Very unstable	Not accurate	Very difficult	It is still in the early stage of development. Possibly used for spoof protection in extreme high security environment

1.2 Basic Functions of Biometrics

Biometrics is primarily used for verification, identification, and watchlist (Table 1.3) [21].

- Verification: It requires the user to input his/her username or ID number, and verifies the person against the one in the database that the user claims. For example, if a person claims himself to be "Smith," the biometric system will try to pull out Smith's data from the system and compare it with yours. The output of the biometric system will be "yes, it is Smith" or "no, it is not Smith." This kind of application is often used in access control or biometric ID.
- Identification: The user does not need to provide his/her username or ID. Instead, he/she only needs to present the biometric data to the system. The biometric system can match the data against all data in the database to identify

Table 1.3.   Basic functions of biometrics

Type	Matching	Solve question	Difficulty level
Verification	One-to-one	Are you who you claim to be?	Hard
Identification	One-to-many	Who are you?	Harder
Watchlist	One-to-a few	Are you a person of interest?	Hardest

this person. The output of the biometric system will be, "yes, it is XXX," or "no, it is not in our database." This kind of system is often seen in remote access control. It is more convenient for the users and more robust against fraud.

- Watchlist: The "watchlist" means a small list of most wanted personals, who are often criminals or terrorists. The watchlist function is very similar to the identification. However, the system often performs identification covertly. In other words, the system does not want the users know that biometric identification is being performed. People in the watchlist usually do not want to be identified and most likely, they will try their best to wear disguise.

1.3 Typical Biometric Systems

A biometric system usually includes two processes: the biometric enrollment process (Fig. 1.2a) and biometric matching process (Fig. 1.2b).

To recognize a person, the first step is to enroll this person in the system. The enroll process acquires the user's biometric data and generates a template to save in a database. The matching process

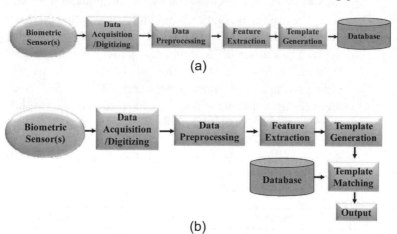

Figure 1.2. Diagram for a typical biometric system: (a) enrollment process and (b) matching process.

acquires new biometric data and generates a template and then matches the template with all templates in the database to find if there is a match.

A biometric enrollment process includes the biometric sensor(s) module, the data acquisition module, the data preprocessing module, the pattern extraction module, the template generation module, and the biometric database module.

In addition to all the modules of enrollment process, a biometric matching process includes the template matching module and the output module.

The biometric sensor(s) module senses data from the user. The senor is usually selected/designed based on the characteristics of the biometric traits. For example, NIR cameras are often used to acquire iris data, digital visible wavelength cameras are typically used to acquire face data, and microphones are used to acquire voice signals. The sensor can be triggered automatically when the biometric traits (identification applications) or username/ID number (verification applications) are presented.

The data acquisition module quantifies biometric data into digital signals (images) and right formats for future processing. In most current biometric systems, the data acquisition module is integrated into the biometric sensor. This module is often used in forensic biometric data where digital data is not available.

The data preprocessing module enhances the signal and reduces the noise effect. It extracts the biometric data from the background. For example, for voice recognition, the human voice signal will be detected and extracted in this module, while other parts (such as silence and background noise) would be eliminated. In addition, the extracted voice signal will be normalized to reduce intensity effect. The accuracy of data preprocessing is very important to the system performance.

The feature extraction module uses mathematical models to analyze the special patterns of individual biometric traits and extract the distinctive features. These features could be some frequency characteristics or spatial correlations. The amount of extractable distinctive features will depend on biometric trait characteristics and the mathematical models used for feature extraction. For example, if heart beat is used as a biometric trait for human identification, the amount of extractable distinctive feature is not high. As a result, the recognition accuracy using heart beat will not be high. If fingerprint is used as a biometric trait for human identification, the amount of extractable distinctive feature is high. The accuracy will be largely affected by the mathematical models used for feature extraction.

The template generation module will encode/quantize the extracted features into templates. The goal of this module is to reduce unnecessary redundancy in the data and to improve the efficiency in matching step.

The templates will be saved in the biometric database for further identification/recognition. Sometimes, for security purpose, the templates will be often encrypted before saved in the database.

The template matching module compares the newly acquired template and the templates inside the database to see how similar/different they are. There are many different mathematical similarity measure models and algorithms that can be used in this step. The selection of proper model/algorithm depends on the characteristics of the templates and system application. The matching strategy depends highly on the characteristics of biometric traits and system requirement. Matching scores are generated in this step.

The output module first performs post-process of the matching scores and decides if there is a match, multiple matches, or nonmatch. The decision can be based on a preset threshold or comparative result. The output format is highly dependent on the system application and characteristics of the biometric data. For example, for face recognition system, the output is often several top matches. It is often based on a comparative result. While for iris recognition system, the output is often based on a preset threshold to decide if there is a match or nonmatch. This is because iris recognition is often more accurate than face recognition.

1.4 How to Evaluate a Biometric System

There are many different kinds of biometric algorithms/methods/systems that are designed/developed every year. To measure the recognition accuracy of a biometric system, the false acceptance rate

(FAR) and the false rejection rate (FRR) are widely used [22]. A biometric system that generates high FAR or high FRR is not reliable and cannot be used.

The FAR measures the percentage of incorrect identification:

$$FAR(\%) = \frac{\text{Number of false acceptance}}{\text{Total number of acceptance by the system}} \times 100\%$$

$$(1.1)$$

The FRR measures the percentage of incorrect rejection:

$$(FAR\%) = \frac{\text{Number of false rejections}}{\text{Total number of rejections by the system}} \times 100\% \quad (1.2)$$

Receiver operating characteristic (ROC) curve is usually used to measure the accuracy of the system performance. An ROC curve is a plot of FAR against FRR. An ROC curve can give a balanced view of FAR and FRR. To compare two ROC curves, equal error rate (ERR) is often used as an important parameter. ERR is defined as the decision threshold of a system that is set so that the proportion of false rejections will be approximately equal to the proportion of false acceptances [2].

For a biometric system, if the output is not an identification result (one-to-many match) but recognition result (few-to-many match), cumulative math characteristic (CMC) curve is usually used to measure the accuracy. The CMC curve is a plot of the accuracy percentage of the system in determining whether a test image is correctly identified in the top n matches, as n is varied. CMC curve is popularly used in analyzing face recognition system performance.

To measure the convenience of a biometric system, the failure-to-enroll rate (FTER) and the retrial rate (RR) can be used. The FTER measures the percentage of unsuccessful enrollment. The unsuccessful enrollment could be because the acquired samples do not contain sufficient quality to create a template. The FTER is defined as:

$$ER(\%) = \frac{\text{Number of unsuccessful enrollment}}{\text{Total number of enrollment attempts}} \times 100\% \quad (1.3)$$

The RR measures, in average, how many times a user needs to try to get correct identification:

$$RR = \frac{\text{Total number of matching attemps}}{\text{Total number of corret identification}} - 1 \quad (1.4)$$

When evaluating a biometric system, the database size, the quality of the data, and the testing environment can play a big role [23]. It is important to evaluate different biometric systems under comparable conditions.

1.5 Summary

Biometrics will be more popularly used in our daily lives to verify and identify a person automatically. In this chapter, we induced some basic concepts of biometrics. The rest of the book provides a more in-depth study of biometric algorithms, systems, and technologies.

References

1. Woodward, J., Orlans, N. M., and Higgins, P. T. (2002) *Biometrics*, Berkeley, CA: The McGraw-Hill Company.
2. Jain, A. K., Ross, A., and Pankanti, S. (2006) Biometrics: A tool for information security, *Information Forensics and Security, IEEE Transactions* **1**(2), 125–143.
3. Kroeker, K. L. (2002) Graphics and security: Exploring visual biometrics, *Computer Graphics and Applications, IEEE* **22**(4), 16–21.
4. Bolle, R. M., Connell, J. H., Pankanti S. *et al.* (2005) *Guide to Biometrics*, New York, NY: Springer.
5. Ives, R. W., Du Y. *et al.* (2005) A multidisciplinary approach to biometrics, *Education IEEE Transactions* **48**(3), 462–471.
6. Ratha, N. K., Connell, J. H., and Bolle, R. M. (2001) Enhancing security and privacy in biometrics-based authentication systems, *IBM Systems Journal* **40**(3), 614–634.
7. Wayman, J. L. (2008) Biometrics in Identity Management Systems, *Security Privacy IEEE* **6**(2), 30–37.
8. Galy, N., Charlot, B., and Courtois, B. (2007) A full fingerprint verification system for a single-line sweep sensor, *Sensors Journal IEEE* **7**(7), 1054–1065.
9. Jain, A. K., Yi, C., and Demirkus, M. (2007) Pores and ridges: High-resolution fingerprint matching using level 3 features, *Pattern Analysis Machine Intelligence IEEE Transactions* **29**(1), 15–27.

10. Mohanty, P., Sarkar, S., and Kasturi, R. (2007) From scores to face templates: a model-based approach, *Pattern Analysis Machine Intelligence IEEE Transactions* **29**(12), 2065–2078.

11. Tae-Kyun, K. and Kittler, J. (2006) Design and fusion of pose-invariant face-identification experts, *Circuits and Systems for Video Technology, IEEE Transactions* **16**(9), 1096–1106.

12. Ke, C. (2005) On the use of different speech representations for speaker modeling, *Systems, Man, and Cybernetics, Part C: Applications and Reviews, IEEE Transactions* **35**(3), 301–314.

13. Kwon, S. and Narayanan, S. (2005) Unsupervised speaker indexing using generic models, *Speech and Audio Processing, IEEE Transactions* **13**(5), 1004–1013.

14. Daugman, J. (2007) New methods in iris recognition, *Systems, Man, and Cybernetics, Part B: Cybernetics, IEEE Transactions* **37**(5), 1167–1175.

15. Zhi, Z., Yingzi, D., and Belcher, C. (2009) Transforming traditional iris recognition systems to work in nonideal situations, *Industrial Electronics, IEEE Transactions* **56**(8), 3203–3213.

16. Xiangqian, W. Zhang, D., and Kuanquan, W. (2006) Palm line extraction and matching for personal authentication, *Systems, Man and Cybernetics, Part A: Systems and Humans, IEEE Transactions* **36**(5), 978–987.

17. Zhang, D., Guangming, L. Wei, L. *et al.* (2009) Palmprint recognition using 3-D information, *Systems, Man, and Cybernetics, Part C: Applications and Reviews, IEEE Transactions* **39**(5), 505–519.

18. Xiaoli, Z. and Bhanu, B. (2007) Integrating face and gait for human recognition at a distance in video, *Systems, Man, and Cybernetics, Part B: Cybernetics, IEEE Transactions* **37**(5), 1119–1137.

19. Zongyi, L. and Sarkar, S. (2006) Improved gait recognition by gait dynamics normalization, *Pattern Analysis and Machine Intelligence, IEEE Transactions* **28**(6), 863–876.

20. Kumar, A., Kanhangad, V., and Zhang, D. A. (2010) New framework for adaptive multimodal biometrics management, *Information Forensics and Security, IEEE Transactions* **5**(1), 92–102.

21. Wayman, A. J. J., Maltoni, D., and Maio D. (2005) Biometric systems, London, UK: Springer.

22. Du, Y. and Chang, C. (2008) 3D combinational curves for accuracy and performance analysis of positive biometrics identification, *Optics and Lasers in Engineering* **46**(6), 477–490.

23. Zhou, Y. D. Z. and Belcher, C. (2009) Transforming traditional iris recognition systesms to work on non-ideal situations, *IEEE Transactions on Industry Electronics* **56**(8), 3203–3213.

Chapter 2

Fingerprint Recognition

Wei-Yun Yau,[a] Zujun Hou,[b] Vutipong Areekul,[c] and Suksan Jirachaweng[d]

[a,b]*Institute for Infocomm Research, A*STAR, Singapore*
[c,d]*Kasetsart University, Bangkok, Thailand*
wyyau@i2r-a-star.edu.sg

2.1 Introduction

Fingerprint is the oldest method of identity authentication. It has been formally accepted as a valid identity authentication method in the court of law and used in forensics since the early 20th century [1]. The fingertips have corrugated skin with line-like ridges flowing from one side of the finger to another. The flow of the ridges is not continuous and forms a pattern as shown in Fig. 2.1. The pattern of ridges and ridge flow (also known as level-1 feature) gives rise to classification pattern of arches, loops, and whorl while the discontinuity in the ridges (also known as level-2 feature) gives rise to feature points, called minutiae. The formation of the minutiae is random, yet the fingerprint, once fully formed at about seven months of fetus development, will not change except due to injuries such

Biometrics: From Fiction to Practice
Edited by Eliza Yingzi Du
Copyright © 2013 Pan Stanford Publishing Pte. Ltd.
ISBN 978-981-4310-88-8 (Hardcover), 978-981-4364-13-3 (eBook)
www.panstanford.com

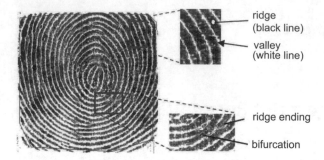

ridge
(black line)

valley
(white line)

ridge ending

bifurcation

Figure 2.1. A sample fingerprint image showing whorl pattern minutiae. See also Color Insert.

as cuts and burns or chemical erosion [2]. These properties make fingerprint an attractive candidate for identity authentication. Automated fingerprint recognition follows four basic steps:

1. Fingerprint acquisition
2. Fingerprint processing
3. Feature extraction
4. Matching

These steps are further elaborated in the following sections.

2.2 Fingerprint Acquisition

The traditional technique used in law enforcement is the off-line or nonlive technique. Black ink is applied to the finger tip which is then pressed against a white paper to obtain the fingerprint image. During crime investigations, latent prints (fingerprints left on the surface such as glass, etc.) are made visible using powder or chemical reagent and then photographed or "lifted" for automated processing. For generic use, the fingerprint image is acquired from a live finger touching a sensor. There are a few variants of live fingerprint acquisition technology available including optical, solid-state, electro-optic, and ultrasound.

In the optical technology, it relies on the use of a prism with a light source (usually red) on one side of the prism. The light is totally reflected internally in the prism and focused onto an imaging sensor such as a CCD or CMOS image sensor. However, when a fingerprint is present at the surface of the prism, the perspiration of the fingerprint introduces water and oil (sebum) which modulates the refraction index. Consequently, the light is not reflected but absorbed at the part where the ridge touches the prism, creating the fingerprint image.

The solid-state technology uses several principles. Among the more popular principles are capacitive, electric field, and pressure. Figure 2.2 shows some examples of the commercially available fingerprint acquisition devices.

- **Capacitive:** Two tiny capacitive sensor plates are constructed for each pixel in the image. A fixed charge is deposited into each of the capacitive sensor plate. Then the capacitance is discharged and a reading is taken after a short duration. When a finger is present, the ridge will be close to the two plates and forms a third plate of the capacitor while the valley will not. This causes variation in the capacitance of the capacitive sensor plates, producing a fingerprint image.
- **Electric field:** An antenna array is used as the sensor together with a drive ring at the circumference of the sensor.

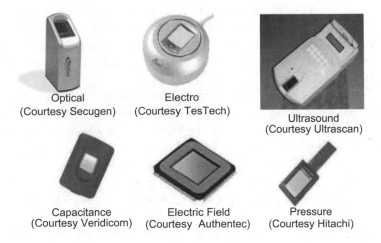

Optical
(Courtesy Secugen)

Electro
(Courtesy TesTech)

Ultrasound
(Courtesy Ultrascan)

Capacitance
(Courtesy Veridicom)

Electric Field
(Courtesy Authentec)

Pressure
(Courtesy Hitachi)

Figure 2.2. Examples of various commercially available fingerprint acquisition devices.

It applies a sinusoidal electric voltage, which flows through the conductive layer of the skin. As the skin is corrugated, the flow is modulated and the antenna will pick up different signal strength depending on whether it is under a ridge or valley. Digitizing the signal forms the fingerprint image.

- **Pressure:** Piezoelectric material which converts pressure into voltage is used as the sensor. The ridge section will have different pressure compared to the valley region, forming the fingerprint image. Alternatively the sensor employs a matrix of microscopic on–off switch which is turned on or off depending on whether the microscopic switch touches the skin.

Electro-optic technology uses a polymer which emits light when properly excited with the proper voltage. The fingerprint in contact with a side of the sensor acts as the ground causing the polymer to emit light at the region where the ridge touches it. The light is then captured by an imaging sensor to form a fingerprint image.

In the ultrasound technology, it uses the echography principle. The sensor emits a focus beam of ultrasound (20 KHz to gigahertz range) by means of a piezoceramic transducer and then measures the reflected beam. The difference between the ridge and valley distance can be measured using the time-of-flight technique. The beam then scans the entire finger to form a fingerprint image. A more detailed explanation of the various acquisition techniques can be found in Ref. [3].

Apart from the acquisition techniques, the method of use may also be different. It can either be touch based where you touch the sensor with your fingertip or swipe based where you swipe your fingertip over the sensor. Parameters to look out for when choosing the sensor includes resolution, imaging area, dynamic range, acquisition speed, size, weight and power consumption. For law enforcement applications, the U.S. Criminal Justice Information Services [4] specify the required specifications of the fingerprint sensors. For general fingerprint use, the ISO document ISO 19794-4 provides the standards for fingerprint image format so that the fingerprint image can be interchangeable [5].

2.3 Fingerprint Processing

The fingerprint images acquired are usually corrupted with noise from dirt, artifact such as scar, latent prints from previous users, etc. There could also be smudges due to higher perspiration than normal or movement of finger during acquisition. The fingerprints may not be clear due to finger dryness or only partially acquired due to imperfect finger placement. Therefore, it is necessary to process the fingerprint images prior to extracting the features. The processing includes segmenting the fingerprint to extract only valid region and to enhance the image. Fingerprint images, unlike any other images, comprise oriented lines of ridges separated by valleys which are almost parallel when viewed in a small local region. Therefore, such information can be used as a basis for both fingerprint segmentation and enhancement.

2.3.1 *Ridge Orientation Estimation*

The aim of ridge orientation estimation is to compute the orientation, θ $(0 \leq \theta < \pi)$, of a local region in the fingerprint. There are several approaches, and these can generally be classified into two, namely piece-wise approach and continuous approach.

In the piece-wise approach, the intensity of the local region is being compared against a projection along a fixed orientation. This is then repeated by changing the orientation of the projection. The orientation of the local region is determined by computing the orientation along which the error is minimum, as in the following equation [6]:

$$K(i, j) = \min \left(\sum_{k=1}^{n} \left[\left| I_p(i_k, j_k) - I(i, j) \right| \right] \quad \forall \, p = 1 \text{ to } P \right),$$

$$(2.1)$$

where n = side length of the window in pixels, $I(i, j)$ = intensity of pixel at point (i, j), $I_p(i_k, j_k)$ = projection in direction p, P = number of orientation (usually 4, 8, or 16), and $K(i, j)$ = orientation at point (i, j).

To increase the robustness of the estimate, the orientation in a local region is obtained using the dominant K from all the $K(i, j)$ in the region. Then replace all other $K(i, j)$ values in the local region with the dominant K. This approach is fast but is not accurate since the orientation is discrete and limited by the number of orientation chosen, P.

In the continuous approach, the image I is divided into blocks of local region $w \times w$. Then compute the gradients $d_x(i, j)$ and $d_y(i, j)$ at each pixel $I(i, j)$ using techniques such as the 3×3 Sobel operator as shown in the following equation:

$$d_x(i, j) = I(i, j) * M_x(i, j)$$
$$d_y(i, j) = I(i, j) * M_y(i, j) \tag{2.2}$$

where M_x and M_y are the Sobel mask for x and y gradient components respectively and $*$ represents convolution. Other possible operators include the Prewitt operator and the integral operator [7]. The local orientation, θ, of each block centered at pixel (i, j) can then be computed using the least square estimate as shown in the following equation [8]:

$$V_x(i, j) = \sum_{u=i-w/2}^{i+w/2} \sum_{v=j-w/2}^{i+w/2} 2d_x(u, v) d_y(u, v),$$

$$V_y(i, j) = \sum_{u=i-w/2}^{i+w/2} \sum_{v=j-w/2}^{i+w/2} \left[d_x^2(u, v) - d_y^2(u, v) \right],$$

$$\theta(i, j) = \frac{1}{2} \tan^{-1} \left(\frac{V_x(i, j)}{V_y(i, j)} \right) \tag{2.3}$$

Since the valid fingerprint region is characterized by the oriented ridges, a simple and effective way to segment the fingerprint into foreground (valid) and background (invalid) region can be done by computing the strength, $c(i, j)$, of the orientation in a local region as given in the following equation [8]:

$$c(i, j) = \frac{1}{w} \cdot \sqrt{\frac{V_x^2(i, j) + V_y^2(i, j)}{V_e(i, j)}},$$

$$V_e(i, j) = \sum_{u=i-w/2}^{i+w/2} \sum_{v=j-w/2}^{i+w/2} \left[d_x^2(u, v) + d_y^2(u, v) \right] \tag{2.4}$$

For each block of size $w \times w$, if its orientation strength, $c(i, j)$, is below a certain threshold, T_s, then the area in this block is marked as background.

2.3.2 *Ridge Orientation Modeling*

The local orientation computed above may not be sufficiently accurate, especially for noisy images. This is difficult to solve using the local orientation estimation approaches since the artifacts such as ridge discontinuities, smudge marks, or fragmented short ridges resulted in non-random perturbation to the original orientation. This reduces the strength of the original orientation while introducing another one or more competing dominant orientations, making determination of the valid orientation non-trivial. However, since the overall fingerprint ridges form a particular pattern of arches, loops, or whorl, then by modeling the orientation, it is possible to correct errors in the local orientation estimation.

A pioneering work in this direction was presented by Sherlock and Monro [9], where the orientation field is described using a pole-zero model. The model is formulated in the complex plane with the core point as zero and the delta point as pole. Taking the image plane as complex plane, and denoting a point in the image plane by z, the zero-pole model is then given by the following equation:

$$p(z) = \sqrt{e^{2j\phi_\infty} \frac{(z - z_{c1}) \dots (z - z_{cm})}{(z - z_{d1}) \dots (z - z_{dn})}},$$

$$\phi(z) = (\arg(p(z))) \bmod \pi \tag{2.5}$$

where ϕ_∞ is a constant correction term, z_{cr} and z_{ds} are the rth core point and the sth delta point, respectively.

This model is almost perfect in regions near the singular points but exhibits error in the other regions. An improvement of the zero-pole model was proposed in Ref. [10] using a piecewise linear approximation model around singular points to adjust the zero and pole's influence. However, it causes imperfection at the singular point regions. To solve this problem, combination model was proposed [11, 12]. A polynomial model was utilized to describe the global orientation pattern and a point-charge model was designed to characterize the orientation pattern near the singular points' region. The entire orientation field of the fingerprint is described through a combination of these two models using an ad hoc weighted function. A unified model was proposed using phase portrait model [13] and quadratic differentials [14]. However, these approaches

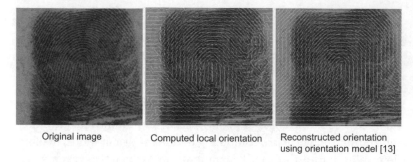

Original image   Computed local orientation   Reconstructed orientation
using orientation model [13]

Figure 2.3. Comparison between local orientation and reconstructed orientation using orientation modeling approach.

assumed that singular points' positions were known. To solve this, Wang *et al.* [15] presented an orientation estimation method using trigonometric polynomials. Figure 2.3 shows the ability to correct the error in the local orientation using the orientation modeling approach.

2.3.3 *Fingerprint Image Enhancement*

The aim of fingerprint image enhancement is to improve the clarity of the ridge and valley. This involves the following:

- Separating falsely connected parallel or different ridges caused by degradations such as smear, latent print, or wet finger
- Joining falsely broken ridges caused by degradations such as dry finger, scar, creases, or faulty sensor
- Maintaining the minutiae characterized by ridge ending and ridge bifurcation

The most commonly used technique for fingerprint image enhancement is based on contextual filters whereby the filter characteristics are changed according to the local context such as the ridge orientation and ridge frequency (number of ridges in the window) [3, 16]. Thus it is crucial to obtain a proper local orientation so that the enhancement does not produce unwanted artifacts which may falsely remove valid minutiae or generate false minutiae, especially in high curvature regions. The filter can be designed using low pass

| Original image | Improper enhancement causes false removal of minutiae | Proper enhancement preserves the minutiae |

Figure 2.4. Fingerprint image enhancement results showing the importance of correct enhancement.

filter along the ridge orientation and band-pass filter normal to the ridge orientation [17] or using Gabor filter [18]. Alternatively, short-time Fourier Transform analysis has also been proposed [19].

2.4 Feature Extraction

An important feature that establishes the uniqueness of a fingerprint is its minutiae comprising ridge endings and bifurcations as shown in Fig. 2.1. Most automated fingerprint recognition systems are based on minutiae matching. Therefore, extracting the minutiae is required prior to matching. A common approach to achieve this is to binarize the enhanced fingerprint image into black and white using thresholding means. Subsequently, thinning algorithm [20] is applied to convert the ridge width into one pixel-wide skeleton. Subsequently, the minutiae can be detected from the skeleton image by computing the transition count $tc(p)$ in a 3×3 window at each pixel p along the skeleton. The transition count is given by the following equation:

$$tc(p) = \sum |p(k+1) - p(k)| \; ; \; 1 \leq k \leq 8 \text{ and } p(9) = p(1),$$

(2.6)

where $p(1), \ldots, p(8)$ are the clockwise sequence in a 3×3 neighborhood of p.

Instead of resorting to binarization and thinning to extract the minutiae, which may introduce spurious minutiae, Maio and Maltoni

[21] pioneered the approach of direct gray scale minutiae extraction. It iteratively moves from a start point at the ridge centre (darkest point in the ridge) along the orientation of the start point in fixed step. Then a new start point is found along the normal to the orientation of that point and continues until it fulfils a termination criterion. The termination criterion is satisfied if either (1) the point reaches the background region, (2) there is excessive bending between the current step and the next step, or (3) when it meets a ridge which has been traced before. Ridge ending is found in criterion (2) while bifurcation is found in criterion (3). Jiang *et al.* [22] improved the tracing speed using an adaptive tracing technique.

Regardless of the extraction approaches, the extracted minutiae from a fingerprint will be used to represent the fingerprints. It is stored in a record, called template. In order to achieve interoperability, a standard data format for the minutia template is specified in the standards document ISO 19794-2 [23].

2.4.1 *Singular Point Detection*

The overall fingerprint exhibits regular flow of ridges with regions where the flow swirls, converges, terminates, or diverges. These regions are called singular regions and can be divided into either core or delta. The centroid of the core and delta, called the core and delta points, are useful as they are distinctive landmarks in the fingerprints and can be used to align the fingerprints as well as serving as additional features for matching. However, detecting these singular points is not easy. Partially captured fingerprints may not contain singular points, and the arch type fingerprints do not have core point. Noise may also obscure the singular points. Automated approaches to detect singular points can be generally classified into three types: pattern based, partition based, and projection based.

Pattern-based approach employs fixed patterns such as the core and delta models and then computes the correlation (or some index parameters) between the defined patterns and the input fingerprints to locate the singular points. Kawagoe and Tojo [24] proposed the use of Poincaré index which can be obtained by summing the orientation differences between the adjacent pixels in a closed window in a counterclockwise direction. Core point will give a summation of 180° while delta point will result in –180°. Improvements to this approach were proposed [25, 26]. Nilsson and Bigun [27] employed the complex symmetrical filters with shapes similar to core and delta in the orientation domain. The singular points are then detected by convolving fingerprint orientation fields with these filter models. The orientation modeling approach can also be used to iteratively detect the singular points by minimizing the orientation error between the original and modeled orientation fields [28, 29].

In partition-based approach, the idea is to partition the fingerprint orientation field or ridges into uniform directional segments and then analyze these partitioning lines to locate the singular points. For example, Huang *et al.* [30] showed that the fault lines, border lines separating two adjacent regions of the same quantized directional fields, converged at the singularities. Iterative clustering scheme is employed to group regions with the same orientation together [31]. The intersection of these cluster boundaries are the fingerprint singularities. Lam *et al.* [32] proposed the symmetry line, a borderline which segment two symmetrical part of fingerprint in order to detect the reference point of arch type fingerprint.

On the other hand, projection-based approach assumes that the normal of the ridge orientations will intersect close to the location of the core point [33]. This can also be obtained using Hough transform [34]. However, it may not be consistent in fingerprints

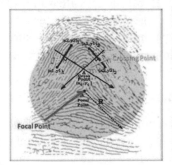

Figure 2.5. Showing the determination of the focal point from the intersection of ridge normals (left) and the use of half concentric lens [16]. See also Color Insert.

having more than one core, such as double loop and whorl. A proposed improvement [6] introduced a half circle window, called half concentric lens model, in which the centroid of the orientation field inside the window is determined. Then the window is moved to the new location found, and a new centroid is computed. The process is repeated until it converges to a stable point, called the focal point. This approach is stable and is able to locate a reference point even for arch type fingerprint which does not have a core point. However, the located reference point may not necessarily coincide with the actual core point.

2.5 Fingerprint Matching

Given two fingerprints, the aim of fingerprint matching is to determine whether both are from the same finger. However, just like other biometric modalities, fingerprint matching is not exact, but gives only a degree of probability or confidence that both are similar. This is because the fingerprint suffers from translation, rotation, partial obscuration, and deformation due to inexact placement of the finger on the sensor, varying skin condition causing variation in the image captured, noise, error in the feature extraction, etc. Therefore, good fingerprint matching algorithms should be able to withstand such variations as much as possible. The fingerprint matching algorithms can be classified according to the features used for matching. The fingerprint features can be classified into three hierarchical levels: level-1 (global ridge flow and pattern type), level-2 (minutiae), and level-3 (permanent ridge details, such as pore, incipient ridge, crease, and scar).

2.5.1 *Level-1 Matching Approach*

The level-1 features such as the global ridge flow pattern, orientation image, ridge spatial relationships, etc., are usually used only for fingerprint classification as the features may not be distinct enough. Nevertheless, there are fingerprint matching algorithms that rely only on these features alone. A famous approach is proposed [35], where a feature vector (called the FingerCode) was extracted using a tessellation pattern. Then the element of the FingerCode was determined based on a Gabor filterbank response of the ridge pattern covered by the cell in the tessellation pattern in an ordered manner. However, most matching algorithms combine the various level-1 features with level-2 feature to improve the matching performance [36–39].

2.5.2 *Level-2 Matching Approach: Minutiae Matching*

This is the most popular approach for fingerprint matching, and is also the most widely used technique in commercial solutions. Each minutia extracted from the fingerprint is represented by a feature vector $g_k = \{x_k, y_k, \theta_k, m_k\}$ where (x, y) is the coordinates of the minutia, θ the minutia angle, and m the type (bifurcation or ridge ending). Then matching two fingerprints reduces to point matching between the two sets of points. Matching the sets in their entirety or global matching can be effectively accomplished using the Hough transform approach [40, 41]. It computes the distance and angle of all possible point pairs (Δx, Δy, $\Delta \theta$), discretizes them, and accumulates the evidence in the discrete space for both fingerprints to obtain the transformation function to align them and finally pairing the minutiae in both images to obtain the matching score. This approach usually results in large template size, and is computationally intensive.

On the other hand, some researchers proposed the use of only information of the minutia and its surrounding minutiae within a local region to perform the matching, called local matching. The local information extracted includes distance between minutiae, relative angle between the minutiae, and the central minutia, ridge count, and occurrence of minutiae type [42, 43]. Such local information is invariant to translation and rotation and is robust to deformation. However, it is not informative enough to achieve good performance. Approaches to combine both local and global approach to harness the advantages of both were proposed [44], where the local structures were used to find the transformation function to align the two fingerprints followed by global matching to obtain the minutiae pairing. The overall matching score can be obtained from just the global matching score or computing a weighted sum of both the local and global matching. Further improvements to the combined local and global matching were proposed [36, 45, 46].

2.5.3 *Level-3 Matching Approach*

Level-3 features such as pore can only be reliably acquired using a high resolution fingerprint sensor ($\geq$1000 dpi). As such, the amount of works is not significant as such sensors are not commonly available. Pores are directly used for fingerprint matching [29] with RANSAC algorithm to refine the pore correspondences. Pores and ridge fragments are used for fingerprint matching [47, 48]. Jain *et al.* [49] further improve the work by utilizing the Iterative Closest Point algorithm to automatically align the pores and the entire ridges. Vatsa *et al.* [50] combined both level-2 and level-3 features for matching by using a two-stage nonlinear registration algorithm to combine all the features together using Taylor series transformation for coarse-scale registration and thin plate spline for fine-scale registration. Then pores and ridge curvatures are extracted and Delauney triangle minutiae added to strengthen the feature vector with support vector machine used for decision making.

2.6 Conclusions

Through many years of intensive research, automated fingerprint recognition systems become commonly available today. It is used from physical access control to automated border control and PC login. The performance of the state-of-the-art fingerprint recognition system is good, especially for good quality fingerprints. However, further research is necessary to improve the matching performance in noisy and deformed fingerprints as well as partial fingerprints and to use richer information to improve the matching reliability to match human performance.

References

1. Babler, W. J. (1991) Embryologic development of epidermal ridges and their configuration, *Birth Defects Original Article Series* **27**(2), 95–112.
2. Bazen, A. M. and Gerez, S. H. (2002) Systematic methods for the computation of the directional fields and singular points of fingerprints, *IEEE Transactions Pattern Analysis & Machine Intelligence* **24**, 905–919.

3. Boonchaiseree, N. and Areekul, V. (2009) Focal point detection based on half concentric lens model for singular point extraction in fingerprint, *Proceedings of the International Conference on Biometrics 2009, LNCS* **5558**, 637–646.

4. Cappelli, R., Lumini, A., Maio, D., and Maltoni, D. (1999) Fingerprint classification by directional image partitioning. *IEEE Transactions Pattern Analysis & Machine Intelligence* **21**(5), 402–421.

5. Chang, S. H., Cheng, F. H., Hsu, W. H., and Wu, G. Z. (1997) Fast algorithm for point pattern-matching: Invariant to translations, rotations and scale changes, *Pattern Recognition* **30**(2), 311–320.

6. Chikkerur, S. S. and Cartwright, A. N., Govindaraju, V. (2005) Fingerprint image enhancement using STFT Analysis, *International Workshop on Pattern Recognition for Crime Prevention, Security and Surveillance* 20–29.

7. Criminal Justice Information Services (1999) *Electronic Fingerprint Transmission Specification Report*, CJIS-RS-0010, vol. 7 (US).

8. Feng, J. (2008) Combining minutiae descriptors for fingerprint matching, *Pattern Recognition* **41**(1), 342–352.

9. Gu, J. and Zhou, J. (2003) A novel model for orientation field of fingerprints. *Proceedings of IEEE Computer Vision and Pattern Recognition* 493–498.

10. Gu, J., Zhou, J., and C. Yang (2006) Fingerprint recognition by combining global structure and local cues, *IEEE Transactions Image Processing* **15**(7), 1942–1964.

11. He, Y., Tian, J., Li, L., Chen, H., and Yang, X. (2006) Fingerprint matching based on global comprehensive similarity, *IEEE Transactions Pattern Analysis & Machine Intelligence* **28**(6), 850–862.

12. Hong, L., Wang, Y., and Jain, A. K. (1998) Fingerprint image enhancement: Algorithm and performance evaluation, *IEEE Transactions Pattern Analysis & Machine Intelligence* **21**(4), 777–789.

13. Hrechak, A. K. and Mchugh, J. A. (1990) Automated fingerprint recognition using structural matching, *Pattern Recognition* **23**(8), 893–904.

14. Huang, C. Y., Liu, L. M., and Hung, D. C. D. (2007) Fingerprint analysis and singular point detection, *Pattern Recognition Letters* **28**(15), 1937–1945.

15. Huckemann, S., Hotz, T., and Munk, A. (2008) Global models for the orientation field of fingerprints: An approach based on quadratic differentials. *IEEE Transactions Pattern Analysis & Machine Intelligence* **30**, 1507–1519.

16. ISO/IEC 19794-2 (2005), *Biometric Data Interchange Formats-Part 2: Finger Minutiae Data* (International Organization for Standardization).

17. ISO/IEC 19794-4 (2005) *Biometric Data Interchange Formats-Part 4: Finger Image Data* (International Organization for Standardization).

18. Jain, A. K., Prabhakar, S., Hong, L., and Pankanti, S. (2000) Filterbank-based fingerprint matching, *IEEE Transactions Image Processing* **9**(5), 846–859.

19. Jain, A. K., Chen, Y., and Demirkus, M. (2007) Pores and ridges: High resolution fingerprint matching using level 3 features, *IEEE Transactions Pattern Analysis & Machine Intelligence* **29**(1), 15–27.

20. Jiang, X. and Yau, W. Y. (2000) Fingerprint minutiae matching based on the local and global structures, *Proceedings of International Conference Pattern Recognition* **2**, 1042–1045.

21. Jiang, X., Yau, W. Y., and Ser, W. (2001) Detecting the fingerprint minutiae by adaptive tracing the gray-level ridge, *Pattern Recognition* **34**, 999–1013.

22. Jiang, X. (2007) Extracting image orientation feature by using integration operator, *Pattern Recognition* **40**, 705–717.

23. Kawagoe, M. and Tojo, A. (1984) Fingerprint pattern classification, *Pattern Recognition* **17**, 295–303.

24. Kryszczuk, K, Drygajlo, A., and Morier, P. (2004) Extraction of level 2 and level 3 features for fragmentary fingerprints, *Proceedings of the 2nd COST275 Workshop* 83–88.

25. Lam, L., Lee, S. W., and Suen, C. Y. (1992) Thinning Methodologies: A comprehensive survey, *IEEE Transactions Pattern Analysis & Machine Intelligence* **14**(9), 869–885.

26. Lam, H. K., Hou, Z., Yau, W. Y., Chen, T. P., Li, J., and Sim, K. Y. (2009) Reference point detection for arch type fingerprint, *Proceedings of the International Conference on Biometrics 2009, LNCS* **5558**, 666–674.

27. Lee, H. C. (2001) *Advances in Fingerprint Technology*, 2nd Ed. (Elsevier Publishing).

28. Lee, D., Choi, K., and Kim, J. (2002) A robust fingerprint matching algorithm using local alignment, *Proceedings of the International Conference Pattern Recognition* **3**, 803–806.

29. Li, J., Yau, W.Y., and Wang, H. (2006) Constrained nonlinear models of fingerprint orientations with prediction, *Pattern Recognition* **39**, 102–114.

30. Li, J., Yau, W.Y., and Wang, H. (2006) Singular points detection using interactive mechanism in fingerprint images, *Proceedings of*

the *International Conference Control, Automation, Robotics and Vision (ICARCV)*, Singapore, 428–433.

31. Li, P., Yang, X., Su, Q., Zhang, Y., and Tian, J. (2009) A novel fingerprint matching algorithm using ridge curvature feature, *Proceedings of the International Conference on Biometrics, LNCS* **5558**, 607–616.

32. Maio, D. and Maltoni, D. (1997) Direct gray-scale minutiae detection in fingerprints, *IEEE Transactions Pattern Analysis Machine Intelligence* **19**(1), 27–40.

33. Maltoni, D., Maio, D. Jain A.K., and Prabhakar, S. (2009) *Handbook of Fingerprint Recognition*, 2nd Ed. (Springer).

34. Mehtre, B.M., Murthy, N.N., and Kapoor, S. (1987) Segmentation of fingerprint images using the directional image, *Pattern Recognition* **20**(4), 429–435.

35. Nanni, L. and Lumini, A. (2008) Local binary patterns for a hybrid fingerprint matcher, *Pattern Recognition* **41**(11), 3461–3466.

36. Nilsson, K. and Bigun J. (2005) Registration of fingerprints by complex filtering and by 1D projections of orientation images, *Proceedings of the Audio-Video Biometric Person Authentication, LNCS* **3546**, 171–183.

37. Ratha, N. K., Chen, S. Y., and Jain, A. K. (1995) Adaptive flow orientation-based feature extraction in fingerprint images, *Pattern Recognition* **28**(11), 1657–1672.

38. Ratha, N. K., Karu, K., Chen, S. Y., and Jain, A. K. (1996) A real-time matching system for large fingerprint databases, *IEEE Transactions Pattern Analysis Machine Intelligence* **18**(8), 799–813.

39. Rerkrai, K. and Areekul, V. (2000) A new reference point for fingerprint recognition, *Proceedings of the International Conference Image Processing* **2**, 499–502.

40. Roddy, A. R. and Stosz, J. D. (1997) Fingerprint features: Statistical analysis and system performance estimates, *Proceedings of the IEEE* **85**(9), 1390–1421.

41. Sherlock, B. G., Monro, D. M., and Millard, K. (1992) Algorithm for enhancing fingerprint images, *Electronics Letters* **28**(18), 1720.

42. Sherlock, B. G., and Monro, D. M. (1993) A model for interpreting fingerprint topology, *Pattern Recognition* **26**, 1047–1055.

43. Vatsa, M., Singh, R., Noore, A., and Singh, S. K. (2009) Crease combining pores and ridges with minutiae for improved fingerprint verification, *Signal Processing* **89**(2), 2676–2685.

44. Vizcaya, P. and Gerhardt, L. (1996) A nonlinear orientation model for global description of fingerprints, *Pattern Recognition* **29**, 1221–1231.

45. Wang, Y., Hu, J., and Phillips, D. (2007) A fingerprint orientation model based on 2D Fourier expansion (FOMFE) and its application to singular point detection and fingerprint indexing, *IEEE Transactions Pattern Analysis Machine Intelligence* **29**, 573–585.

46. Wahab, A., Chin, S. H., and Tan, E. C. (1998) Novel approach to automated fingerprint recognition, *IEE Proceedings – Vision, Image, and Signal Processing* **145**(3), 160–166.

47. Zhao, Q., Zhang, L., Zhang, D., and Luo, N. (2009) Direct pore matching for fingerprint recognition, *Proceedings of the International Conference on Biometrics, LNCS* **5558**, 597–606.

48. Zhou, J. and Gu, J. (2004) A model-based method for the computation of fingerprints' orientation field. *IEEE Transactions Image Processing* **13**, 821–835.

49. Zhou, J., Chen, F., and Gu, J. (2009) A novel algorithm for detecting singular points from fingerprint images, *IEEE Transactions Pattern Analysis Machine Intelligence* **31**(7), 1239–1250.

50. Nilsson, K. and Bigun, J. (2005) Registration of fingerprints by complex filtering and by 1D projections of orientation images, *Proceedings of the Audio-Video Biometric Person Authentication, LNCS* **3546** 171–183.

51. Novikov, S. O. and Kot, V. S. (1998) Singular feature detection and classification of fingerprint using Hough transform, *Proceedings of the SPIE International Workshop on Digital Image Processing and Computer Graphics: Applications in Humanities and Natural Sciences* **3346**, 259–269.

Chapter 3

Face Detection and Recognition

Huiyu Zhou

ECIT, Queen's University Belfast,
Belfast, BT3 9DT, United Kingdom
H.Zhou@ecit.qub.ac.uk

In this chapter the state-of-the-art face detection and recognition algorithms are reviewed. Several classical face detection approaches including AdaBoost, Gabor neural network, neural network, rank deficiency, and SNoW are introduced. Their performance is evaluated against a publicly accessible database. The evaluation results demonstrate that SNoW algorithm has the best accuracy while AdaBoost is the fastest face detector. Afterwards, face recognition algorithms, i.e., Eigenface, Fisherface, and Tensorface algorithms are summarized and evaluated over publicly available face databases.

3.1 Introduction

Like other security systems, facial image acquisition and assurance systems can be used for applications like robotics, access control, and identity authentication and intruders detection. In practice, a face detection and recognition system must be reliably working to various changes onto the faces. However, the existing systems are

Biometrics: From Fiction to Practice
Edited by Eliza Yingzi Du
Copyright © 2013 Pan Stanford Publishing Pte. Ltd.
ISBN 978-981-4310-88-8 (Hardcover), 978-981-4364-13-3 (eBook)
www.panstanford.com

reluctant to meet this requirement and hence further developments are immense.

Face detection is one of the challenging problems in computer vision. The goal of face detection is to determine whether or not there is any face in the image and the location of each face if there is. This topic attracts popular attention because of its wide range of applications. For example, intelligent video surveillance systems and human-computer interface have been closely linked to the industrial applications where face detection plays a key role.

A number of face detection algorithms have been established till date. A comprehensive survey on face detection can be found in [1, 2]. These available techniques mainly deal with the challenges that are summarized as follows:

1. Lighting condition: Lighting change brings new cast shadow that may lead to extra computation complexity.
2. Facial expression: This may result in a completely different appearance of the facial structure.
3. Occlusion: Evidence shows that occluded faces are difficult to be detected due to unavailability of facial entities.
4. Pose variations: This action may result in 1, 2, and 3.

Research intention has been continuously focused on face detection in a single gray or colorful image. This is an area that appears completely different from the face tracking–based approaches, which have fully taken advantage of smoothness and consistency constraints over a short period. In this chapter, we will only discuss the case of face detection on a single image.

Referring to the description in Ref. [1], we summarize the recent developments made in the topic of face detection in the following sections by categorizing the existing techniques into four groups: knowledge-based, feature invariant, template matching, and appearance-based methods. Of these established approaches, knowledge-based approaches are based on the rules that can be used to associate different features together for localizing faces [3, 4]. Feature invariant schemes attempt to discover structural features that present rotation-, zoom- or translation-invariant properties in different circumstances [5, 7]. Template matching methods have been developed by comparing the real images and the template counterparts that have been stored in the database [6, 7]. Appearance-based methods enable the face models to be learnt from a number of training data that captures the representative variability of facial appearance. These models are then applied to the real images so as to generate discrimination [19].

Following the summary of the face detection algorithms, we introduce three established face recognition algorithms, which include Eigenface, Fisherface, and Tensorface algorithms. For decades studies on face recognition have addressed the problem of interpreting faces by machine, their efforts over time leading to a considerable understanding of this research area, and rich practical applications. However, in spite of their impressive performance, the established face recognition systems to some extent exhibit deficiency in the cases of partial occlusion and illumination changes. This is due to the fact that these systems mainly rely on the low-level attributes (e.g., color, texture, shape, and motion), which may change significantly in the presence of image occlusions or illumination variations.

The entire chapter is organized as follows: In the next section we summarize the recent progress in face detection, which consists of knowledge-based, feature-invariant, template-matching, and appearance-based approaches. Section 3.3 reveals several frequently used face detection algorithms and their exemplar applications. This is followed by a comprehensive evaluation of these approaches based on a publicly accessible database. Section 3.4 summarizes three face recognition algorithms with their evaluations over two face databases. Finally, conclusions and scope for future work are given in Section 3.5.

3.2 Literature Review

3.2.1 *Face Detection*

The established face detection approaches can be briefly reviewed in the following subsections. As mentioned earlier, knowledge-based, feature-invariant, template-matching, and appearance-based approaches will be introduced subsequently.

3.2.1.1 Knowledge-based methods

They are top-down techniques based on the rules that have been derived from the common knowledge of human faces. For example, the facial structure with two eyes and one nose has often been used to identify possible candidates in a large amount of inputs. However, one significant weakness of these methods is the lack of capability of translating human knowledge into computational rules that can be utilized to distinguish different faces and non-faces.

Yang and Huang [3] presented a hierarchical knowledge-based method to detect faces. This system has three levels of rules. The top level observes that possible face candidates are found by sliding a window over the input image and applying a set of rules at each location. At level 2, local histogram equalization was performed on the face candidates. Survivors of the faces will then be examined using the rules, where facial features corresponding to the eyes and mouth were used in the evaluation. To enhance the efficiency of the entire strategy, a coarse-to-fine scheme was applied. On the other hand, Kotropoulos and Pitas [4] proposed a project method to generate facial features that can be used to outline the boundary of a face.

Hsu *et al.* [14] proposed a face detector for color images in the presence of varying lighting conditions as well as complex backgrounds. Based on a lighting compensation technique and a nonlinear color transformation, the method detected skin regions over the entire image and then generated face candidates based on the spatial arrangement of these skin patches. This algorithm constructed eye, mouth, and boundary maps for verifying each face candidate.

3.2.1.2 Feature-based methods

This is a different case from the knowledge-based algorithms. The strategy is of a bottom-up style. Yow and Cipolla [5] introduced a feature-based method that used a large number of evidence from the image and its contextual evidence: (1) A second derivative Gaussian filter was applied and (2) the edges around the interest points were examined and then grouped together. This method can detect faces at different orientation and poses.

Saber and Tekalp [7] described an algorithm for face detection. This approach started from a supervised pixel-based color classifier that was employed to mark all pixels that are falling in a predefined region of skin color. This region was computed from a training set of skin patches. This color map was then smoothed using the Gibbs random field model-based filters to determine the skin regions. An ellipse model was then fit to disjoin skin regions. Finally, the centre of the eyes, tip of nose and centre of mouth were searched by solving symmetry-based cost functions.

Dai and Nakano [8] introduced a method for full face detection. Face feature were extracted using space gray-level dependence matrix and the face texture model. A color information application in combination with the face texture features was investigated. Using the face-texture model the orange-like parts were enhanced by utilizing the components of YIQ color system.

Viola and Jones [9] presented a new face detection approach including three key contributions. The first one is the introduction of a new image representation called the "Integral Image," which allows the features used by our detector to be computed very quickly. The second is a learning algorithm, based on AdaBoost, which selects a small number of critical visual features from a larger set and yields extremely efficient classifiers. The third contribution is a method for combining increasingly more complex classifiers in a "cascade" which allows background regions of the image to be quickly discarded while spending more computation on promising object-like regions. The cascade can be viewed as an object specific focus-of-attention mechanism, which unlike previous approaches, provides statistical guarantees that discarded regions are unlikely to contain the object of interest.

A novel learning procedure called FloatBoost was proposed for learning a boosted classifier for achieving the minimum error rate [18]. FloatBoost learning used a back-track mechanism after each iteration of AdaBoost learning to minimize the error rate directly, rather than minimizing an exponential function of the margin as in the traditional AdaBoost algorithms. A second contribution is a novel statistical model for learning best weak classifiers using a stage wise approximation of the posterior probability.

In Ref. [10], a novel Bayesian discriminating features (BDF) method for multiple frontal face detection was presented. First, feature analysis generated a discriminating feature vector by combining the input image, its 1-D Harr wavelet representation, and its amplitude projections. While the Harr wavelets produced an effective representation for object detection, the amplitude projections captured the vertical symmetric distributions and the horizontal characteristics of human face images. Second, statistical modeling estimated the conditional probability density functions, or PDFs, of the face and non-face classes, respectively. While the face class is usually modeled as a multivariate normal distribution, the non-face class is much more difficult to model due to the fact that it includes "the rest of the world." The estimation of such a broad category is, in practice, intractable. However, a subset of the non-faces was produced that lies closest to the face class, and then modeled this particular subset as a multivariate normal distribution. Finally, the Bayes classifier applied the estimated conditional PDFs to detect multiple frontal faces in an image.

Hadid *et al.* [25] introduced a novel discriminative feature space which was efficient not only for face detection but also for recognition. The face representation was based on local binary patterns (LBP), and consists of encoding both local and global facial characteristics into a compact feature histogram. The proposed representation was invariant with respect to monotonic gray scale transformations and could be derived in a single scan through the image. Considering the derived feature space, a second-degree polynomial kernel SVM classifier was trained to detect frontal faces in gray scale images.

3.2.1.3 Template-matching methods

Wu and Zhou [11] reported an efficient face candidate selector for face detection. Eye-analogue segment at a given scale were discovered by finding regions which were roughly as large as real eyes and were darker than their neighborhoods. Then a pair of eye-analogue segment were hypothesized to be eyes in a face and combined with a face candidate if their placement is consistent with the anthropological characteristic of human eyes.

A system was developed for finding un-occluded vertical frontal views of human faces in images [12]. This approach modeled the distribution of face patterns by means of a few prototype clusters, and learnt from examples a set of distance parameters for distinguishing between "face" and "non-face" test patterns. The proposed model was capable to automatically learn thresholds and parameters.

One deformable template approach was introduced to model the nonrigid elements of faces or facial subfeatures [13]. The parameterized curves and surfaces were fixed elastically to a global template frame to allow for minor positional variations between two facial features. The matching process was to align the template with one or more preprocessed images, e.g., peak, valley, and edge maps. An energy functional constrained alignment by attracting the parameterized curves and surfaces to corresponding features, while penalizing configuration

Jin *et al.* [6] reported a new face detection algorithm. Firstly, a luminance conditional distribution model of skin color information was used to discover the skin pixels from the image. Morphological operations were then used to extract skin-region rectangles. Finally, template matching based on a linear transformation was used to detect faces in each skin-region rectangles.

A scheme for detecting faces in color images was proposed in Ref. [15]. It utilized the skin color method with a new approach to detecting skin color pixels in the RGB color space. The edge information was used to increase the distinction between the skin-colored face patches and the background. This is followed by a scan line candidate determination algorithm. A method combining profiles, geometrical moments, the use of the $R-B$ color subspace and gray level images for eyes localization was presented. The verification was finally made based on a template matching approach.

In Ref. [16] a new method was reported to detect faces in color images based on the fuzzy theory. Two fuzzy models were created to describe the skin color and hair color, respectively. In these models, a perceptually uniform color space was used to describe the color information to increase the accuracy and stableness. These two models were used to extract the skin color regions and the hair color regions, and then comparing them with the prebuilt head-shape models by using a fuzzy theory based pattern-matching method to detect face candidates.

In Ref. [17], a template-matching approach was proposed for face verification, which neither synthesized the face image nor built a model of the face image. Template matching was performed using an edginess-based representation of the face image. The edginess-based representation of face images was computed using 1-D processing of images. An approach was proposed based on auto-associative neural network models to verify the identity of a person.

3.2.1.4 Appearance-based methods

Phimoltares *et al.* [19] presented an algorithms for all types of face images in the presence of several image conditions. In the first stage, the faces were detected from an original image by using Canny edge detection, and proposed average face templates. Second, a proposed neural visual model (NVM) was used to recognize all possibilities of facial feature positions. Input parameters are obtained from the positions of facial features and the face characteristics that are low sensitive to intensity change. Finally, to improve the results, image dilation was applied for removing some irrelevant regions.

A kernel machine based approach was proposed in Ref. [20] to the provision of an effective view-based representation for multiview face detection and pose estimation. Assuming that the view is partitioned into a number of distinct ranges, one nonlinear view-subspace is learned for each (range of) view from a set of example face images of that view (range), by using kernel principal component analysis (KPCA). Projections of the data onto the view-subspaces are then computed as view-based nonlinear features. Multiview face detection and pose estimation are performed by classifying a face into one of the facial views or into the non-face class by using a multiclass kernel support vector classifier (KSVC).

Robinson [21] investigated high-dimensional statistical models using appearance-based strategies. He argued for regularized covariance estimation and introduces a new method suitable for appearance-based image processing. The reported method was demonstrated for face detection, where a maximum likelihood classifier trained with regularized covariances achieve discrimination and detection results comparable to those of complicated multimodal and nonlinear classifiers.

Waring and Liu [22] presented a face detection method using spectral histograms and support vector machines (SVMs). Each image window was represented by its spectral histogram, which was a feature vector consisting of histograms of filtered images. Using statistical sampling, the representation groups face images together. By using an SVM trained on a set of 4500 face and 8000 non-face images, a robust classifying function was obtained for face and non-face patterns. With an effective illumination-correction algorithm, this system reliably discriminated face and non-face patterns in images under different kinds of conditions.

A multiple-model approach (MMA) for top-down, model-based attention processes was proposed [23]. The advantages offered by this proposal for space-variant image representations are discussed. A simple but representative frontal-face detection task is given as an example of application of the MMA. The combination of appearance-based features and a linear regression-based classifier proved very effective.

Sebe *et al.* [24] presented a theoretical analysis of semi-supervised learning and show that there was an overlooked fundamental difference between the purely supervised and the semi-supervised learning paradigms. While in the supervised case, increasing the amount of labeled training data is always seen as a way to improve the classifier's performance; the converse might also be true as the number of unlabeled data is increased in the semi-supervised case. The impact of this theoretical finding on Bayesian network classifiers was studied with the goal of avoiding the performance degradation with unlabeled data.

3.2.2 *Face Recognition*

Classical image-based face recognition algorithms can be categorized into appearance and model based. The former normally consists of linear (using basis vectors) and nonlinear analysis. These approaches represent an object using raw intensity images, being considered as high-dimensional vectors. For example, Beymer [40] described a pose estimation algorithm to align the probe images to candidate poses of the gallery subjects. Pentland *et al.* [41] compared the performance of a parametric eigenspace with view-based eigenspaces. The latter includes 2-D or 3-D model–based schemes, where the facial variations with prior knowledge are encoded in a model to be constructed. Examples can be found in [42–44].

As one of the linear appearance algorithms, the well-known Eigenface algorithm [45] uses the principal component analysis (PCA) for dimensionality reduction in order to find the best vectorized components that represent the faces in the entire image space. The face vectors are projected to the basis vectors so that the projection coefficients are used as the feature representation of each face image [45]. Another example of the linear appearance approaches is the application of independent component analysis (ICA). ICA is very similar to PCA except that the distribution of the components is assumed to be non-Gaussian. One of these ICA-based algorithms is the FastICA scheme that utilized the InfoMax algorithm [46]. The Fisherface algorithm [47], derived from the Fisher linear discriminant (FLD), defines different classes with different statistics. Faces with similar statistics will be grouped together by FLD rules. Tensorface [48] recruits a higher-order tensor to describe the set of face images and extend singular value decomposition (SVD) to the higher-order tensor data.

3.3 Classical Face Detection Algorithms

A number of face detection algorithm have been established. Due to their stability and accuracy, AdaBoost [9], neural network [26], Gabor neural network [27], SNoW [28], rank-deficient-based [29], and coarse-to-fine [30] face detection algorithms are popular in the community. Here, we will summarize their principles followed by performance demonstration.

3.3.1 *AdaBoost Face Detection*

There are three contributions of the AdaBoost algorithm [9]. The first contribution is the formation of a new image representation namely an integral image that permits fast feature evaluation. The second contribution is the design of a simple classifier that is built for selecting a small number of important features from the overall potential features. The third contribution is the development of a method for combining some complex classifiers in a cascade style in order to increase the speed of the face detector. We provide more details as follows.

AdaBoost uses simple features such as Harr basis functions [31]. Figure 3.1 illustrates example rectangle features relative to the enclosing detection window. The value of a two rectangle feature is the difference between the sums of the pixels within two rectangular regions. A three rectangle feature refers to the sum within two outside rectangles subtracted from the sum in a center rectangle. A four rectangle feature allows the difference between diagonal pairs of rectangles to be computed.

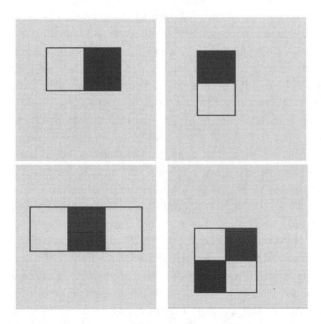

Figure 3.1. Example rectangle features are shown relative to the enclosing detection window. The sum of the pixels which lie within the white rectangle is subtracted from the sum of pixels in the black rectangles.

Rectangle features can be computed quickly using a technique called "integral image." The integral image at location x, y is the sum of the pixels above and to the left of x, y, using the following recurrences:

$$s(x, y) = s(x, y - 1) + i(x, y) \qquad (3.1)$$

$$ii(x, y) = ii(x - 1, y) + s(x, y) \qquad (3.2)$$

where $s(x, y)$ is the cumulative row sum.

Given a feature set (see the above), a dimensional reduction of the feature set must be proposed in order to maintain computational efficiency. A variant of AdaBoost was used both to select the features and to train the classifier reported [32]. The AdaBoost classifier improves the performance of a simple learning algorithm by combining a collection of weak classification functions to form a stronger classifier. After each round of learning, the results will be re-weighted so as to emphasize those which have not been correctly classified by the previous weak classifier.

The conventional AdaBoost approach can be treated as a greedy feature selection process. The challenge is to associate a large weight with each good classification function and a smaller weight with poor functions. To achieve this, the weak learning algorithm is designed to select the single rectangle feature which best separates the positive and negative examples. For each feature, the weak learner determines the optimal threshold classification function such that there are a minimum number of examples to be misclassified. In practice, features that are selected early in the process generate error rates between 0.1 and 0.3. Features selected in later process yield error rates between 0.4 and 0.5.

The weak classifier selection algorithm work like this: For each feature, the examples are sorted based on feature value. The AdaBoost optimal threshold for that feature can then be computed in a single pass over this sorted list. For each element in the sorted list, four sums are computed: the total sum of positive example weights, the total sum of negative example weights, the sum of positive weights below the current examples, and the sum of negative weights below the current example. The error for a threshold which divides the range between the current and previous example in the sorted list is the minimum of the error of labeling all examples below the current examples negative and labeling the examples above positive versus the error of the converse [9].

3.3.1.1 Attentional cascade

This is to describe an algorithm for constructing a cascade of classifiers while achieving increased detection performance. Simpler classifiers can be used to reject most of the subwindows before more complex classifiers are adopted to reduce the false positive rates. Starting with a two-feature strong classifier, a face filter can be obtained by adjusting the strong classifier threshold to minimize false negatives. A degenerate decision tree namely "cascade" [33] is used in the face detection. A positive result from the first classifier can trigger the process of a second classifier that has been adjusted to perform high-detection rates. A positive result from the second classifier triggers a third classifier, etc.

A training process for a cascade of classifiers is necessary. The overall training process has two types of tradeoffs. In general, an optimization framework is sought while determining the number of classifier stages, the number of features of each stage, and the threshold of each stage. In practice, a simple framework is used to produce an effective classifier which is highly efficient. The user defines the maximum, acceptable rates for the cascaded classifiers. If the overall target false positive rate has not been met yet, then another layer is added to the cascade.

Figure 3.2 illustrates some face images with detection results by the AdaBoost detector. These face images are part of a publicly accessible database created in University College Dublin of Ireland (http://ee.ucd.ie/~prag/). Among these nine example images, there is only one image where a face has been missed by the AdaBoost detector.

3.3.2 *SNoW Face Detection*

SNoW (Sparse Network of Winnows) is a space network of linear functions that utilizes the Winnow update rule [28]. SNoW is tailored for learning in the domain in which the potential number of feature taking part in decision is large but may not be known a priori.

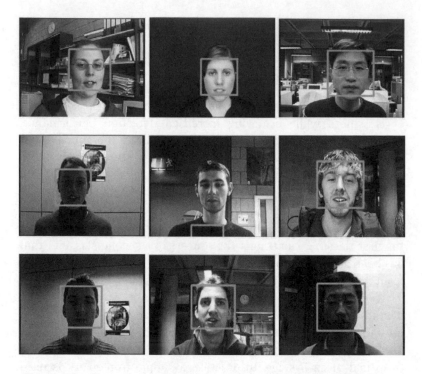

Figure 3.2. Example images demonstrate the performance of AdaBoost.

Nodes in the input layer of the network represent simpler relations over the input, and are being used as the input features. Each linear unit is a target node and stands for relations where only two target nodes are used: one is a representation for a face pattern and the other for a non-face pattern.

Given a set of relations (i.e., types of features) that is extracted in the input image, each input image is mapped into a set of features which are active in it. This representation is presented to the input payer of SNoW and propagates to the target nodes. Target nodes are linked via weighted edges to input features. A single SNoW unit includes two subnetworks, one for each of the targets is used. A given example is treated autonomously by each target subnetwork. An image labeled as a face is used as a positive example for the face target and as a negative example for the non-face target, and vice versa.

The learning policy is on-line and mistake driven. Several update rules can be used within SNoW. The best one and the only used in this work is a variant of Littlestone's Winnow update rule, a multiplicative update rule tailored to the situation in which the set of input features is not known a priori, as in the infinite attribute model [34]. This model is implemented via the sparse architecture of SNoW. This includes: (1) input features are allocated in a data driven style, where an input node for feature i is allocated only if this feature is active in the image and (2) a link (a nonzero weight) exits between a target node t and feature i if and only if i has been active in the image labeled i.

The Winnow update rule has in addition to the threshold θ_t at target t, two update parameters: a promotion parameter $\alpha > 1$ and a demotion parameter $0 < \beta < 1$. These are used to update the current representation of the target t only when a mistake in prediction is made. Winnow is known to learn efficiently any linear threshold function and to be robust in the presence of various kinds of noise and in cases where no linear thresholds function can make perfect classification, and still maintain its dependence on the number of total and relevant attributes [35]. Once target subnetworks have been learned and the network is being evaluated, a winner-takes-all mechanism selects the dominant active target node in the SNoW structure to produce a final prediction.

More than 1000 face images have been used to train the SNoW face detector with various pose, facial expression, and lighting condition. More than 8000 non-face examples consisting of landscapes, trees, buildings, etc., are used as negative examples. The SNoW-based face detector utilizes Boolean features that encode the positions and intensity values of pixels. Let the pixel at (x, y) of an image with width w and height h have intensity $I(x, y)$. This information is encoded as a feature whose index is $256(yw + x) + I(x, y)$. This representation ensures that different points in the position and intensity space are mapped to different features. Only 400 of those features are active in each example. This sparseness generates great efficiency that releases the algorithmic complexity.

Multiscale information can be represented using the Boolean features in the SNoW paradigm. To produce multiscale features, the mean and variance of a multiscale pixel in addition to the position are used. The learning problem can be simplified using this multiscale feature that does not require many pixel-based features. Uninformative multiscale features will e assigned low weights by the learning algorithm and will not degrade the system performance. Each face image is normalized to be a rectangular image of the same size. It is fair to generate features with regards to the means and variances of their intensity values.

Instead of using the absolute values of the mean and variance when encoding the features, these values can be divided into a predefined number of classes. The distribution of the mean value and variance values are normal and therefore the division is quite close to the means of the distributions. The total number of values is empirically determined to be 100. Mapping from the position/intensity mean and variance space to the Boolean feature space is carried out for four different sub-image scales, i.e., 1×1, 2×2, 4×4 to 10×10 pixels. The number of active features in each example is $400 + 100 + 25 + 4$ in spite of a larger number of the overall features.

Figure 3.3 demonstrates a few images with corresponding facial detection. Clearly, all the faces have been correctly detected in these examples. This is due to the fact that SNoW allows each subregion to be classified accurately.

3.3.3 *Rank-Deficient Face Detection*

SVMs have provided state-of-the-art accuracy in object detection. However, these have limited use due to the expensive computation in decision functions. The main constraints consist of two facts. First, the complexity of an SVM is proportional to the number of support vectors (SVs). Second, the similarity computation between the input and an SVM is proportional to the number of operations needed.

Kienzle *et al.* [29] reported a new approach to address the second issue where the high computational cost of the kernel function needs to be reduced. The simplicity of gray value correlations with the speed advantage of more sophisticated image representations was concerned. To this end, the reduced set vectors (RSVs) are constrained to have a special structure and can be evaluated via separable convolution. The average computational complexity of the

Figure 3.3. Example images demonstrate the performance of SNoW face detector.

RSV evaluations can be reduced from $O(hw)$ to $O(r(h+w))$, where r is a small number that can be used to balance speed and accuracy, h and w are the image size.

Assume that an SVM has been successfully trained on the data. Let $\{X_1, \ldots, X_m\}$ denote the set of SVs, $\{\alpha_1, \ldots, \alpha_m\}$ the corresponding coefficients, $k(\cdot)$ the kernel function, and b the bias of the SVM solution. The decision rule for a test pattern $\mathbf{X}$ is:

$$f(\mathbf{X}) = \text{sgn}\left(\sum_{i=1}^{m} y_i \alpha_i k(\mathbf{X}_i, \mathbf{X}) + \mathbf{b}\right) \qquad (3.3)$$

The decision surface induced by f corresponds to a hyperplane in the kernel Hilbert space associated with k. The resulting RS decision function f' is then given by

$$f'(\mathbf{X}) = \text{sgn}\left(\sum_{i=1}^{m'} \beta_i k(\mathbf{Z}_i, \mathbf{X}) + b\right) \qquad (3.4)$$

where β_i and reduced set $\mathbf{Z}_i$ can be determined using a gradient-based optimization technique [36].

Considering a 2-D convolution, if $\mathbf{I}$ is an input image and $\mathbf{H}$ is the impulse response (filter mask), we then have the output image as follows:

$$\mathbf{J} = \mathbf{I} \times \mathbf{H} \tag{3.5}$$

The SVD of the $h \times w$ matrix $\mathbf{H}$ can be expressed as:

$$\mathbf{H} = \mathbf{USV}^{\mathrm{T}} \tag{3.6}$$

where $\mathbf{U}$ and $\mathbf{V}$ are orthogonal matrices of size $h \times h$ and $w \times w$, respectively, $\mathbf{S}$ is diagonal (the diagonal entries are the singular values) and has size $h \times w$. Now let $r_0 = \mathrm{rank}(\mathbf{H})$. Since $\mathrm{rank}(\mathbf{S}) = \mathrm{rank}(\mathbf{H})$, we can have

$$\mathbf{H} = \sum_{i=1}^{r_0} s_i \mathbf{u}_i \mathbf{v}_i^T \tag{3.7}$$

where s_i denotes the ith singular value of $\mathbf{H}$ and $\mathbf{u}_i$ and $\mathbf{v}_i$ are the ith columns of $\mathbf{U}$ and $\mathbf{V}$. Therefore, we shall have the result as follows after a weighted convolution has been performed:

$$\mathbf{J} = \sum_{i=1}^{r_0} s_i [\mathbf{I} * \mathbf{u}_i] * \mathbf{v}_i^T \tag{3.8}$$

The speed benefit depends on r_0. Assume g is an arbitrary function and $c(\mathbf{H},\mathbf{X})$ denotes the correlation between images $\mathbf{X}$ and $\mathbf{H}$. We then have a kernel of the form

$$k(\mathbf{H}, \mathbf{X}) = g(c(\mathbf{H}, \mathbf{X})) \tag{3.9}$$

For example, a Gaussian kernel leads to

$$k(\mathbf{H}, \mathbf{X}) = \exp(\gamma(c(\mathbf{X}, \mathbf{Y}) - 2c(\mathbf{H}, \mathbf{X}) + c(\mathbf{H}, \mathbf{H}))) \tag{3.10}$$

The middle term is the correlation that will be evaluated using separable filters. The first term is independent of the SVs while the last term is a constant scalar. The correlation of image pixels can be evaluated using the squared Euclidean distance:

$$||\mathbf{x} - \mathbf{z}||^2 = ||\mathbf{X} - \mathbf{Z}||_{\mathrm{F}}^2 \tag{3.11}$$

where the dot product equals to

$$x^T z = 0.5 \left(||\mathbf{X}||_{\mathrm{F}}^2 + ||\mathbf{Z}||_{\mathrm{F}}^2 - ||\mathbf{X} - \mathbf{Z}||_{\mathrm{F}}^2 \right) \tag{3.12}$$

where $\mathbf{X}$ and $\mathbf{Z}$ are the corresponding image patches and $||\blacksquare||_{\mathrm{F}}$ is the Frobenius norm.

Z_is can be replaced by their SVD:

$$\mathbf{Z}_i \leftarrow \mathbf{U}_i \mathbf{S}_i \mathbf{V}'_i \qquad (3.13)$$

The first r diagonal elements of $\mathbf{S}_i$ can be made to be nonzero. Therefore an approximation can be reached as follows:

$$\Psi'_r = \sum_{i=1}^{m'} \beta_i k \left(\mathbf{U}_{i,r}\mathbf{S}_{i,r}\mathbf{V}_{i,r}^T\right) \qquad (3.14)$$

where $\mathbf{S}_{i,r}$ being $r \times r$ (diagonal) and $\mathbf{U}_{i,r}$ and $\mathbf{V}_{i,r}$ being $h \times r$ and $w \times r$ matrices, respectively.

Fixing m' and $\mathbf{S}_{i,r}$, $\mathbf{U}_{i,r}$, $\mathbf{V}_{i,r}$ and β_i can be found as they are used to minimize the approximate error $||\psi - \psi'_r||^2$. This minimization problem can be solved using a gradient decent approach. When computing the gradients for $\mathbf{S}_{i,r}$ and β_i, one needs to pay more attention to the orthogonality of $\mathbf{U}_{i,r}$ and $\mathbf{V}_{i,r}$. Therefore, during each gradient loop re-orthogonalization must be undertaken.

Figure 3.4 illustrates the face detection results of using this rank deficient algorithm. It shows that two of the faces have been missed while one has not been detected at all.

3.3.4 *Gabor-Based Neural Networks*

Gabor features have been increasingly used in face recognition [37]. This is due to the fact that they model the response of human visual cortical cells [38]. Gabor wavelets provide a better understanding to the orientation and spatial frequency selective properties of simple cortical neurons. Using Gabor features we can remove certain variations in lighting and contrast while reducing intrapersonal variations. These Gabor-based features are robust against small shifts and small object deformations.

Let $I(z)$ be the gray level distribution of the input image. Gabor wavelet transform on $I(z)$ can be written as a convolution of $I(z)$ with a family of kernels K_k:

$$G(z) = I(z) * K_k(z) \qquad (3.15)$$

where * denotes the convolution operator and $G(z)$ is the convolution result at k. the Gabor wavelets is determined using a Gaussian envelope function [39]:

$$K_k(z) = \frac{||k||}{\sigma^2} e^{-||k||^2||z||^2/(2\sigma^2)} \left[e^{ikx} - e^{\frac{-\sigma^2}{2}} \right] \qquad (3.16)$$

Figure 3.4. Example images demonstrate the performance of rank deficient face detector.

where k determines the wavelength and orientation of the kernel $K_k(z)$ in image coordinates. The first term in the bracket is an oscillation part, and the second one is a DC part. k is estimated as

$$k(\omega, \mu) = k_\mu e^{i\varphi_\mu} \qquad (3.17)$$

where ω and μ are the orientation and scale of the Gabor kernels with

$$k_\mu = k_{\max} ax / f^\mu \qquad (3.18)$$

$$\varphi_\mu = \pi \mu / 8 \qquad (3.19)$$

$k_{\max}$ is the maximum frequency, and f is the spacing factor between the kernels in the frequency domain.

Evidence shows that good results can be obtained using Gabor wavelets of five different scales and eight orientations [39]. Therefore, $V \in \{0, \ldots, 4\}, \omega \in \{0, \ldots, 7\}, \sigma = 2\pi, k_{\max} = \pi/2$, and $f = \sqrt{2}$. The down-sampled Gabor wavelet transform is performed by the factor of 64 to form a feature vector. In the implementation, people normally divide the input image into blocks with smaller size. Then each block is investigated in order to obtain its mean. Networks can be shaped if each pixel is subtracted by the mean in the block. Once Gabor features have been fully extracted, a neural network approach will be called to classify the image blocks for facial parts. A full story about a neural network will be independently introduced in the next subsection.

Figure 3.5 denotes image examples and their results using the Gabor-based neural network face detector. Clearly, this approach suffers from the clutters that distract the face detector, and lighting change also deteriorates the performance of the detector.

3.3.5 *Neural Network-Based Face Detection*

This strategy has been well recognized since its birth in 1998. Rowley *et al.* [26] introduced face detector that consists of two

Figure 3.5. Example images demonstrate the performance of neural network face detector.

stages: the first stage is to apply a set of neural network-based filters to an image and the second stage is to combine the outputs using an arbitrator.

A pyramid of images is generated from the original image using scaling steps of 1.2. Each 20 × 20 pixel window of each level of the pyramid passes through several processing stages. First, the window is preprocessed using histogram equalization, and given to a router network. The rotation angle returned by the router is then used to rotate the window with the potential face to an upright position. Finally, the de-rotated window is preprocessed and passed to one or more detector networks which will decide whether or not the window contains a face.

The first stage is to apply the route network. This network assumes the input window contains a face, and is trained to estimate its orientation. The inputs to the network are the intensity values in a 20 × 20 pixel window of the image. The output angle of rotation is represented by an array of six output units, in which each unit i represents an angle of $10i$ (degree). To reflect the angle θ of the face, each output is trained to have a value of $\cos(\theta - 10i)$. Each output can be interpreted as a weight for a vector in the direction indicated by the output number i. The training examples are generated from a set of manually labeled images containing 1048 faces. The eyes, tip of the nose, and the corners and centre of the mouth in each face are labeled. The labeled faces are then aligned to one another using an iterative process. Firstly, the average location of each labeled feature over the entire training set. Each face is then aligned with the average feature locations, computing the rotation, translation and scaling that minimizes the distances between the corresponding features. The best alignment can be sought using an overconstrained linear system. The architecture of the router network includes three layers: an input layer of 400 units, a hidden layer of 15 units, and an output layer of 36 units.

After the router network has been applied to a window of the input, the window is de-rotated to make any face that may present upright. Then the topic changes to decide whether or not the window contains an upright face. A linear function is fitted; the linear function approximates the overall brightness of each part of the window and can be subtracted to compensate for a variety of lighting conditions. Secondly, histogram equalization is performed which expands the range of intensities in the window. The detector networks are trained to produce an output of $+1$ if a face is present and -1 otherwise.

The detectors have two sets of training examples: face images and non-face images. Unlike face recognition, where the classes to be discriminated are different faces, the two classes to be separated in face detection are "images with faces" and "images without any face."

A post-processing heuristic is employed to rectify the inconsistencies where there are different orientations at adjacent pixel locations. Each face detection consists of a 4-D space where the dimensions are the x and y positions of the centre of the face, the level in the image pyramid at which the face was detected, and the angle of the face with increments of $10°$. For each detection, the number of detections within four units along each dimension (4 pixels, 4 pyramid levels, or $40°$) is available. This number can be interpreted as a confidence measure and a threshold is applied.

Although this heuristic has been found to be effective at eliminating false detections, a single detection network still produces an unacceptable high false detection rate. To further reduce the number of false detections, two independently trained detector networks will be arbitrated. Each network is given the same set of positive examples, but starts with different randomly set initial weights. To use the outputs of these two networks, the post-processing heuristics mentioned above are applied to the outputs of each network, and then the detections from these two networks are combined in a logic and style. The specific preprocessing thresholds used in the experiments are empirical.

Figure 3.6 shows some example images with detected faces within individual images. Although all the faces have been detected, there are significant errors in the localization of faces. This is possibly due to the lighting condition and pose changes that affect the estimation.

3.3.6 *Evaluation Work*

To evaluate the performance of the previously summarized face detectors, we use the VALID database that is the courtesy of

Figure 3.6. Illustrations of the performance of Gabor-based neural network face detector.

University College Dublin of Ireland (http://ee.ucd.ie/~prag/). This database consists of five recording sessions of 106 subjects over a period of one month. Among the 106 subjects, 77 male and 29 female subjects were employed in different poses and lighting conditions. Thirty-eight subjects were with spectacles and 8 were with facial hair. The entire database was recorded using a Canon 3CCD XM1 PAL digital video camcorder, which has a sensor resolution of 3.2k pixels and records in the PAL DV propriety format. The image frames come up with a pixel resolution of 576×720 and pixel depth of 24 bits.

There are a total of 340 frontal images to be processed in this evaluation. The computer comprises Intel® Xeon® CPU at 2.4 GHz with a RAM of 4 GB. The evaluation targets can be categorized into three folds: (1) detection accuracy, (2) detection efficiency, and (3) further analysis. The algorithms included in this evaluation contain: AdaBoost [9], neural network (NN) [26], Gabor neural network (GNN) [27], SNoW [28], and rank-deficient (RD) based [29]. In the evaluation of detection accuracy, we utilize the following equations:

$$\text{Precision} = tp/(tp + fp)$$
$$\text{Recall} = tp/(tp + fn)$$

where tp is true positive, fp is false positive, and fn is false negative.

First of all, Table 3.1 shows the statistics of comparing different face detection algorithms. Among them, the SNoW algorithm has the best recalls and precision while the GNN approach has the worst performance. In the meantime, it also reveals that SNoW missed the least number of missed face detections.

Secondly, taking a look at Table 3.2, we observe that GNN takes the most computational efforts while AdaBoost is the fastest approach to obtain the detection results. The complexity behind GNN is due to the computation of Gabor feature extraction.

Table 3.1. Statistics of face detection: accuracy and missed detections (R = recall, P = precision)

Algorithms	Accuracy		Missed detections
	R	P	
AdaBoost	84.3	91.7	11
NN	89.6	93.1	9
GNN	71.4	82.0	34
SNoW	97.8	99.2	5
RD	74.7	84.5	27

Table 3.2. Computational costs of different face detectors (per image)

Algorithms	Time (s)	Ratio (%)
AdaBoost	0.07	0.06
NN	0.41	0.37
GNN	108.20	98.88
SNoW	0.63	0.58
RD	0.12	0.11

Figure 3.7. Image examples and performance using Gabor-based neural network.

To further analyze the performance of the best face detector SNoW, we here use more example images. Figure 3.7 illustrates a few examples where the SNoW face detector fails to obtain correct detection. The first two examples show that lengthy necks may have side-effects on the final performance. The last example denotes that the performance of this face detector needs to be improved in the presence of background clutters and poor illuminations.

We now look at the case of neural network-based face detection. Figure 3.8 demonstrates some failure examples using the neural net-

Figure 3.8. Example images demonstrate the failure of the SNoW face detector.

Figure 3.9. Example images demonstrate the failure of neural network face detector.

work approach. This is probably due to the neck areas that possess the image components, which bias the appearance estimation in the model.

3.4 Classical Face Recognition Algorithms

3.4.1 *Eigenface*

Eigenface is a set of eigenvectors used for human face recognition. This approach was originally developed by Turk and Pentland [45]. The eigenvectors can be derived from the covariance matrix of the probability distribution of the high-dimensional vector space of possible faces of people. Let a face image $I(x, y)$ be a two-dimensional $N \times N$ array of intensity values. An image can also be treated as a vector of dimension N^2. An image is then mapped to this huge vector space. Principal component analysis is then used to find the vectors that most fits the distribution of the face image within this space. Examples of face images are illustrated in Fig. 3.9.

Let the training set of the face images be $T_1, T_2, T_3, \ldots, T_M$. The mean of this training data set is required in order to calculate the covariance matrix or eigenvectors. The average face is calculated as $\Psi = (1/M) \sum_1^M T_i$. Each image in the data set has dissimilarity to the average face expressed by the vector $\Phi = T_i - \Psi$. The covariance matrix is

$$C = (1/M) \sum_1^M \phi_1 \phi_1^T = AA^1, \tag{3.20}$$

where $A = [\phi_1, \phi_1, \ldots, \phi_M]$. The matrix C is a N^2 by N^2 matrix, and will generate N^2 eigenvectors and eigenvalues. It is very difficult to

Figure 3.10. Example images of face images in ORL database.

Figure 3.11. Eigenfaces of the faces shown on Fig. 3.10.

achieve calculation on an image of size 256×256 or even less due to the computational efforts.

A computationally feasible method is to compute the eigenvectors instead. If the number of images in the training set is less than the number of pixels in an image (i.e., $M < N^2$), then we can solve an $M \times M$ matrix instead of solving a N^2 by N^2 matrix. Consider the covariance matrix as $A^T A$ instead of AA^T. Now the eigenvector v_i can be calculated as follows,

$$AA^T v_i = \mu_i A v_i, \tag{3.21}$$

where μ is the eigenvalue. Here the size of covariance matrix is $M \times M$. We then have m eigenvectors instead of N^2. Multiplying Eq. (3.21) by A, we have

$$AA^T A v_i = \mu_i A v_i. \tag{3.22}$$

The right-hand side of the above equation brings us M eigenfaces of N^2 by 1. Such a process leads to an image space of dimensionality M.

Since an approximate reconstruction of the face is intended, we can reduce the dimensionality to M' instead of M. This is performed by selecting M' eigenfaces, which have the largest associated eigenvalues. These eigenfaces now span an M'-dimensional subspace instead of N^2.

A new image T is transformed into its eigenface components (projected into the "face space") by the following operation:

$$w_k = \mu_k^T (T - \psi) \tag{3.23}$$

where $k = 1, 2, \ldots, M'$. The weights obtained as above constitute a vector $\Omega^T = [w_1, w_2, w_3, \ldots, w_M]$ that describes the contribution of each eigenface in representing the input face image. This vector can be used in a standard classification algorithm to explore the best shot in the database that describes the income face image. The face class in the database is formulated by averaging the weight vectors for the images of one individual. In some cases, subjects may have spectacles. In this situation, classification must be correctly made. The Euclidean distance of the weight vector of the new image from the face class weight vector can be calculated as follows,

$$\epsilon_k = ||\Omega - \Omega_k|| \tag{3.24}$$

where Ω_k is a vector representing the kth face class. Euclidean distance formula can be found in [45]. The face is classified as belonging to class k when the distance ϵ_k is below some threshold value $\theta\varepsilon$. Otherwise the face is classified as unknown. Also it can be found whether an image is a face image or not by simply finding the squared distance between the mean adjusted input image and its projection onto the face space.

$$\epsilon^2 = ||\phi - \phi_f|| \tag{3.25}$$

where ϕ_i is the face space and $\Phi = T_i - \Psi$ is the mean adjusted input. Using this criterion, we can classify the image as known face image, unknown face image, and not a face image.

3.4.2 *Fisherface*

Fisherface works in a combinatorial scheme, where one performs dimensionality reduction using linear projection and then applies Fisher's Linear Discriminant (FLD) [49] for classification in the reduced feature space. This approach intends to find an optimal projection where the ration of the between-class scatter and the within-class scatter is maximized [47]. Let the between-class scatter matrix be

$$S_B + \sum N_i(\mu_i - \mu)(\mu_i - \mu)^T \tag{3.26}$$

and the within-class scatter matrix is defined as

$$S_w = \sum_{i=1}^{c} \sum_{X_k \in X,} (X_k - \mu_i)(X_k - \mu_i)^T \tag{3.27}$$

where μ_i is the mean image of class X_i, and N_i is the sample number in class X_i. If S_W is nonsingular, the optimal projection W_o will be the one with orthonormal columns that satisfy the following equation,

$$W_0 = \arg\max_W \frac{|W^T S_B W|}{|W_T S_W W|} = [W_1, \ldots, W] \qquad (3.28)$$

where W_i $(i = 1, 2, \ldots, m)$ is a set of generalized eigenvectors of S_B and S_W corresponding to the m largest eigenvalues λ_i, equivalently,

$$S_B W_i - \lambda_i S_W W_i, i = 1, 2, \ldots, m. \qquad (3.29)$$

In real cases of face recognition, the within-class matrix SW is normally singular. This is due to the fact that rank of SW is at most $N - c$, and the number of images in the learning set N is smaller than that of image pixels. To tackle this problem, Fisherfaces uses PCA to reduce the dimension of the feature space to $N - c$, and then employs a standard FLD scheme to reduce the dimension to $c - 1$. Therefore, the optimal projection matrix is

$$W_0^T = W_{FLD}^T W_{PCA}^T \qquad (3.30)$$

where

$$W_{PCA} = \arg\max_W |W^T S_T W|$$
$$W_{FLD} = \arg\max_W \frac{|W^T W_{PCA}^T S_B W_{PCA} W|}{|W^T W_{PCA}^T S_W W_{PCA} W|} \qquad (3.31)$$

W_{PCA} is optimized over $[n, (N - c)]$ matrices with orthonormal columns while W_{FLD} is optimized over $[(N - c), m]$ matrices with orthonormal columns. Figure 3.11 illustrates the exemplar outcomes of Fisherface.

Figure 3.12. Fisherfaces of the faces shown on Fig. 3.10.

3.4.3 *Tensorface*

Let us start with the problem of linear dimensionality reduction. One of the common approaches is the use of Laplacian eigenmap with the objective function as follows:

$$\min \sum (f(x_i) - f(x_j))^2 S_{ij} \tag{3.32}$$

where S denotes the similarity matrix and x is the functional variables, e.g., image vectors.

Let the face data set be $\mathbf{X}_1, \ldots, \mathbf{X}_m$ in the space $R^{n_1} \oplus R^{n_2}$. If a face image $\mathbf{X}$ matches its template $\mathbf{Y}$ in the database, then we can decompose $\mathbf{Y}$ into the multiplication of $\mathbf{U}$, $\mathbf{V}$, and $\mathbf{X}$, where $\mathbf{U}$ and $\mathbf{V}$ have size $n_1 \times l_1$ and $n_2 \times l_2$, respectively. In fact, we shall have $\mathbf{Y}_i = \mathbf{U}^T \mathbf{X}_i \mathbf{V}$.

Given m data points from the face submanifold $\mathbf{M} \in R^{n_1} \oplus R^{n_2}$, we intend to find a nearest graph $\mathbf{G}$ to simulate the geometry of $\mathbf{M}$. The similarity matrix S can be

$$if \|x_i - x_j\| \le \eta, \tag{3.33}$$

where c is a constant and $\| \cdot \|$ is the Frobenius form.

Let D be a diagonal matrix with $D_u = \sum_i S_{i,j}$. Then we can have the following representation:

$$\left(\sum_i \|U^T X_i V - U^T X_i V\|^2 S_{ij} \right) /2 = tr \left(U^T (D_V - S_V) U \right) \tag{3.34}$$

where

$$D_v = \sum_i D_u X_i^T V V^T X_i^T$$

and

$S_v = \sum_i S_{ii} X_i^T V V^T X_j^T$. Similarly, we have

$$\left(\sum_i \|U^T X_i V - U^T X_i V\|^2 S_{ii} \right) /2 = tr \left(V^T (D_U - S_U) V \right) \tag{3.35}$$

where

$$D_U \sum_i D_{ii} X_i^T U U^T X_i^T \tag{3.36}$$

and

$$S_U = \sum_i S_{ii} X_i^T U U^T X_i^T \tag{3.37}$$

To find an optimal face match, we have to minimize $tr(V^T(D_v - S_v)V)$ together with $tr(V^T(D_U - S_U)V)$.

Large global variance on the manifold may help the discrimination of different data sets. As a result, during the face recognition amplify the similarity distance in the feature space. This leads to the following relationship:

$$\text{var}(Y) = \sum_i ||Y_i||^2 D_i - tr(V^T D_U V) \qquad (3.38)$$

Assuming a zero mean distribution, we also have another similar form as follows:

$$\text{var}(Y) = \sum_i tr(Y Y_i^T) D_{ii} = tr(U^T D_V U) \qquad (3.39)$$

Through the analysis above, a matched face in the database is subject to the following constraint

$$\left\{ \min UV \left(\frac{tr(U^T(D_v - S_v)U)}{tr(U^T D_v U)} \right) \min UV \left(\frac{tr(V^T(D_U - S_U)V)}{tr(V^T D_U V)} \right) \right.$$

$$(3.40)$$

A simpler solution to the optimization problem has been found as follows. Firstly, U is fixed; V can be computed by solving a generalized eigenvector problem:

$$(D_U - S_U)\hat{V} = \lambda D_U \hat{V} \qquad (3.41)$$

Once V is available, we then update U by this eigenvector process: d, V can be computed by solving a generalized eigenvector problem,

$$(D_U - S_V)\hat{U} = \lambda D_V \hat{U} \qquad (3.42)$$

Repeating this procedure, we eventually have an appropriate solution. Note that initially U is set to be identity matrix. Figure 3.12 shows the Tensorface examples.

Finally, these reported face recognition algorithms are compared to have statistics in Table 3.3. It shows that for this database Tensorface has the best performance in terms of accuracy and efficiency.

Figure 3.13. Tensorfaces of the faces shown on Fig. 3.10.

Table 3.3. Statistics of different face recognition algorithms for PIE database

Algorithms	Time (s)	Errors (%)
Eigenface	0.83	66.8
Fisherface	1.62	32.6
Tensorface	0.61	28.9

3.5 Conclusions and Outlook

In this chapter, we review the current state-of-the-art technology in face detection and recognition. Afterwards, we mainly summarize the established face detection/recognition algorithms. The performance of these algorithms has been compared against each other for frontal face databases.

The comparison results show that SNoW has the best performance in terms of face detection accuracy. AdaBoost holds a good compromise of face detection accuracy and efficiency. Gabor neural network provides the worst performance in accuracy and efficiency. This is possibly due to the less capability of Gabor feature extraction. On the other hand, Tensorface algorithm has the best performance in the used database.

In the future, the research stream is still to be directed towards the improvements of accuracy while reducing computational complexity. Such a target is driven by the fact that a real time implementation is necessary in the facial assurance system.

Acknowledgments

This work was initiated when the first author worked in the School of Engineering and Design, Brunel University, United Kingdom.

References

1. Yang, M.-H., Kriegman, D. J., and Ahuja, N. (2002) *IEEE Transactions Pattern Analysis and Machine Intelligence* **24**, 34–58.

2. Zhao, W., Chellappa, R., Phillips, P. J., and Rosenfeld, A. (2003) *ACM Computing Surveys* **35**, 399–458.

3. Yang, G. and Huang, T. S. (1994) *Pattern Recognition* **27**, 53–63.

4. Kotropoulos, C. and Pitas, I. (1997) *Proceedings of the International Conference Acoustics, Speech and Signal Proceessing* 4.

5. Yow, K. C. and Cipolla, R. (1997) *Image and Vision Computing* **15**, 713–735.

6. Jin, Z., Lou, Z., Yang, J., and Shun, Q. (2007) *Neurocomputing* **70**, 794–800.

7. Saber, E. and Tekalp, A. M. (1998) *Pattern Recognition Letters* **19**, 669–680.

8. Dai, Y. and Nakano, Y. (1996) *Pattern Recognition* **29**, 1007–1017.

9. Viola, P. and Jones, M. (2001) *Proceedings of IEEE Conference on Computer Vision and Pattern Recognition*.

10. Liu, C. (2003) *IEEE Transactions Pattern Analysis and Machine Intelligence* **25**, 725–740.

11. Wu, J. and Zhou, Z.-H. (2003) *Pattern Recognition*, 1175–1186.

12. Sung, K.-K. and Poggio, T. (1998) *IEEE Transactions PAMI* **20**, 39–51.

13. Yuille, A. Hallinan, P., and Cohen, C. (1992) *International Journal of Computers* **8**, 99–111.

14. Hsu, R.-L., Abdel-Mottaleb, M., and Jain, A. K. (2002) *IEEE Transactions PAMI* **24**, 1010–1025.

15. G. Kukharev and A. Nowosielski, *Machine Graphics & Vision* **13**, 377–399, (2004).

16. Wu, H., Chen, Q., and Yachida, M. (1999) *IEEE Transactions PAMI* **21**, 557–563.

17. Sao, A. K. and Yeqnanarayana, B. (2007) *IEEE Transactions Information Forensics and Security* **2**, 636–641.

18. Li, S. Z. and Zhang, Z. (2004) *IEEE Transactions PAMI* **26**, 572–581.

19. Phimoltarest, S., Lursinsap, C., and Chamnongthai, K. (2007) *Image and Vision Computing* **25**, 741–753.

20. Li, S. Z., Gu, L., Scholkorf, B., and Zhang, H.-J. (2001) *International Conference on Computer Vision*.

21. Robinson, J. A. (2005) *British Machine Vision Conference*.

22. Waring, C. A., and Liu, X. (2005) *IEEE Transactions SMC, Part B*, **35**, 467–476.

23. Traver, V. J., Bernardino, A., Moreno, P. and Santos-Victor, J. (2004) *Proceedings of the International Conference on Image Analysis and Recognition*.

24. Sebe, N., Cohen, I., Huang, T. S., and Gevers, T. (2005) *IEEE Conference on Computer Vision and Pattern Recognition.*

25. Hadid, A., Pietikainen, M., and Ahonen, T. (2005) *IEEE Conference on Computer Vision and Pattern Recognition.*

26. Rowley, H. A., Baluja, S., and Kanade, T. (1996) *IEEE Conference on Computer Vision and Pattern Recognition.*

27. Sahoolizadeh, H., Sarikhanimoghadam, D., and Dehghani, H. (2008) *World Academy of Science, Engineering and Technology*, 45.

28. Roth, D., Yang, M.-H., and Ahuja, N. (2000) *Advanced in Neural Information Processing Systems*, 855–861.

29. Kienzle, W., Bakir, G., Franz, M., and Scholkopf, B. (2005) *Advanced in Neural Information Processing Systems*, 673–680.

30. Fleuret, F. and Geman, D. (2001) *International Journal of Computer Vision* **41**, 85–107.

31. Papageorgiou, C., Oren, M., and Poggio, T. (1998) *International Conference on Computer Vision* 555–562.

32. Freund, Y. and Schapire, R. E. (1995) *Computational Learning Theory: Eurocolt'95*, 23–37.

33. Quinlan, J. (1986) *Machine Learning* **1**, 81–106.

34. Blum, A. (1992) *Machine Learning* **9**, 373–386.

35. Kivinen, J. and Warmuth, M. K. (1995) *Proceedings of the Annual ACM Symposium on the Theory of Computing.*

36. Burges, C. J. C. (1996) *Proceedings of International Conference on Machine Learn* 71–77.

37. Duc, B., Fischer, S., and Bigun, J. (1999) *IEEE Transactions Image Processing* 504–516.

38. Jones, J. and Palmer, L. (1987) *Journal of Neurophysiology*, 1233–1258.

39. Lades, M., Vorbruggen, J. C., Buhmann, J., Lange, J., von der Malsburg, C., Wurtz, R. P., and Konen, W. (1993) *IEEE Transactions On Comput.* 300–311.

40. Beymer, D. (1993) *Technical Report AIM-1461*, MIT AI Laboratory.

41. Pentland, A., Moghaddam, B., and Starner, T. (1994) *Proceedings of theIEEE Conferenceon Computer Visionand Pattern Recognition* 84–91.

42. Cootes, T., Wheeler, G., Walker, K., and Taylor, C. (2002) *Image and Vision Computing* **20**, 657–664.

43. Lanitis, A., Taylor, C., and Cootes, T. (1997) *IEEE Transactions Pattern Analysis and Machine Intelligence* **19**(7), 743–775.

44. Romdhani, S., Gong, S., and Psarrou, A. (1999) *Proceedingsof 10th British Machine Vision Conference* 483–492.

45. Turk, M. and Pentland, A. (1991) *Journal of Cognitive Neuroscience* **3**(1), 71–86.

46. Draper, B., Baek, K., Bartlett, M., and Beveridge, J. (2003) *Computer Vision and Image Understanding* **91**(1–2), 115–137.

47. Belhumeur, P., Hespanha, J., and Kriegman, D. (1996) *Proceeding of European Conference on Computer Vision* 45–58.

48. Vasilescu, M. and Terzopoulos, D. (2003) *Proceedings of Inernational Conferenceon Computer Vision and Pattern Recognition* 93–99.

49. Fisher, R. A. (1936) *Annals of Eugenics* **7**, 179–188.

Chapter 4

Iris Recognition

Robert W. Ives, Randy P. Broussard, Ryan N. Rakvic, and Steven B. Link

ECE and WSE Depts., U.S. Naval Academy,
Annapolis, MD 21402, USA
ives@usna.edu

The iris is the colored portion of the eye that lies between the pupil and the sclera (the white part of the eye). The fibrous patterns contained within the iris are randomly created and remain stable throughout life from an early age. The patterns contained in a person's left and right eyes are distinct from each other, and also distinct from any other person's eyes. Since the iris is very unique to an individual, it can serve to identify them with a high degree of confidence.

The science of iris recognition combines a number of fields of research: computer vision, pattern recognition, mathematics, statistics, and human factors. Compared with other distinctive features used for human identification such as face and fingerprints, iris patterns are more stable and reliable. Iris recognition systems are non-invasive to their users, but in current systems, they do require a cooperative subject.

Biometrics: From Fiction to Practice
Edited by Eliza Yingzi Du
Copyright © 2013 Pan Stanford Publishing Pte. Ltd.
ISBN 978-981-4310-88-8 (Hardcover), 978-981-4364-13-3 (eBook)
www.panstanford.com

4.1 Introduction

Figure 4.1 is an example of an iris image. The iris has color as a result of the amount of pigment (melanin) contained in the different regions of the iris. Specifically, the eye color is due to the amounts of eumelanin (brown/black melanins) and pheomelanin (red/yellow melanins). More of the eumelanin is found in brown-eyed people, and more of the pheomelanin is found in blue- and green-eyed people.

The function of the iris is to control the amount of light entering the eye by varying the size of the pupil opening. The iris contracts and expands, depending on the amount of light present. By regulating the size of the pupil, the iris varies the amount of light directed onto the retina. With more light directed toward the eye, the pupil contracts, so the iris enlarges. In a dark room, the pupil expands to let more light into the eye, so the iris is smaller. The pupil itself appears dark because of the absorbing pigments in the retina. The sclera, commonly referred to as the white part of the eye, surrounds the pupil and forms a part of the support structure for the eyeball [1].

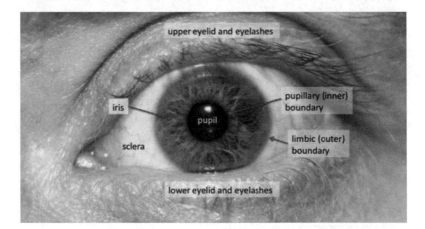

Figure 4.1. An example of an iris image. Notice that the pupil and the iris boundaries appear almost circular. If you look closely, you can see that the center of the pupil lies to the left of the center of the iris. See also Color Insert.

The patterns contained within the iris are created prior to birth, are random in nature, and it is postulated that as long as the eye suffers no trauma or disease, the patterns remain stable throughout life [2]. The randomness of the patterns and the stability over a lifetime make the iris a good basis for human identification.

4.2 Iris Recognition Algorithms

The concept of using the iris for identification dates back to the late 1980s, when ophthalmologists first noted from clinical experience that every iris had a highly detailed, unique texture that remained stable after age one. In 1987, Flom and Safir were awarded a patent that described methods and a system for iris recognition based on iris features seen under visible light [2, 3]. They are the first to propose the use of iris as a means for human identification. Their technique required adjustments to the intensity of the light that is applied to the eye until the pupil reached a predetermined size. The iris was then compared with stored image information from an eye with the same pupil size. The requirement of needing the same pupil size when comparing irises made implementation of their iris recognition system challenging to implement.

In 1994, Dr. John Daugman was awarded a patent for a human identification system based on the information contained within the iris [4, 5]. His development was the first automatic iris recognition system. In his method (called iris2pi), Daugman used Gabor wavelets to extract the distinctive information contained within the iris, and transform iris images into "iris codes." His method proved to take advantage of the uniqueness of the iris in an efficient manner, and is now the predominant algorithm used in commercial iris recognition systems worldwide.

The general steps to iris recognition are shown in the block diagram in Fig. 4.2. The process of iris recognition includes: image acquisition, preprocessing, feature extraction, template generation, and matching/identification. Identification is achieved by comparing two templates: known iris templates from an enrollment database and the template of an unknown iris image. The steps are described in the following sections.

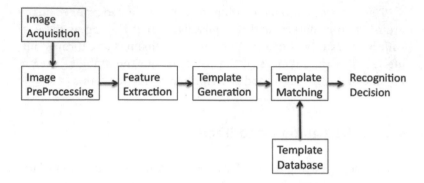

Figure 4.2. The general algorithmic steps in iris recognition.

4.2.1 *Image Acquisition*

Image acquisition involves capturing a digital image of a human iris. In commercial systems used for secure access, images are collected from an input live video stream. In research applications, images can be individually collected from a camera and stored for later use as part of an iris database. There are a number of iris databases that have been made available for research use, and are available over the Internet. These images are typically collected with the subject's head pointed toward the camera and the eye looking into the camera, from a distance of approximately 12 inches from eyeball to camera. Two areas of current research in iris recognition involve (1) recognition if the subject's head and/or eye is not pointed toward the camera (called "off-axis," see Section 4.4.1) and (2) iris recognition at greater distances between the eye and the camera (see Section 4.4.2).

In most commercial systems, the images are collected under near-infrared (NIR) illumination, using light with a wavelength somewhere between 700 nm and 900 nm. NIR lighting is commonly used since it brings out the distinctive features of the iris which may not be so apparent under visual light. This is particularly true for individuals with very dark-colored irises, brown for example. There is current research into the use of other wavelengths of light for iris recognition, and that will be discussed more in Section 4.4.3. An NIR iris image of the eye in Fig. 4.1 is shown in Fig. 4.3.

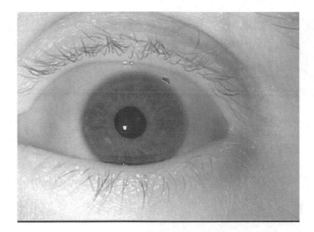

Figure 4.3. The same iris as in Fig. 4.1, but captured here under NIR illumination.

4.2.2 *Preprocessing*

The preprocessing step primarily involves segmentation of the iris from the remainder of the image. This step begins by locating the boundaries of the iris. In particular, it determines the inner (pupillary) boundary of the iris, separating the iris and the pupil, and also determines the outer (limbic) boundary of the iris, which separates the iris from the sclera. In many iris recognition algorithms, these boundaries are assumed to be circular, as that is the simplest approach. In fact, the pupil and iris are usually not quite circular, and in many cases are very noncircular.

There are different approaches to finding the inner and outer boundaries. For example, assuming a circular model for the pupil and iris can allow circular edge detection (e.g., Hough transform) to locate these boundaries. Once the center and radius of each of these circles are determined, the iris image can be transformed into polar coordinates. Here, the relatively donut-shaped iris region of the image is "unwrapped" into a rectangular grid. Each row of the unwrapped image represents an annulus around the pupil; the top row is the annulus closest to the pupil's center, and the bottom one is the farthest from the pupil. Each column in the unwrapped image represents an angular wedge from the pupil's center outwards at a

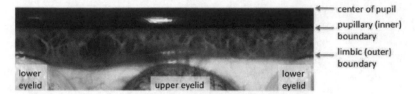

Figure 4.4. The unwrapped iris image from Fig. 4.1 now in polar coordinates. Here, the unwrapping process used the center of the pupil as the reference location. Since this pupil is almost circular, the inner boundary of the iris is now almost horizontal. Since the center of the iris is offset from the center of the pupil, the outer boundary is not horizontal. See also Color Insert.

given angle with a fixed angular width. Unwrapping the iris to polar coordinates allows common digital image processing techniques to be applied to the image for further analysis. Figure 4.4 is an example of an iris image in polar coordinates. This image is unwrapped to polar coordinates using the center of the pupil as the point of reference. Note that this figure shows more than just the iris region of the image to give a better example of the unwrapping process. In an iris recognition algorithm, only the region between the pupil and the outer boundary of the iris are unwrapped.

Once the image is unwrapped, additional segmentation can be applied to detect noise in the iris, such as the presence of glare from the illumination source and the detection of eyelids and eyelashes which may cover portions of the iris. It is important for the sake of accuracy that their presence be detected, since when comparing two irises, it is desired that only the information within the iris be considered.

Another consideration in the preprocessing stage is that the size of the same iris taken at different times may be variable in the image as a result of changes in the camera-to-eye distance, the amount and type of illumination, and due to the natural dilation of the eye even in constant illumination (called *hippus*). These factors will change the distance between the inner and outer boundaries of the iris. Iris preprocessing usually involves a linear normalization of the distance between the inner and outer boundaries of the iris, called the "rubber sheet" model.

4.2.3 *Feature Extraction*

Feature extraction involves processing an iris image to find and exploit the relevant (distinctive) information that can be used to tell one iris from another. In the Daugman iris2pi method, the unwrapped (polar) image is filtered with two-dimensional complex-valued Gabor wavelets, and the phase of the filtered result is used as the features of the iris. Another approach to feature extraction is found in the Ridge-Energy-Direction (RED) algorithm [6], where the unwrapped iris is processed with contrast-limited adaptive histogram equalization (CLAHE), and then subjected to a number of filters that are sensitive to different orientations (directions) of ridges within the iris. CLAHE is performed to allow the ridges to stand out more. For each pixel in the unwrapped iris, the predominant ridge direction at each pixel location is recorded, if the ridge was strong enough. Here, the ridge directions are the features extracted.

4.2.4 *Template Generation*

Template generation is the processing of the feature information so as to create a viable representation of the iris that can be compared to other irises. In the Daugman iris2pi method, the Gabor wavelet-filtered polar image is transformed into an 8-row by 256-column image (template), where each pixel in the template represents the quadrant of the phase from the Gabor wavelet-filtered iris [4]. Using four quadrants of phase means that each pixel in the template is quantized into 2 bits. In the iris2pi algorithm, the template is referred to as the iris code. In the RED algorithm, each pixel in the template represents the identity of the directional filter that produced the strongest output at that location in the unwrapped image. If only two directions are used to make the template, then each direction is represented by a single bit. If four directions are used, then each direction is represented by two bits, etc.

In addition, there can be certain regions of the iris image that are within the boundaries of the iris but are not actually part of the iris. This includes eyelids, eyelashes, and glare, and is commonly referred to as noise. In the RED algorithm, if a directional ridge is not strong enough at any location in the unwrapped iris image, this is considered noise. In order that noise is not considered in the identification process, a binary mask is created that distinguishes between pixels that should be compared and those that should not. The representation of an iris, then, has two parts: (1) the iris template determined from the feature extraction process and (2) a mask that indicates the regions of the template that provide a valid comparison in the identification process. An overview of the template generation process for the RED algorithm is shown in Fig. 4.5.

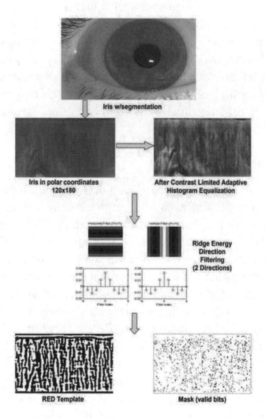

Figure 4.5. An overview of the template generation process in the RED algorithm. Here, feature extraction is accomplished using only two directional filters, vertical and horizontally oriented, resulting in a binary iris template. The two filters are displayed (looking down, and with a cutaway view). In addition, the mask is used to identify noise, such as locations where no ridges were present.

4.2.5 *Template Matching*

Template matching compares two representations of irises to determine if they are from the same iris or not. As mentioned in Section 4.2.4, a template and a mask usually represent the iris. In the iris2pi algorithm, the matching metric used is the fractional Hamming distance. The fractional Hamming distance (also called the raw Hamming distance, HD) is computed in the following equation:

$$HD = \frac{\|(\text{template A} \otimes \text{template B}) \cap \text{mask A} \cap \text{mask B}\|}{\|\text{mask A} \cap \text{mask B}\|}. \qquad (4.1)$$

In Eq. (4.1), we compare two templates, A and B. The $\otimes$ symbol represents binary EXCLUSIVE OR, and the $\cap$ symbol binary AND. The $\| \cdot \|$ symbol represents a summation of 1-bits within its argument. Overall, the numerator counts the number of bits in the iris template that do not match, but the masks ensure that only valid bits are compared (i.e., noise is not included). The denominator counts the number of bits that were compared. The value of HD then is the fraction of valid bits that do not match between two iris images. A fractional HD of 0.0 indicates that all valid bits in both irises are the same, while a fractional HD of 1.0 indicates that all of the bits in one template are the exact opposite of all the valid bits in the other template.

Another matching metric used in iris systems is the modified fractional Hamming distance (HD'). This metric takes into account the number of valid bits in the comparison. For example, a low fractional Hamming distance (i.e., a good match) computed using only 10 valid bits is likely not as accurate as a low fractional Hamming distance based on a comparison of 1000 valid bits.

$$HD' = 0.5 - (0.5 - HD)\sqrt{\frac{N}{911}}. \qquad (4.2)$$

In Eq. (4.2), N is the total number of bits compared. The equation was empirically determined to adjust the statistics of the modified HD score distribution to allow a stable decision rule. This equation is the basis of matching in the iris2pi algorithm, but many other algorithms also use fractional Hamming distance for matching two irises.

4.2.6 *Performance*

How "close" do two iris images have to be before they are called a match? Placing a threshold on the matching metric forces a decision on whether two iris images are of the same eye or not, and so determines performance in iris recognition systems. Algorithm performance can be determined by applying the algorithm to a database of iris images. Here, templates are created for each image in the database, and every template is compared against every other template. When the true identity of each template is known a priori, then it is known whether each comparison involves same-eye templates (a genuine match) or different-eye templates (an imposter match). Hamming distance values can be collected for all of the same-eye matches and for all of the different-eye matches separately, and a histogram created for each resulting distribution of HD scores. Dividing the histogram of the same-eye comparisons by the total number of same-eye comparisons leads to the probability mass function (PMF) of the genuine distribution, and dividing the histogram of the different-eye comparisons by the total number of different eye-comparisons generates the PMF of the imposter distribution. These two curves can be plotted against HD as shown in Fig. 4.6.

Comparisons of the same eye should result in lower HD scores, since one expects there to be fewer bits in disagreement between the two templates of the same eye. Also, comparisons of different eyes should result in higher HD scores because one expects more of the bits to be in disagreement. This is evidenced by the curves in Fig. 4.6. One thing to note is that the imposter distribution does not have a mean value of 0.5, which might be expected. The mean of the imposter distribution is actually lower, because in the matching process any relative rotation of the two eyes in the images compared is accounted for. Since the left and right edges of the unwrapped iris are actually connected, when comparing the templates, we can shift one of the templates left and right and compute the HD at each shift. We then use the lowest HD from all of the shifts as the score for this match. In this way, if comparing two images of the same eye and one of the images involved a tilt of the head, we have a better chance of making a correct identity decision. PMF curves can be used to gage how well a system will do in determining identity.

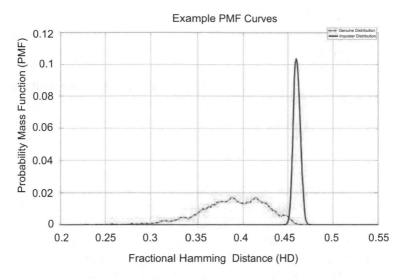

Figure 4.6. The general shape of probability mass function (PMF) curves for a collection of same-eye (genuine) and different-eye (imposter) matches.

In a recognition system, there are two types of correct decisions and two types of incorrect decisions. System performance is typically described in terms of the incorrect decisions. Performance can be measured in terms of false acceptance rate (FAR) and false reject rate (FRR). The FAR is the rate at which two irises are decided to be from the same eye when they are in fact not from the same eye; and FRR is the rate at which two irises are decided to be not from the same eye when in fact they are. These two measures are calculated as follows.

$$\text{FAR} = \frac{\text{\# of false acceptances}}{\text{Total \# of comparisons of different-eye templates}}. \quad (4.3)$$

$$\text{FRR} = \frac{\text{\# of false rejections}}{\text{Total \# of comparisons of same-eye templates}}. \quad (4.4)$$

Consider choosing a threshold value of HD to make an identity decision; visualize this with a vertical line applied to Fig. 4.6 that can be shifted left or right. The area under the imposter PMF curve that lies to the left of the threshold represents the FAR, and the area under the genuine PMF curve that lies to the right of the threshold represents the FRR. As the threshold used in the matching is adjusted higher or lower (vertical line moved left or right), the number of false acceptances (and the FAR) and false rejections (and the FRR) changes.

Ideally, there would be a distinct separation between the two PMF curves, so that a threshold may be chosen that results in no false accepts and no false rejects. In real systems, there is usually some overlap between the two distributions (as in Fig. 4.6) such that some errors are expected. The goal of algorithm developers is to create a system that will improve performance by either (1) moving the PMF curves farther apart (for iris systems, we desire to move the genuine distribution more to the left) or (2) making the PMF curves more compact to minimize overlap between the distributions. Both of these goals will result in fewer identification errors.

Another display of system performance is found in the receiver operating characteristic (ROC) curve, which is a plot of FRR vs. FAR. An example can be seen in Fig. 4.7. Using a plot like this, we can estimate what the FRR would be for any desired FAR, and vice-versa. Also, we can determine the system's equal error rate point, where FRR = FAR. Together, Figs. 4.6 and 4.7 can help determine the system

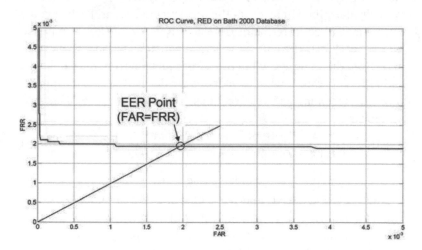

Figure 4.7. An example of an ROC curve. This curve was derived by applying the RED algorithm to the University of Bath 2000 image iris database [7]. From this curve, we see that the EER is equal to approximately 1.9×10^{-3}.

operation point, which is based on the threshold on HD chosen for identification.

4.3 Some Applications of Iris Recognition

Like any young technological product, iris recognition systems have been drastically evolving, driven both by consumer demands and technological improvements. A differentiating factor amongst iris recognition systems today is the variance in the form factor. Current iris recognition systems vary in terms of size, weight, focal distance, and hardware and software portability. The advancement of technology has dramatically impacted iris recognition systems, providing the opportunity to create smaller, more portable au-tonomous systems. However, the need for larger, more powerful traditional systems still exists. For example, in an airport setting where space and power are not limitations, the primary objective is having the most secure system possible. The current deployment of iris recognition systems ranges from government to commercial to even private use. We now give a brief overview of different form factors of iris recognition systems while giving specific examples in each domain.

4.3.1 *PC-Tethered Systems*

A very popular form factor for iris recognition devices is tethered to a PC in order to restrict or grant access to a computer or computer's applications. The Panasonic Authenticam™ DT120 is an iris recognition system that is lightweight and compact. It is designed to work with a host PC, preventing unauthorized access using what is called Private ID™ recognition software. Another PC-based iris recognition system is the Jiris JPC1000 (shown in Fig. 4.8).

4.3.2 *Wall-Mount Systems*

Another popular form of iris recognition systems is to provide door access, and hence most of these systems are mounted on a wall. The IRISPASS-M [8] (see Fig. 4.9) recognizes at approximately 1–2 feet

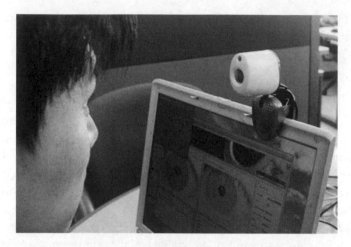

Figure 4.8. An example of the JIRIS1000 (from http://www.engadget. com/2006/03/06/jiris-jpc1000-brings-iris-scanning-home/).

Figure 4.9. An example of the IRISPASS-M (from http://www.oki.com/ jp/FSC/iris/en/m_features.html).

while examining at a height of 57–78 inches, and the system weighs 11 lbs. The interface is intuitive as it provides voice guidance. This specific model is currently being used by a private bank in Geneva, Switzerland [8].

4.3.3 *Walk-Through Portal Systems*

Allowing the human of interest to continue walking while providing highly accurate recognition may be the most attractive form factor

Figure 4.10. An example of the iris on the move (from http://www. sarnoff.com/products/iris-on-the-move).

for future iris recognition systems. As the name indicates, Iris on the Move™ (IOM) [9] provides iris detection and recognition at the "speed of life." Physically, the system permits a person to walk through a portal (shown in Fig. 4.10), with normal walking speed, for iris detection and capture. It does not require people to stop or to remove their glasses. It has the ability to capture 20 moving subjects per minute. IOM's applications include transportation facilities, government buildings, courthouses, or power plants.

4.3.4 *Portable Systems*

Governments around the world have expressed vested interests in portable iris recognition systems. The HIIDE™ [10] is known as the world's first multi-modal hand-held enrollment and recognition device. Illustrated in Fig. 4.11 is the small and lightweight HIIDE™ Series 4. The Series 4 model weighs only 2 lbs, 3 ounces and the focal distance is 8–10 inches. Because this series was first designed for the US Department of Defense, it can enroll up to 10,000 biometric portfolios. The developers claim that this model is "ideal for mobile identification of individuals on the battlefield, at border checkpoints,

Figure 4.11. An example of the L-1 HIDE Series 4 (from http://www. l1id.com/images/stories/solutions/hiide_product_sheet.pdf).

in airports, in detention centers, and for checking individuals against known watch lists in addition to naval and coast guard applications" [10].

The PIER™-T [11] is a "rugged" hand-held device providing both enrollment and identification functions. The system weighs only 12 ounces, while incorporating state-of-the-art lenses, dual-band illumination, a high-resolution video sensor, and a liquid crystal display screen. This popular and capable system is employed in a wide range of locations, including the Department of Defense (DOD), Biometric Fusion Center (BFC), the Office of Law Enforcement Technology Commercialization (OLETC), and the Space and Naval Warfare Systems Command (SPAWAR). The PIER™ 2.3, illustrated in Fig. 4.12, handles iris recognition on the handheld unit. The system weighs only 16.5 ounces with a focal distance of 4–6 inches. It has also been utilized for security purposes. It has been incorporated into the Biometric Application Toolset (BAT), a multi-biometric security platform developed by the U.S. Army, Battle Command Lab. Accordingly, the BAT is being utilized by the Navy, Marines, Army and other DOD and non-DOD agencies [11].

Finally, the IrisGuard IG-H100 [12] is a versatile handheld iris recognition camera weighing only 26.5 ounces. The focal distance is between 4 and 12 inches. The IrisGuard IG-H100 is utilized around the world in many high-level security venues including the United Arab Emirates: "The United Arab Emirates (UAE) interior ministry has claimed continuing success for its nation-wide iris-recognition network, which includes the country's airports in its coverage. The

Figure 4.12. An example of the PIER 2.3 (from http://www.securimetrics. com/solutions/pier.html).

system, which uses a single-eye H-100 camera supplied by UK-based company IrisGuard, was introduced in 2003 and has since expanded to include 140 iris-recognition stations in 22 enrollment centers and 35 land, sea, and air border points across the UAE. The nationwide system has 1.1 million irises stored in its database, according to the interior ministry, and has performed 21 million iris searches for 10.5 million persons over the past three years, which makes it the largest search iris database in the world. Using this information, the UAE identified 124,435 individuals who were trying to return to the country illegally with forged documents after deportation." [12]

4.4 Current Research Areas

Iris recognition is an active field of research. Researchers are actively looking into ways to make iris recognition systems more accurate when a non-cooperative subject is involved to operate at longer distances and under a wide variety of light wavelengths. These are just three of the areas of current research, and each are briefly described below.

4.4.1 *Off-Axis Iris Recognition*

Noticeably absent from the above-mentioned systems are methods for handling iris images gazing in a direction other than the camera (off-axis). While this section does not provide an in depth examination into the various algorithms, it is worth discussing how certain mathematical processing can be incorporated to improve off-axis identification.

One approach is to apply a special transformation against the captured image before it undergoes the coding process. The simplest transformation is an affine rectification. Such transformations are "analogous to rectification of oblique aerial images to place them in a map-like spatial coordinate system" [13]. In order to apply this concept it is important to estimate the subject's direction of gaze. Various methods have been proposed for accomplishing this task, and two in particular are worth noting. The first includes continuously applying multiple rectification constants to a series of captured images. The second involves implementing a Dual Purkinje Image (DPI) tracker. The first proposal could be accomplished very easily with the use of an offset camera. Rather than having to apply numerous rectification parameters to a series of images until the best Hamming Distance is acquired, an offset camera could be stationed so the angle of gaze is known. If images were purposely taken at designated angle then specific transformations would already exist and could be quickly applied [13]. The DPI requires more specialized hardware to capture the necessary layered images. Purkinje images represent reflections given off from increasingly deeper layers of the eye. When the eye undergoes a translation, the two images would move together. But when the eye is fixed at a gaze the distances between images become separated, yielding a specific angular measurement [14].

4.4.2 *Iris Recognition at a Distance*

Current commercial systems require a cooperative subject and have iris images captured at relatively short distances (approximately 8–12" from the camera for wall-mounted and portable systems, and approximately 3 m for a portal system). This translates into a short-range capture volume from which acceptable iris images can be captured. There is research into developing systems that can expand the capture volume and allow recognition to be performed at longer distances.

Retica Systems has developed an iris recognition prototype named "Eagle-Eye" that is capable of capturing useable iris images at a distance and within an area far greater than the current commercial products. It is noted that a solution for increasing the capture volume with current technology lies within coupling a wide field of view camera and a narrow field of view camera "mounted on a pan/tilt stage" [13]. The Eagle-Eye system takes this concept and integrates three separate cameras with hierarchically ordered field of views (FOV) in order to capture both face and iris biometric data. A fixed camera first surveys a volume (3 m × 3 m × 2 m) until a person is found. The tracking and person acquisition events are stored to avoid repeatedly focusing on the same subject. Mounted above this camera on a pan/tilt unit (PTU) are the face and iris cameras. Once a person is found the next camera utilizes a facial recognition algorithm in order to capture a high resolution image of the face. Once this has been accomplished, the iris camera and illumination source are turned on. This system is unique in the way an iris is illuminated. Rather than use fixed lighting sources, a laser illuminator mounted on the PTU sends a collimated light source towards the iris. This type of illumination can adequately provide quality images over a greater distance.

Like the IOM, subjects can remain in motion and still be identified. "The velocity of the PTU assembly and subject are matched such that their relative positions coincide at predicted future times/locations" [15]. A handheld version has also been developed and is named Mobile-Eyes.

Other "iris at a distance" systems have been designed with reasonably successful results. Frederick *et al.* [16] incorporated a hierarchical FOV system as well, but did not implement a tracking system. Their experimentation primarily revolved around capture time and reported (based on a steady stream of subjects) an average time of 7.1 s before an individual was verified by the system. Further standoff distances have been reported capturing images up to 10 m away [17], but this requires heavy constraints on the user's position.

Currently, a stand off system is being developed at the US Naval Academy, which can capture quality images from 25 + m away. Progress is being made to automate the system with the goal of significantly relaxing subject constraints.

4.4.3 *Multispectral Iris Recognition*

As alluded to in earlier sections, irises look differently when illuminated under different wavelengths of light. This is evident in Fig. 4.13. In terms of recognition, this means that different features become evident depending on the illumination. This area of research seeks to determine the best wavelength(s) of light to use in iris recognition, and possibly how to combine the information from different wavelengths to improve recognition performance. Some preliminary analysis of multispectral iris recognition can be found in the literature [18–20].

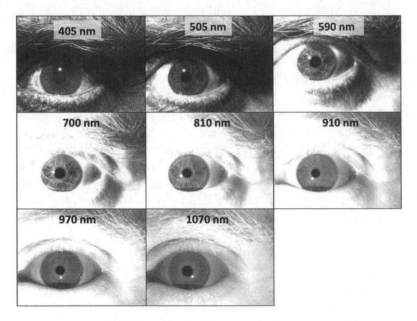

Figure 4.13. The same eye from Fig. 4.1 illuminated with different wavelengths. Most commercial iris systems use illumination in the range from 700 to 900 nm in wavelength.

References

1. Gross Anatomy of the Eye, http://webvision.med.utah.edu/anatomy.html, 17 Dec. 2009.

2. Woodward, J., Orlans, N. M., and Higgins, P. T. (2002) *Biometrics*, The McGraw-Hill Company, California, CA.

3. Flom, L. and Safir, A. United States Patent No. 4,641,349 (issued February 3, 1987), Iris Recognition System, Washington D.C.: U.S. Government Printing Office.

4. Daugman, J. (1994). How iris recognition works, *JIEEE Transactions On Circuits and Systems for Video Technology* 14(1), 21–30.

5. Daugman, J. United States Patent No. 5,291,560 (issued March 1, 1994). Biometric Personal Identification System Based on Iris Analysis. Washington D.C.: U.S. Government Printing Office.

6. Ives, R., Broussard, R., Rakvic, R., and Etter, D. Iris recognition using the ridge energy direction (RED) algorithm, *Proceedings of the 42nd Annual Asilomar Conference on Signals, Systems and Computers* 1219–1223.

7. Monro, D. M., Rakshit, S., and Zhang, D, University of Bath, U.K. Iris Image Database, http://www.bath.ac.uk/elec-eng/pages/sipg/irisweb, 27 Dec. 2009.

8. OKI Corporation, http://www.oki.com/jp/FSC/iris/en/, 27 Dec. 2009.

9. Sarnoff Corporation, www.sarnoff.com/products/iris-on-the-move, 27 Dec. 2009.

10. L-1 Identity Solutions, http://www.l1id.com/pages/47-hiide-series-4, 27 Dec. 2009

11. L-1 Identity Solutions, http://www.l1id.com/pages/48-pier-2-4, 27 Dec. 2009.

12. Irisguard Corporation, www.irisguard.com, 27 Dec. 2009.

13. Matey, J. R., Ackerman, D., Bergen, J., and Tinker, M. (2007) "Iris Recognition in Less Constrained Environments," in *Advances in Biometrics* 10, 107–131.

14. Morimoto, C. and Mimica, M. (2004) Eye Gaze Tracking Techniques for Interactive Applications. *Computer Vision and Image Understanding* 98, 4–24.

15. Bashir, F., Casaverde, P., Usher, D., and Friedman, M. (2008) Eagle-Eyes: A System for iris Recognition at a Distance, *2008 IEEE Conference on Technologies for Homeland Security*, 426–431.

16. Frederick, A., Perera, A., Abramovich, G., Yu, B., and Tu, P. (2008) Stand-Off Iris Recognition System, *2nd IEEE Conference on Biometrics: Theory, Applications and Systems* 1–7.

17. Fancourt, C., Bogoni, L., Hanna, K., Guo, Y., Wildes, R., Takahashi, N., and Jain, U. (2005) Iris Recognition at a Distance, *Audio- and Video-Based Biometric Person Authentication, 5th International Conference.*

18. Boyce, C., Ross, A., Monaco, M., Hornak, L., and Li, X. (2006) Multispectral Iris Analysis: A Preliminary Study, *Proceedings of Computer Vision and Pattern Recognition Workshop on Biometrics* 51–60.

19. Ross, A., Pasula, R., and Hornak, L. (2009) Exploring Multispectral Iris Recognition beyond 900 nm, *Proceedings of the 3rd IEEE Inernational Conference on Biometrics: Theory Applications and Systems* 1–8.

20. Ngo, H., Ives, R., Matey, J., Dormo, J., Rhoads, M., and Choi, D. (2009) Design and Implementation of a Multispectral Iris Capture System, *Proceedings of the 43rd Asilomar Conference on Signals, Systems and Computers.*

Chapter 5

Speaker Recognition for Biometric Systems

Ravi Sankar and Tanmoy Islam

iCONS Research Lab, Department of Electrical Engineering,
University of South Florida, Tampa, Florida, USA
sankar@usf.edu

5.1 Introduction

Speech is one of the most natural and efficient modes for human communication. Speech contains many different levels of information that are communicated to its listener. It not only conveys a message of spoken words, but also at other levels conveys information about the language being spoken, the emotion, gender, and the identity of the speaker. Over the years, the ability to communicate with machines using speech has gradually improved. Speech recognition systems deal with the identification of spoken language at different levels from phoneme, words, to continuous sentences. An automatic speaker recognition system extracts the feature of an individual speaker, then characterizes and classifies the information in the speech signal to decide the speaker identity.

Biometrics: From Fiction to Practice
Edited by Eliza Yingzi Du
Copyright © 2013 Pan Stanford Publishing Pte. Ltd.
ISBN 978-981-4310-88-8 (Hardcover), 978-981-4364-13-3 (eBook)
www.panstanford.com

5.2 Modes of Operation

Speaker recognition comprises of two primary tasks. They are *speaker identification* and *speaker verification.* Speaker identification is to identify who is talking from a set of known voice patterns previously enrolled in the system database. The unknown person does not make any identity claim and the system decides who the speaking person is by performing a 1 to N classification. This process is depicted in Fig. 5.1.

Speaker verification (also known as speaker authentication) is the task of determining claimed identity of a person from his voice [1]. This is a binary decision (yes/no) about the claimed identity. A claimed speaker's identity is compared to a previously trained and saved speaker's template. Once a comparison is made, a decision can be reached. Depending on the level of user cooperation, control in an application and the algorithm used for the identification, the verification task can further be divided into *text-dependent* and *text-independent* systems. In a text-dependent system, the spoken text is known. Thus it clearly requires cooperative users. A user requires a specific pass phrase to use this system. A text-independent system on the other hand prompts a random phrase. This dissuades any potential imposter trying to use a pre recorded pass phrase to gain access to the system. Unlike text-dependent systems, in a text-independent application, the system has no prior information

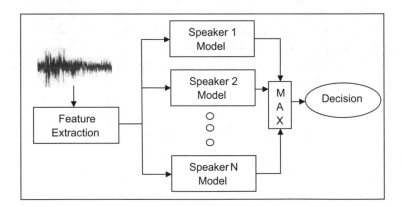

Figure 5.1.   Speaker identification system.

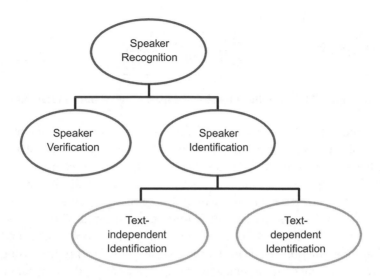

Figure 5.2. Speaker identification taxonomy.

of the spoken text. This type of systems allows verification of a speaker while the speaker is carrying conversation. It reflects on a more real world model where speech is unrehearsed. Without prior knowledge of the spoken text, the task of recognition becomes more difficult. The prior knowledge and constraint of the text can greatly boost performance of a recognition system. Hence, most text-dependent speaker recognition/verification systems perform better than text-independent systems. The distinction between text-independent and text-dependent applications will decrease as the recognition accuracy improves and speaker and speech recognition systems merge. This taxonomy is represented in Fig. 5.2.

5.3 Voice-Based Recognition Systems

In any speaker identification or verification system, the process involves two phases. The first phase is the speaker enrollment, where speech samples are collected from the speakers. Then, they are used to train and generate their models. In the enrollment phase, these features are modeled and the enrolled speaker models

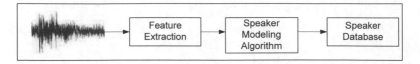

Figure 5.3. Enrollment phase of a speaker recognition system.

are then stored in a reference database. This process is shown in Fig. 5.3. The second phase is the identification/verification phase, where a test sample from an unknown speaker is compared to the existing speaker models stored in the database. Again the features are extracted and a model is created for the unknown speaker before comparison with reference database. This process is shown in Fig. 5.4. Both phases include, preprocessing and feature extraction, as the initial processing steps. The preprocessing involves signal conditioning and analog to digital (A/D) conversion. This is generally the front end of any digital signal processing system. Feature extraction is used to extract speaker dependent characteristics from the speech data. It reduces the amount of test data while retaining speaker discriminative information.

The performance of identification or verification algorithms cannot be measured without successful enrollment and modeling algorithms. Not all pattern recognition processes use speaker modeling. Speaker comparison can be done in feature space instead of model space. Template matching algorithm using dynamic time warping (DTW) method is one such approach that does not require

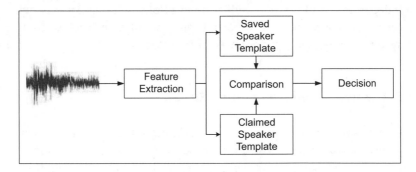

Figure 5.4. Identification/verification phase of a speaker recognition system.

speaker modeling. Instead test features to reference features are compared and classified using distance measures. Further details can be found in Section 5.6.

5.4 Preprocessing Algorithms

First, the analog speech signal captured by the microphone needs to be preprocessed. This involves signal conditioning including amplification and low-pass filtering to prepare the signal for further processing. The signal is then send to a CODEC which performs the A/D conversion. The digital speech signal then goes through some common preprocessing algorithms including pre-emphasis filtering and windowing before desired features are extracted from the voice samples. The usual preprocessing steps are the following.

5.4.1 *A/D Conversion and Pre-emphasis*

Once the analog speech signal is acquired it must be converted into a digital signal. Sampling rate varies, based on the acquisition hardware. Generally it is 8 kHz but can be set higher. As the speech is radiated from the speaker's mouth/lips, there is about 6 dB/octave decay as frequency increases. Further the high-frequency unvoiced speech tends to be much lower in energy than the low-frequency voiced speech. By using a pre-emphasis filter, a first-order high-pass filter of the form $1 - az^{-1}$, where $a = 0.9 - 0.95$, the weak high-frequency components can be emphasized or boosted. The magnitude and phase responses of this filter with $a = 0.95$ is shown in Fig. 5.5. Figure 5.6 shows the effect of the pre-emphasis filter on a speech signal. The original signal's amplitude is spectrally flattened once the signal passes through the filter.

5.4.2 *Framing and Windowing*

A speech signal can be assumed to be *quasistationary* when analyzed over a small frame or samples of data. A speech signal is generally segmented into short blocks called frames with a typical frame size of 10–50 ms so as to perform short time processing. Each frame

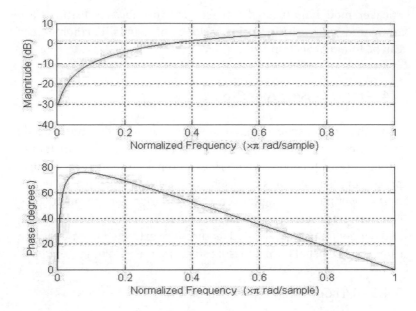

Figure 5.5. Frequency response of pre-emphasis filter.

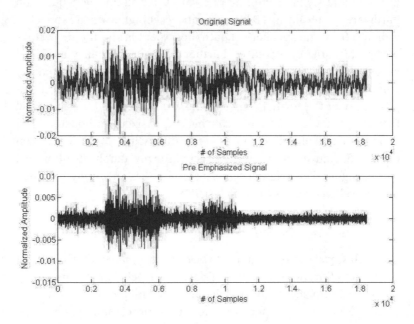

Figure 5.6. Speech signal before and after pre-emphasis.

of data is then windowed before it goes through feature extraction and analysis or modeling or recognition. There are various types of windows such as boxcar, Bartlett, Hamming, Hann, Blackman, Tukey, and Kaiser [2] that can be used for this purpose of framing. The simplest window would be a boxcar or rectangular window in which the signal is not scaled or weighted. In order to reduce the spectral leakage, each frame of samples is multiplied by a smoother window such as Hamming window. The consecutive frames are overlapped in order to have signal continuity and prevent data loss at the frame edges.

Hamming window is defined by

$$w(n) = \begin{cases} 0.54 - 0.46 \cos(2\pi n/N - 1), & n = 0, 1, \ldots, N - 1 \\ 0, & n \text{ otherwise} \end{cases}$$

where n is the sample time and N is the total length of the window. Figure 5.7 shows a 30 ms (frame length = 1323 samples) of a Hamming window when the sampling frequency = 44,100 Hz.

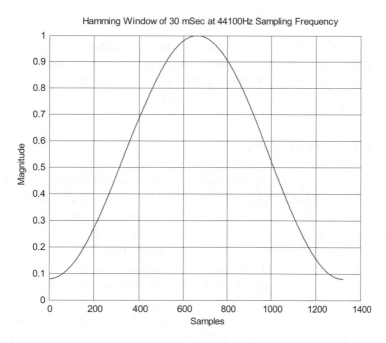

Figure 5.7. Hamming window (frame size = 30 ms).

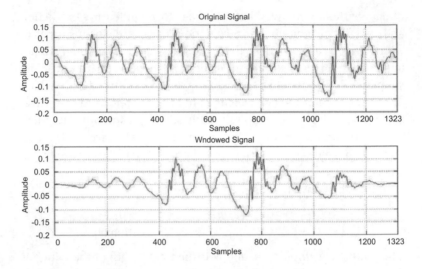

Figure 5.8.   Hamming windowed speech signal (frame size = 30 ms).

Figure 5.8 shows the effect of a hamming window on a speech original signal. Due to the cosine nature of the window, the edge of the signal is flattened, however the middle of the signal is preserved.

5.5 Feature Extraction

The acoustic speech signal conveys information about the speaker that humans can detect with ease, accent, emotion, and/or identity of the speakers. However for automatic recognition system, recognizable information has to be presented to the algorithm so as to discern the source of the features, i.e., the characteristics of the speaker. Then the identity of the speaker can be recognized. A feature generally can be either a time domain or a frequency domain parameter. Many properties of speech signal can be used as features, such as pitch, energy, formant frequencies, vocal tract model parameters, linear prediction (LP) model coefficients, and cepstral coefficients.

5.5.1 *Short-term Analysis*

As mentioned earlier, a speech signal is considered to be quasi-stationary over a short period of time window, say 30 ms, where it has stable acoustic characteristics. A small window is moved along the signal with each successive window, overlapping the other (usually 30–50% of the window length). The signal processing algorithm is applied on each small windowed frame of data and the feature vector is extracted. Hence there will be one set of features that will represent each frame. Figure 5.9 shows a speech signal is segmented with an overlapping hamming window. Then for each frame the corresponding feature vector $\mathbf{X}_n$ is extracted. Many different techniques exist for extracting features from each frame. In speaker recognition area, most widely used features are the LP coefficients, cepstral coefficients, and their variants, such as linear prediction cepstral coefficient (LPCC) and mel frequency cepstral coefficients (MFCC). These are discussed in the following section.

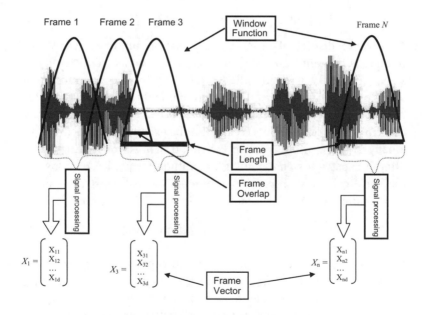

Figure 5.9. Short-term analysis.

5.5.2 *Cepstral Analysis*

Cepstral analysis has been used to transform output speech response of a linear time-invariant system signal that is obtained by convolution of its impulse response with the input excitation into summed signal components, i.e.,

$$s(n) = x(n) * h(n)$$

where $s(n)$ is the output response (speech signal), $x(n)$ is the input excitation, $h(n)$ is the impulse response of the vocal tract system, and * represents the convolution.

Then by taking the discrete Fourier transformation, the equation in the frequency domain can be expressed as a product

$$S(e^{j\omega}) = X(e^{j\omega}).H(e^{j\omega}),$$

where $S(e^{j\omega})$, $X(e^{j\omega})$ and $H(e^{j\omega})$ are the output, input and system frequency responses, respectively. By taking logarithm, the multiplying Fourier signal can be transformed into individual additive signals, as shown in the following equation

$$\log|S(e^{j\omega})| = \log|X(e^{j\omega})| + \log|H(e^{j\omega})|.$$

An inverse discrete Fourier transformation on this logarithmic frequency domain signal is termed *cepstrum* which represents the signal in a new domain called *quefrency*. In this domain using *lifter*, low-quefrency cepstral signal components (related to the vocal tract impulse response) can be separated from the high-quefrency cepstral signal components (related of the excitation or pitch) [3, 4]. Finally, by computing discrete Fourier transform on the low-time liftered cepstrum signal, the log magnitude frequency response of the vocal tract system can be obtained. The real cepstrum can be represented in a more general term with the following equation

$$\hat{s}[n] = \frac{1}{2\pi} \int_{-\pi}^{\pi} \log|S(e^{j\omega})|e^{j\omega n} d\omega.$$

Both linear prediction coding (LPC) and cepstral techniques have been widely used to model the vocal tract spectrum. Cepstral coefficients have been found to be robust, reliable feature set in the application of speech and speaker recognition area. Once we have spoken speech, cepstrum analysis helps us separate the different components of the speech, which we can use to create features of the original speaker. Great success has been achieved in speech/speaker recognition area by using cepstral coefficients converted from the LP parameters [5] and by mel frequency cepstrum [6], which are described below.

5.5.3 *Linear Prediction*

LP is used to predict present and/or future sample values by linear weighted combination of the past signal samples. The objective is to find the LP weights or coefficients of this predictive filter so that the mean-square error (MSE) between the predicted and the actual sample data is minimized. Hence it is known as LPC or autoregressive (AR) modeling. The theory of LPC is well known and utilized in the area of speech and speaker recognition [7–9]. LPC is popular because the algorithm is based on an *all-pole model* that represents the spectrum of the voiced signal very well. LPC is also very simple to implement and yet the performance is comparable to or better than other complex methods, such as filter bank approach [10]. People perceive the magnitude information better than the phase information and the LPC all-pole model of sufficient filter order can preserve magnitude dynamics in the spoken words from a speaker with minimal error.

LP approximation depends on the linear weighted combination of the past sample values as given by the following equation

$$\hat{s}(n) = \sum_{k-1}^{p} a_k * s(n - k)$$

where $\hat{s}(n)$ is an approximation of the present output, $s(n-k)$ are the past output samples, p is the prediction order, and a_k are the model weights or LP coefficients.

$$\hat{e}(n) = s(n) - \hat{s}(n)$$

where $e(n)$ is the prediction error between, predicted error signal $\hat{s}(n)$ and actual signal $s(n)$. One method of computing LPC is the Yule–Walker or autocorrelation method that can be implemented efficiently using Levinson–Durbin recursion. For a pth order filter, the autocorrelation method requires solving p simultaneous equations for solving the LP coefficients and one equation to computer the MSE. This is given in matrix form as follows:

$$
\begin{bmatrix}
r(0) & r(1) & \cdots & r(p-1) \\
r_n(1) & r(0) & \cdots & r(p-2) \\
\vdots & \vdots & \ddots & \vdots \\
r(p-1) & r(p-2) & \cdots & r(0)
\end{bmatrix}
\begin{bmatrix}
a_1 \\
a_2 \\
\vdots \\
a_p
\end{bmatrix}
=
\begin{bmatrix}
r(1) \\
r(2) \\
\vdots \\
r(p)
\end{bmatrix}
$$

$$
\mathbf{Ra} = \mathbf{r}
$$

Here, p is the prediction order of the LPC, $a = [a_1 a_2 \ldots a_p]^t$ is the LPC coefficient vector, $r = [r(1)r(2)\ldots r(p)]^t$ is the autocorrelation vector of the speech signal and $\mathbf{R}$ is the $p \times p$ Toeplitz autocorrelation matrix. Thus solution to LPC coefficient can be given by

$$
\mathbf{a} = \mathbf{R}^{-1}\mathbf{r}
$$

and the least mean squared error of the prediction is given by

$$
E = \sum_n e^2(n) = A^t \mathbf{R} A
$$

where, $A = [1 a_1 a_2 \ldots a_p]^t$. Though the general equation calls for computationally expensive metric inversion, it can be avoided using QR decomposition or Levinson–Durbin recursion.

Using mapping transformation, the cepstral coefficients can be computed from these LP coefficients given by the following equations [4, 8]

$$
\mathbf{c}_0 = r(0),
$$

$$
\mathbf{c}_m = a_m + \sum_{k=1}^{m-1} \frac{k}{m} \, \mathbf{c}_k a_{m-k}, \qquad \text{where } 1 \leq m \leq p
$$

$$
\mathbf{c}_m = \sum_{k=1}^{m-1} \frac{k}{m} \mathbf{c}_k a_{m-k}, \qquad \text{where } m > p
$$

Here, c_m are the cepstral coefficients, a_m are the LPC coefficients, p is the prediction order filter of the LPC. Once extracted, cepstral coefficients can be used as the feature set for the speech signal.

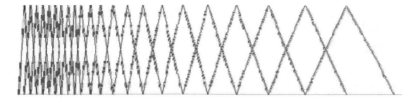

Figure 5.10.   Triangular filters used to compute mel cepstrum.

5.5.4 *Mel Frequency Cepstrum*

Mel frequency cepstrum coefficients (MFCC), originally proposed by [6], suggests that the frequencies of the lower band are phonetically more important to humans. Hence by following human perception modeling, the filter components in MFCC are linear up to 1 kHz and exponential thereafter.

MFCC feature extraction is similar to cepstrum calculations with one difference. The frequency axis is warped according to the mel scale [11], which is the perceived pitch by our ear. Mel scale is represented in a logarithmic frequency axis as shown in Fig. 5.10. Each triangular filter is used for each desired mel frequency component. This is given as

$$m = 2595 \log_{10} \left(\tfrac{f}{700} + 1 \right)$$

where f is frequency in Hz, m is warped frequency in mel scale. Figure 5.11 shows the frequency warped in mel scale. It can be seen that up to 1000 Hz mel scale has fairly a linear relationship to its corresponding frequency scale and exponential thereafter.

A windowed (framed) time signal is converted to frequency domain by taking a Fourier transformation. This frequency domain signal is then scaled by a bank of triangular filters. Triangular filter is equally spaced on a logarithmic frequency axis (see Fig. 5.10). Then, the logarithm of the sum of the magnitude coefficient is computed. Discrete cosine transformation (DCT) is then applied to extract the cepstral coefficients. DCT is used instead of inverse DFT for computational efficiency. If N is the number of triangular band pass filter and M is the number of cepstrum coefficients, then MFCC

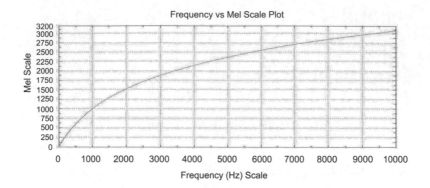

Figure 5.11. Frequency vs. mel scale mapping.

can be described by the following equation:

$$\text{MFCC}_i = \sum_{k=1}^{N} X_k \cos\left[i \bullet \left(k - \frac{1}{2}\right) \frac{\pi}{N}\right],$$

where $i = 1, 2, 3, \ldots M$, X_k, $k = 1, 2, \ldots, N$, represents the log-energy output of the kth filter. Figure 5.12 shows the block diagram of the MFCC feature extraction algorithm.

Variations of MFCC have been introduced. For example, human factor cepstral coefficient (HFCC) [12], which modifies the bandwidth of the MFCC filter bank, using Moore and Glasber's approximation equivalent rectangular bandwidth (ERB) [13]. This is given by

$$\text{ERB} = 6.23 f_c^2 + 93.39 f_c + 28.52 \text{ (Hz)}$$

where f_c is the center frequency in kHz, in the range of 0.1 and 6.5 kHz.

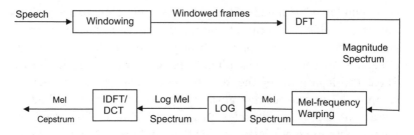

Figure 5.12. Computation flow chart of mel cepstrum.

5.5.5 *Intersession Variability*

Intersession variations in a speakers voice and in the communication channel are a major problem for the application of speaker recognition in general. The problem must be dealt with also in other applications of speech processing (e.g., speech recognition), but is particularly acute for speaker recognition. Typically the enrollment speech has been recorded in a single session. However, testing data will be most often collected under different microphone and environment. This creates a mismatch that poses a major challenge [14].

Acoustic channel introduces additive distortion in the log spectral domain and also in the cepstral domain [15]. Once feature vector has been acquired, it can be normalized using techniques such as cepstral mean subtraction (CMS) [16], RelAtive SpecTrAl (RASTA) filtering [17], and feature mapping [18]. Both CMS and RASTA have proven to be very effective methods when it comes to feature normalization and removing intersession variability.

5.6 Speaker Modeling

Once an appropriate set of feature vectors has been extracted from speech signal, there are two ways to save them in a database so that a claimed person's identity can be verified. The two main approaches for solving the classification problem in the speaker recognition are: template matching and stochastic matching/modeling.

Template matching is a deterministic process that compares the training feature vector X_t to stored reference (imposters) feature vectors X_i in a database. Examples of template matching techniques are DTW [19], vector quantization (VQ) [20], *nearest neighbor* (NN) or k-NN-based clustering [21], *support vector machine* (SVM) [22], and *artificial neural network* (ANN) [23, 24]. In contrast, stochastic matching uses probabilistic approach to modeling and classification. Stochastic matching gives us a probability $P(\mathbf{O}|\lambda)$ of an observation $\mathbf{O}$ (test feature) given a model λ (training feature/model). Examples of stochastic matching techniques are *hidden Markov model* (HMM), *Gaussian mixture model* (GMM), *GMM likelihood ratio* (GMMLR), etc.

There are many different sub models which also combine above mentioned algorithms.

5.6.1 *Dynamic Time Warping*

DTW was first introduced in the early 60's [19] for feature matching where there is a temporal variation possible between training and test subject. DTW has since been used in speech recognition, handwriting recognition, gesture recognition or any other time series data mining problem. In speech and speaker recognition area DTW was used to account for temporal variations in the spoken word [25, 26], i.e., normalizing different speaking rates among the speakers to the same time scale. In DTW, this is done by stretching or compressing the feature vectors of the test speaker by making a frame-by-frame comparison to the reference templates.

DTW is an efficient time series comparison algorithm. DTW algorithm aligns the test and reference sequences in such a way that the total distance (time distortion) is minimized. Figure 5.13 shows an example of a DTW; the optimum warping path through the grid space warps the time axis of the reference sequence with respect to the time axis of the test sequence. The objective is to find the optimal

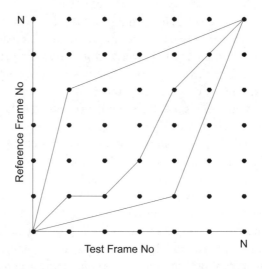

Figure 5.13. Example of dynamic time warping.

warping path $m = w(n)$ in the (n, m) plane which minimizes the total accumulated distance between the test sequence $T(n)$ and the ith reference template, $R_i(m)$

$$\hat{D}_i(n, m) = \min_{w(n)} \left\{ \sum_{n=1}^{N} d(T(n)), R_i(w(n)) \right\}$$

where $d(.)$ is the localized distance measure. Instead of squared Euclidean distance measure, Itakura–Saito distance has been widely used as a measure of similarity between LP vectors [7, 27] and is given by

$$d = \frac{(\mathbf{a} - \mathbf{b})^t \mathbf{R} (\mathbf{a} - \mathbf{b})}{\mathbf{a}^t \mathbf{R} \mathbf{a}}$$

where $\mathbf{R}$ is the autocorrelation matrix of the test frame, $\mathbf{a}$ and $\mathbf{b}$ are the LPC vectors of the test and reference frames.

5.6.2 *Vector Quantization*

VQ involves quantizing a block of signal samples or a block of signal parameters or features. The algorithm maps feature vectors to a finite number of regions on a vector space. Thus VQ approximates data within the region. These regions are called clusters or cells and represented by their correspond centroids. A set of centroids, which represents the whole vector space, is called a *codebook*.

One of the more commonly used VQ algorithm is LBG VQ [20]. The algorithm begins with the size of *codebook*. An initial codebook is chosen as the average of the code vectors. Then this codebook is split into two, by an ascending order of their values.

$$\mathbf{c}_i^0 = (1 + \varepsilon) \mathbf{c}_i^*$$
$$\mathbf{c}_{N+i}^0 = (1 - \varepsilon) \mathbf{c}_i^*$$

where $i = 1, 2, 3, \ldots, N$. Size of the vector is $2N$. Now an iterative process is run with these two as initial codebook, and their distances from the rest of the vectors are measured. Test vector that produces the minimum distance among these two code vectors, will belong to its corresponding codebook. Then the final two codebooks will be split again and the process is repeated until the desired number of codebooks is achieved.

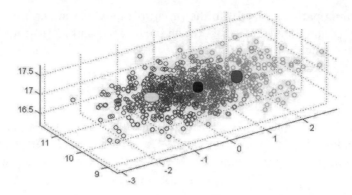

Figure 5.14. Three centroids for three different feature sets. See also Color Insert.

VQ is applied to the set of feature vectors extracted from the speech sample and as a result, the speaker codebook is generated. Such codebook has a significantly smaller size than extracted vector set and is referred to as a speaker model. Figure 5.14 shows multiple feature sets and how VQ can represent the features as their own centroids. By comparing the centroids from a set of data sets to another, a similarity matrix can be created.

The *quantization distortion* (quality of quantization) is usually computed as the sum of squared distances between vector and its representative (centroid). The well-known distance measures are *city block*, *Euclidean*, and *weighted Euclidean*. During matching, a matching score is computed between extracted feature vectors and every speaker codebook enrolled in the system. Commonly it is done as a partitioning extracted feature vectors, using centroids from speaker codebook, and calculating matching score as a quantization distortion. The final identification decision is made based on the matching score: speaker who has a model with the smallest matching score is identified as one who spoke the test speech.

5.6.3 *Hidden Markov Model*

HMM has been widely used for modeling speech recognition systems. There are many ways HMM can be used. However, its usage/solution can be summarized in following three categories:

- Given the observation sequence **O** and a model λ, how do we compute $P(\mathbf{O}|\lambda)$?
- Given the observation sequence **O** and the model λ, how do we choose a corresponding state sequence q that is optimal?
- How do we adjust the model parameters λ to maximize $P(\mathbf{O}|\lambda)$?

In speaker recognition tasks we are most interested in the solution to the third problem.

In order to use HMM in speaker recognition area, we want to be able to create a model (λ) given the observation features **O**.

Let an observation sequence be $\mathbf{O} = (o_1, o_2, \ldots, o_T)$ and its HMM model be $\lambda = (A, B, \pi)$. Where A denotes state transition probability, B denotes output probability density functions, and π is the initial state probabilities. We can iteratively optimize the model parameters λ, so that it best describes the given observation O. Thus the likelihood (expectation), $\mathbf{P}(\mathbf{O}|\lambda)$ is maximized. This can be achieved using Baum–Welch method [28]. For the solution this problem, Baum–Welch method is exactly identical to expectation maximization (EM) algorithm.

To re-estimate HMM parameters, $\xi_t(i, j)$ is defined as the probability of being in state i at time t, and state j at time $t + 1$, given the model and the observation sequence,

$$\xi_t(i, j) = \frac{\alpha_t(i)a_{ij}b_j(O_{t+1})\beta_{t+1}(j)}{\sum_{i=1}^{N}\sum_{j=1}^{N}\alpha_t(i)a_{ij}b_j(O_{t+1})\beta_{t+1}(j)}$$
$$= \frac{P(q_t = i, q_{t+1} = j|O, \lambda)}{P(O|\lambda)}.$$

Using the above formula, we can re-estimate HMM parameter from an initial model parameter $\lambda = (A, B, \pi)$ given by

$$\bar{\pi}_j = \gamma_1(i)$$

$$\bar{a}_{ij} = \frac{\sum_{t=1}^{T-1}\xi_t(i, j)}{\sum_{t=1}^{T-1}\gamma_t(i)}.$$

$$\bar{b}_j(k) = \frac{\sum\limits_{\substack{t=1 \\ s.t.o_t=v_k}}^{T} \gamma_t(j)}{\sum\limits_{t=1}^{T} \gamma_t(j)}$$

$$\gamma_t(i) = \sum_{j=1}^{N} \xi_t(i, j).$$

Thus we can iteratively find optimal HMM parameter λ. This procedure is also viewed as training and by using optimal HMM parameter model we can later compare a testing set of data or observation **O** by calculating the likelihood **P(O|λ)**.

5.6.4 *Gaussian Mixture Modeling*

GMM is a stochastic modeling technique and is based on the modeling of statistical variation of the features. It provides a statistical representation of how a speaker produces sounds. A *Gaussian mixture density* is a weighted sum of component densities, as represented in the following equation [1, 29].

$$p(x) = \sum_{i=1}^{M} w_i g\left(X|\mu_i, \sum_i\right)$$

X is a D-dimensional vector. w_i ($i = 1, 2, 3, \ldots, M$), are the weights for the Gaussian mixtures. The sum of mixture weight will be $\sum_{i=1}^{M} w_i = 1$. g($X|\mu_i, \sum_i$)1, 2, 3, $\ldots$, M, are the Gaussian densities. Each density is a Gaussian function of the form,

$$g\left(X|\mu_i, \sum_i\right) = \sum_{i=1}^{m} a_i \frac{1}{(2\pi)^{D/2}\left|\sum_i\right|^{1/2}} \exp$$

$$\times \left(-\frac{1}{2}(x - \mu_i)^T \sum_i^{-1} (x - \mu_i)\right)$$

where, μ_i is the mean vector and $\sum_i$ is the covariance matrix. In order to ensure a proper density mixture, the prior probabilities should be chosen to sum to unity (Speech Recognition Tutorial). Each component density is given by the following equation:

$$p(x|M) = \sum_{i=1}^{m} a_i \frac{1}{(2\pi)^{D/2}\left|\sum_i\right|^{1/2}} \exp\left(-\frac{1}{2}(x - \mu_i)^T \sum_i^{-1} (x - \mu_i)\right)$$

where $p(x|M)$ is the likelihood of **x** given the mixture model, M. The mixture model consists of a weighted sum over m unimodal Gaussian densities, each parameterized by the mean vectors, μ_i, and covariance matrices, $\sum_i$. The coefficients, a_i, are the mixture weights, which are constrained to be positive and must sum to one. The coefficients, a_i, are the mixture weights, which are constrained to be positive. The parameters of a GMM, $a_i \sum_I \mu_i$ for $i = 1, 2, \ldots, m$ may be estimated using the maximum likelihood criterion using the iterative expectation maximization (EM) algorithm [30]. Maximum likelihood estimates (MLE) problem can be solved using various well-known techniques, e.g., gradient descent, conjugate descent, Gauss–Newton [31]; however, most popular algorithm so far is EM.

5.6.4.1 Expectation maximization

EM is an iterative algorithm. Once feature vector has been obtained, we wish to find its GMM, hence the GMM parameter λ. N-dimensional feature vector $X = \{x_1, x_2, \ldots, x_N\}$, which is then assumed to be independent. Thus it can be represented as

$$\log p(X|\lambda) = \sum_{N=1}^{N} \log p(x_N|\lambda). \tag{5.1}$$

Using iterative methods described in [30], parameters can be estimated. In order to compute EM, an initial model is required so that the recursion can start. Usually this initial model $\lambda_{i=0}$ can be obtained by estimating parameters from the clustered feature vectors where proportions of vectors in each cluster can serve as a mixture weights w_i. Means, μ_i, and covariances, $\sum_I$, are estimated from the vectors in each cluster, where $i = 0$, for the initial model parameters. Thus we can begin an initial model λ_0 and by iteration estimate a new model λ_1 such that

$$p(X|\lambda_1) \geq p(X|\lambda_0).$$

Now in the next iteration, model λ_1 becomes the initial model and a new model λ_2 is estimated. This process continues until some convergence criterion is met. In general, fewer than 10 iterations of the EM algorithm will provide sufficient parameter convergence. Training GMMs using EM leads to a generative model. GMMs are analogous to VQ in that the mean of each Gaussian density can be thought of as a codebook vector.

A GMM is trained using maximum likelihood, to estimate the probability density function, $P(x_i|M)$, of the client speaker. The probability, $P(X|M)$, that an utterance, $X = \{x_1, x_2, \ldots, x_N\}$, is generated by the model, M, is used as the utterance score. It is estimated by the mean log likelihood over the sequence,

$$S(X) = \log P(X|M) = \frac{1}{N} \sum_{i=1}^{N} \log P(x_i|M)$$

5.6.5 *GMM Likelihood Ratio*

Another way to model/compare speaker feature is to use two GMMs instead of one. The first GMM is used to model the client as above. The second GMM is a speaker independent universal model, also known as a global background model (GBM) or universal background model (UBM) and it is usually a large GMM (2000 mixtures or more) [32, 33]. The UBM is trained on a large number of background speakers and is therefore a general model of speech. The basic idea is that the second GMM should model the properties of speech signals that are common to all speakers. In speaker verification it is desirable to assign high scores to frames, x_i, that are specific to the client and low scores to frames that are common to most speakers.

This may be achieved by taking the ratio of the client model, M, likelihood to the UBM, Ω, likelihood on the frame level. This is equivalent to computing the difference between the client and UBM's mean log likelihood scores for the full sequence,

$$S(X) = \frac{1}{N} \sum_{i=1}^{N} \log \frac{P(x_i|M)}{P(x_i|\Omega)}$$
$$= \log P(X|M) - \log P(X|\Omega).$$

Consider a frame of data that has a high likelihood of being generated by the client model. If that frame is common in most speech then the UBM should have a high likelihood of generating it also. Dividing the client model likelihood by the UBM likelihood reduces the score of this frame. As a result, frames that are common to all speakers contribute less to the utterance score. On the other hand, if the frame is specific to the client then the UBM likelihood will be small. Computing the likelihood ratio will yield a high score and the contribution to the utterance score will be large. In this respect, this method, which we call the GMM likelihood ratio (GMM-LR), may be seen as a simple way of obtaining discrimination from two generative models. The GMM-LR method is better than the GMM method in that the former takes into account the general distribution of speech and scores the utterance according to properties that are specific to the client while avoiding properties that are common to many speakers. It may also be said that the two GMMs are trained from two different data sets, therefore each model contains information that the other does not, thereby increasing the accuracy of the system [8].

5.7 State of the Art in Speaker Recognition Systems

Speaker recognition system can be used for various biometric applications, such as access control, person authentication, etc. Characterizing various algorithms is difficult because conditions that affect algorithm performance can differ from one published report to another. National Institute of Science and Technology (NIST) holds speaker recognition evaluation (SRE), where a data set is given to each participant and an evaluation plan is published for each year. For more information on NIST SRE visit http://www.itl.nist.gov/iad/mig/tests/sre/.

Detection error tradeoff (DET) has been used as a performance measure in NIST SRE [34], since 1997. A DET curve plots false acceptance rate (FAR) vs. false rejection rate (FRR) on x and y axes, respectively. DET curve is normally plotted using logarithmic axes. On a DET curve where FAR $=$ FRR is called the equal error rate (EER) [34]. An ideal algorithm would have FAR $=$ FRR $= 0$. But realistically we would want as small EER as possible. By comparing this EER value we can compare performances of two algorithms. Another performance measure that has been used by NIST is called minimum decision cost function (minDCF) [35] that is described by following equation:

$$\min DCF = \min_{\theta} \ 0.1 \, P_{\text{miss}}(\theta) + 0.99 \, P_{\text{FA}}(\theta),$$

where $P_{\text{miss}}(\theta)$ and $P_{\text{FA}}(\theta)$ are the probability of miss (false rejection) and false acceptance, respectively at the detection threshold, θ.

Participants of NIST 2008 evaluation plan [36] were given two data sets. One set was used for training and the other set was for testing. For training, six different types of data were given:

- 10-Sec: A two-channel telephone conversation, estimated length of 10 s speech.
- Short2: One two-channel telephone conversational excerpt, of approximately 5 min total duration.
- 3Conv: Three two-channel telephone conversations.
- 8conv: Eight two-channel telephone conversations.
- Long: Single-channel microphone-recorded conversation, 8 min or longer.
- 3summed: Three summed channel conversation, by sample summing of their two sides.

For testing, four different data sets were given:

- 10-Sec: A two-channel telephone conversation, estimated length of 10 s speech.
- Short3: A two-channel telephone conversational excerpt, of approximately 5 min total duration.
- Long: Single channel microphone recorded conversation, 8 min or longer.
- Summed: Summed channel conversation, by sample by sample summing of their two sides.

Various combinations of training and testing data sets can be used to evaluate the performance of the speaker recognition algorithm. NIST SRE required participants to publish results at least using *Short2* training data and *Short3* testing data. Excellent results based on these standard data sets have been reported by [37–41]. To provide a glimpse of one of the algorithm's performance, results reported by [39] are shown in Table 5.1.

Table 5.1. Published reports for NIST 2008 core results

Training data *short2*	Testing data *short3*	EER	minDCF
Interview	Interview	2.80%	0.105
Interview	Telephone	4.30%	0.178
Telephone	Interview	4.30%	0.171
Telephone	Microphone	4.10%	0.171
Telephone	Telephone	5.30%	0.280

A variant of GMM-based speaker recognition algorithm was used to achieve the reported results. It should be noted that in Table 5.1, low EER was achieved by fusing score generated from multiple algorithm, with equal weight. Fusion of intermodal and intra modal algorithms is an excellent way to increase performance accuracy as shown in [42], where scores generated from face recognition algorithm and voice recognition algorithm were fused together to achieve a higher recognition rate, when compared to either of the algorithms alone. Fusion of different algorithms has also been used in [43] where video segmentation was enhanced by using speaker recognition system. Similar improvement has been reported in [44] by fusing scores from multiple algorithms for voice recognition system. In [45], accent has been fused with speaker recognition algorithm to increase recognition accuracy. This provides us with information about the current state of the art in speaker recognition systems and performances that are achievable.

5.8 Summary

In this chapter, we presented a detailed overview of speaker recognition for biometric systems. Various modes of operation, taxonomy, and the process of speaker recognition systems were discussed in the first few sections of the chapter. Then we described each of the various blocks of the system and the algorithm components associated to those blocks. This included preprocessing, feature extraction, and speaker modeling, classification and recognition. In the feature extraction we presented some of the widely used feature sets including LPC, cepstum, and MFCC. With the basics of speaker recognition covered, template matching techniques such as DTW and VQ and speaker modeling approach using HMM and GMM were described. Finally, current state-of-the-art speaker recognition system performances and their evaluation benchmarks using standard NIST data sets have been presented.

More research is needed in understanding the noise characteristics, performance degradation due to mismatch in data sets and operational conditions, and channel variability, in order to make speaker recognition/verification systems more robust and better performing for biometric applications. Future direction should include exploitation of higher level information, fusion of multiple algorithms, and emphasis on unconstrained tasks. Recent studies has also shown that fusion of multiple modalities such as fusing confidence scores from, face, voice and finger print recognition algorithms can produce robust person/speaker authentication engine for biometric systems.

References

1. Atal, S. (1976) Automatic recognition of speakers from their voices, *Proceedings IEEE* **64**(4), 460–475.

2. Baum, L. and T. Petrie (1966) Statistical inference for probabilistic functions of finite state Markov chains, *The Annals of Mathematical Statistics* **37**(6), 1554–1563.

3. Bellman, R. and Kalaba, R. (1959) On adaptive control processes, *IRE Transactions* on *Automatic Control* **4**(2), 1–9.

4. Bogert, B., Healy, M. J. R., and Tukey, J. W. (1963) The quefrency alanysis of time series for echoes: Cepstrum, pseudo-autocovariance, cross-cepstrum, and saphe cracking, in *Time Series Analysis* (Rosenblatt, M., ed.), pp. 209–243.

5. Carey, J., Parris, S., and Bridle, S. (1991) A speaker verification system using alpha-nets, *Proceedings IEEE International Conference on Acoustics, Speech, and Signal Processing (ICASSP)* I, 397–400.

6. Cooley, J. and Tukey, J. (1965) An algorithm for the machine computation of complex Fourier series, *Mathematical Computation* **19**, 297–301.

7. Cortes, C. and Vapnik, V. (1995) Support-vector networks, *Machine Learning* **20**, 273–297.

8. Cover, T. and Hart, P. (1967) Nearest neighbor pattern classification, *IEEE Transactions on Information Theory* **13**(1), 21–27.

9. Dalmasso, E., Castaldo, F., Laface, P., Colibro, D., and Vair, C. (2009) Loquendo: Politecnico di Torino's 2008 NIST speaker recognition evaluation system, *Proceedings IEEE International Conference Acoustics, Speech and Signal Processing (ICASSP)*, April 4213–4216.

10. Davis, S. and Mermelstein, P. (1980) Comparison of parametric representations for monosyllabic word recognition in continuously spoken sentences, *IEEE Transactions Acoustics, Speech, and Signal Processing* **28**(4), 357–366.

11. Dempster, A., Laird, N., and Rubin, D. (1977) Maximum likelihood from incomplete data via the EM algorithm, *Journal of the Royal Statistical Society* **39**(1), 1–38.

12. Guo, W., Long, Y., Li, Y., Pan, L., Wang, E., and Dai, L. (2009) iFLY system for the NIST 2008 speaker recognition evaluation, *Proceedings IEEE International Conference Acoustics, Speech and Signal Processing (ICASSP)*, April, 4209–4212.

13. Harris, F. J. (1978) On the use of windows for harmonic analysis with the discrete Fourier transform, *Proceedings IEEE* **66**(1), 51–83.

14. Hermansky, H., Morgan, N., Nayya, A., and Kohn, P. (1992) RASTA-PLP speech analysis technique, *Proceedings IEEE International Conference Acoustic on Speech and Signal Processing (ICASSP)* I, 121–124.

15. Ruan, H. and Sankar, R. (1995) Applying neural network to robust keyword spotting in speech recognition application, *Proceedings International Conference on Neural Networks (ICNN)*, November, 2882–2886.

16. Islam, T., Mangayyagari, S., and Sankar, R. (2007) Enhanced speaker recognition based on score-level fusion of Ahs and Hmm, *IEEE Proceedings SoutheastCon,* 14–19.

17. Itakura, F. (1975) Minimum prediction residual principle applied to speech recognition, *IEEE Transactions on Acoustics, Speech and Signal Processing* **23**(1), 67–72.

18. Itakura, F. and Saito, S. (1968) Analysis-synthesis telephone based on the maximum-likelihood method, *Proceedings 6th International Congress on Acoustics* C, 17–20.

19. Kajarekar, S., Scheffer, N., Graciarena, M., Shriberg, E., Stolcke, A., Ferrer, L., and Bocklet, T. (2009) The SRI NIST 2008 speaker recognition evaluation system, *Proceedings IEEE International Conference Acoustic on Speech and Signal Processing (ICASSP)*, April, 4205–4208.

20. Linde, Y., Buzo, A., and Gray, R. (1980) An algorithm for vector quantizer design, *IEEE Transactions on Communications* **28**, 84–94.

21. Mangayyagari, S., Islam, T., and Sankar, R. (2008) Enhanced speaker recognition based on intra-modal fusion and accent modeling, *Proceedings 19thInternational Conference on Pattern Recognition (ICPR)*, December.

22. Martin, A. and Przybocki, M. A. (1998) Speaker recognition evaluation plan, National Institute of Standards and Technology (see NIST's speaker recognition http://www.nist.gov/speech/test.htm).

23. Martin, A., Doddington, G., Kamm, T., Ordowski, M., and Pryzbocki, M. (1997) The DET curve in assessment of detection task, performance, *Proceedings of the European Conferenceon Speech, Communication, and Technology* **4**, 1895–1898.

24. McLachlan, G. (1988) Mixture models, Marcel Dekker, New York, NY.

25. Mokbel, C., Paches-Leal, C. R., Jouvet, D., and Monn, J. (1994) Compensation of telephone line effects for robust speech recognition, *Proceedings Third International Conference on Spoken Language Processing (ICSLP)*, 987–990, September.

26. Moore, B. and Glasberg, B. (1983) Suggested formula for calculating auditory-filter bandwidth and excitation patterns, *Journal of Acoustic Society of America* **74**, 750–753.

27. Myers, C., Rabiner, L., and Rosenberg, A. (1980) Performance tradeoffs in dynamic time warping algorithms for isolated word recognition, *IEEE Transactions on Acoustics, Speech, and Signal Processing* **28**(6), 626–635.

28. Nosratighods, M., Thiruvaran, T., Epps, J., Ambikairajah, E., Bin, M., and Haizhou, L. (2009) Evaluation of a fused FM and cepstral-based speaker recognition system on the NIST 2008 SRE, *Proceedings IEEE International Conference Acoustics, Speech and Signal Processing (ICASSP)*, 4233–4236.

29. Oppenheim, A., Schafer, R., and Stockham, T. (1968) Nonlinear filtering of multiplied and convolved signals, *Proceedings IEEE* **56**(8), 1264–1291.

30. Philips, P. J., Martin, A., Wilson, C. L., and Przybocki M. (2000) An introduction to evaluating biometric systems, *Computers* **33**(2), 56–63.

31. Rabiner, L. and Juang, B. (1993) Fundamentals of speech recognition, Prentice-Hall, Inc., Upper Saddle River, NJ.

32. Rabiner, L. and Levinson, S. (1981) Isolated and connected word recognition: Theory and selected applications, *IEEE Transactions on Communications* **29**(5), 621– 659.

33. Reynolds, D. (2003) Channel robust speaker verification via feature mapping, *Proceedings IEEE International Conference Acoustics, Speech and Signal Processing (ICASSP)* II, 53–56.

34. Reynolds, D. (1997) Comparison of background normalization methods for text-independent speaker verification, *Proceedings – European Conferenceon Speech, Communication, and Technology*, 963–967.

35. Rosenberg, A., Lee, E. C., and Soong, F. (1994) Cepstral Channel Normalization Techniques for HMM-Based Speaker verification, proceedings of the third international conference on spoken language processing (ICSLP), september, 1835–1838.

36. Sakoe, H. and Chiba, S. (1978) Dynamic programming algorithm optimization for spoken word recognition, *IEEE Transactions on Acoustics, Speech, and Signal Processing* **26**(1), 43–49.

37. Sankar, R. and Patravali, S. (1994) Noise immunization using neural net for speech recognition,*Proceedings IEEE International Conferenceon Acoustics, Speech and Signal Processing (ICASSP)* II, 685–688.

38. Skowronski, M. and Harris, J. (2004) Exploiting independent filter bandwidth of human factor cepstral coefficients in automatic speech recognition,*Journal of Acoustical Society of America* **116**(3), 1774–1780.

39. Smith, S., Volkman, J., and Newman, E. (1937) A scale for the measurement of the psychological magnitude of pitch, *Journal of the Acoustical Society of America* **8**(3), 185–190.

40. Sturim, D., Campbell, W., Karam, Z., Reynolds, D., and Richardson, F. (2009) The MIT Lincoln Laboratory 2008 speaker recognition system, *Proc of Interspeech*, September.

41. The 2008 NIST Speaker Recognition Evaluation Plan (2008) http://www.itl.nist.gov/iad/mig//tests/spk/2008/sre08_evalplan_release4.pdf.

42. Vajaria, H., Islam, T., Mohanty, P., Sarkar, S., Sankar, R., and Kasturi, R. (2007) Evaluation and analysis of a face and voice outdoor multi-biometric system, *Pattern Recognition Letters* **28**(12), 1572–1580.

43. Vajaria, H., Islam, T., Sarkar, S., Sankar, R., and Kasturi, R. (2006) Audio segmentation and speaker localization in meeting videos, *Proceedings 18th International Conference on Pattern Recognition (ICPR)* **2**, 1150–1153.

44. Wayman, J. (1999) Error rate equations for the general biometric system, *IEEE Robotics and Automation Magazine* **6**(9), 35–48.

Chapter 6

Palm Recognition

Mike Beale

Department of Electrical and Computer Engineering, Indiana University-Purdue University at Indianapolis, 723 W. Michigan Street Room 160, Indianapolis, Indiana 46202, USA
mpbeale@iupui.edu

6.1 Introduction

Hands are in the most primal sense what mankind uses to create; therefore, it is logical that for thousands of years man has used hand imprints or outlines to show what he has created and where he has been [1]. Even today, movie stars stamp their hand prints in the Hollywood Walk of Fame to honor their achievement. It is no surprise that the hand has become an anatomical feature used to identify a person. There are several characteristic of the hand that can be used as biometrics: fingerprints [2], veins in the palm [1, 3, 4], hand geometry [1, 2, 5], and palm recognition. This chapter is going to focus on palm recognition, but the other subjects will come up again when multimodal biometrics is discussed.

Although using the palm as a marker or signature is ancient, modern automated palm recognition technology is an up-and-

Biometrics: From Fiction to Practice
Edited by Eliza Yingzi Du
Copyright © 2013 Pan Stanford Publishing Pte. Ltd.
ISBN 978-981-4310-88-8 (Hardcover), 978-981-4364-13-3 (eBook)
www.panstanford.com

coming topic in biometrics. Palm recognition relies on the unique characteristics of the human palm to distinguish people.

There are three different characteristics covered in this chapter. The minutiae of the human palm consist of ridges, like the ridges in fingerprints. The principal lines of the hand are the deep creases that run across the hand. The third is the texture of the palm.

The system-wide approach is the next part to be examined. This will cover the hardware and some of the algorithms used in segmenting and comparing images of palms. Finally, the future of palm recognition will be theorized.

6.1.1 *History*

Palm recognition biometrics is the oldest form of biometrics; it was first used in a commercial setting in 1858 by Sir William Herschel. Herschel needed a way to track his employees; this was difficult because they were illiterate. Herschel's solution was to take hand prints of all of his employees in order to verify that pay was going to the correct employee [6].

The first commercial automated palmprint recognition was possible in the mid to late 1990s. These were systems similar to Automatic Fingerprint Identification System (AFIS) for fingerprints, except that it was for the palm. In Rhode Island, Connecticut, and California[6], these system where offline, i.e., the print was made a medium and then scanned into the system. Companies such as NEC and Motoral make devices that compare palmprints for forensic applications [1].

6.2 Methods

There are several characteristics of the palm that provide good biometric data (see Fig. 6.1). First are the wrinkles or texture on the palm. The second characteristic is the minutiae on the palm [6, 7]. The minutiae are similar to fingerprints. The next feature that can be extracted is the principal lines of a hand. Principal lines are the deep wrinkles running the length of the hand [8, 9]. The wrinkles or texture of the palm could also be used as biometric information.

Valleys

Principal Lines

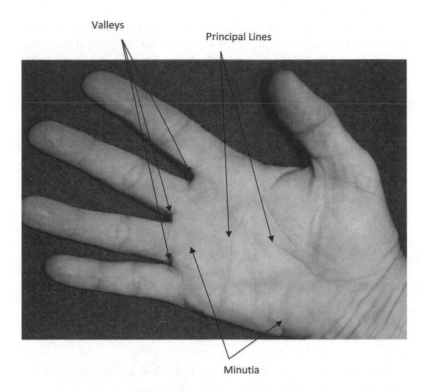

Minutia

Figure 6.1. Image of palm.

This method includes information about the large principal lines, and also about the smaller wrinkles [10–13].

6.2.1 *Minutiae*

The minutiae of the palm are very similar to the minutiae on fingerprints. Palm minutiae consist of ridges. Everybody has slightly different ridge endings, pore locations, and bifurcations (points at which ridges join each other).

The minutiae of the palm were first incorporated into an automatic biometric system in the mid-1990s [14]. This was an offline system used for forensics similar to AFIS. By the late 1990s many states added palmprints to their AFIS system [6].

There are three ways to analyze palm minutiae points [6]. The first is correlation; this simply means lining up the two prints being tested to see how well they match. The next is by looking at the location and direction of the minutiae points. Minutiae points are described below. The final method involves looking at ridge pattern markings.

The minutiae of the palm share several of the advantages of fingerprint recognition. Like fingerprint recognition, using minutiae is very well researched and reliable. The minutiae on the hand are stable and do not change over the course of a person's life [6].

Using minutiae has some disadvantages. First, the minutiae on the palm can be difficult or impossible to acquire for several reasons. Oftentimes, this data degrades if a person has heavy calluses on his or her hands. Another disadvantage of using minutiae is that a relatively high resolution image is required in order to accurately read the information on the palm. Minutiae recognition requires an image with 400 dots per inch (dpi), while other forms of palm recognition require as little as 100 dpi. Minutiae require a large area to scan unlike other forms of biometrics [11].

Because a very high-quality image is needed to use minutiae on a palmprint, this techneque is mostly used in forensic situations.

6.2.2 *Principal Lines*

Principal lines are the deep creases in middle area of the palm. These lines are synonymous with palm readers because these are supposed to tell fortunes. Now, this same physiological trait is used to identify people. This form of biometrics is much newer than minutiae recognition, and it is very promising. Principal lines identification has the advantage of using much lower-resolution images to perform the identification.

Using principal lines for palm recognition has one main advantage: it has a small template size [8]. The primary lines can be represented as a binary image; this means that it can be stored in files. This also allows for faster results when trying to identify a palmprint.

6.2.3 *Texture of Palm*

The texture of the palm is unique for each person, and one way to identify someone is to look at all the texture information available on the palm. Rather than separating out specific data texture, identification looks at the palm from a holistic point of view. The techniques used to compare palms using texture are similar to those used to compare faces. These algorithms take a larger set of data and project it on to smaller subspace, therefore making the data easier to compare. Two such techniques are eigenpalm [12] and fisherpalm [10, 13].

The advantage in using texture is that it allows for identification using a relatively low-resolution image. Another advantage is that there is no extra noise created by an extensive feature extraction process like in principal line extraction and minutiae extraction. The disadvantage is that the algorithms for identifying a palm are complicated and require a great deal of computational power.

6.3 System

In this overview of system, the first thing that is covered is the hardware that is used to acquire the data from the palm. Next, in the software section, I will discuss several of the methods used to extract usable information from the data gathered from palm data. The basic design of a palmprint recognition system is similar to all other forms of biometric systems.

6.3.1 *Palm Acquisition*

Palm acquisition is where the data is actually gathered from hand; this could be done with any number of different sensors. This includes optical, capacitive, thermal, and ultrasonic sensors [6]. An optical scanner from cross-match is pictured in Fig. 6.2 [15].

There are two different kinds of data that are entered into the biometric system. The first is enrollment data, and the second is identification data. The information gathered for enrollment is stored in the database. The information gathered from the identification is compared to the information already in the database [1].

Figure 6.2. Optical scanner (1).

6.3.2 *Palmprint Recognition*

After the data is acquired it is sent for preprocessing. In the preprocessing stage, the palmprint data is formatted so that the important information is easier to obtain. This stage includes accounting for slight variations that are caused by the way people interact with the sensor. In system without pegs, the palmprint could be rotated and stretched; it is critical that the palmprints be normalized in order for the match results to be accurate. One method to orientate the palm is to find and measure the gaps between the fingers called valleys [7, 11, 16, 17].

Next, the feature extraction stage background noise is eliminated and the essential features are isolated. For example, in principal line identification the extraction stage would result in an image of just the black and white lines. Template generation involves taking the feature extracted from the feature stage and storing them in a form that can be easily compared. Oftentimes, this involves doing a transform so that the data is in a form that is easier for matching the algorithm to be used [12, 13, 18, 19].

The final step of the palmprint recognition system is the matching process. There are two basic matching methods. The first is verification; in this method, the system is presented with the

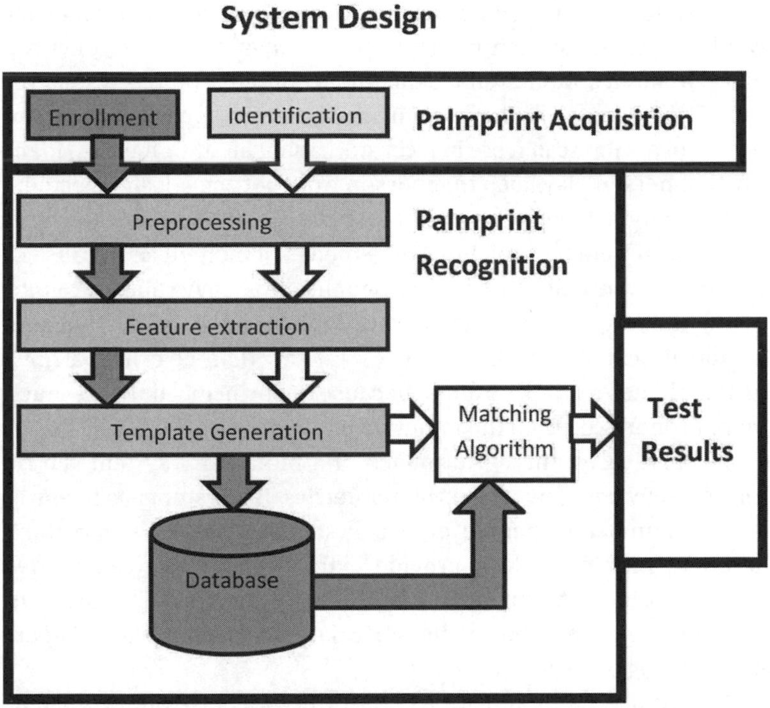

System Design

Figure 6.3. System schematic of palm recognition system.

ID of the subject and the subject's biometrics information. The system then decides if the biometric data that the subject presents the system is similar enough to be a match. The other method of matching is identification; in this method, the system is only given the biometric information. The system then finds the ID of the subject by finding the set of biometric information that is most similar to the biometric data presented to the system.

6.4 The Future of Palm Recognition

6.4.1 *Multimodal*

Multimodal biometrics is a method of biometrics that uses two or more different traits to establish the identity of a person [1]. Using palm identification in conjunction with another mode of biometrics would make the system better in many ways. Using two or more different modes would reduce the impact of noise on the system results. For example, if someone hurt their palm in such a way that the results of a palm scan were inaccurate, having another mode to identify that person may keep that person from getting falsely rejected.

Multimodal biometrics also has advantage of being able to enroll people who cannot enroll into some modes of biometrics because of physical abnormality. Oftentimes, people with heavy calluses cannot enroll into fingerprint system because the minutiae on their fingers are too difficult to read. In this case, it is likely that the principal lines on their hands can still be found because the principal lines are much more pronounced then the minutiae on the fingertip.

In most cases, the performance of a biometrics system can be improved by using two forms of biometrics. If a system has to enroll a large number of people or if a system has to have very high accuracy, multimodal can provide extra performance capabilities [2]. If another different kind of biometrics was used, it could help differentiate people whose biometric data is too similar to tell apart by just using one system.

Finally, it is more difficult to spoof (provide false information to a biometric system) if a system is looking at two forms of data [20].

6.4.1.1 Vein and palm

Vein recognition is a new area of biometrics. It relies on near-infrared light to get thermal information in order to map the veins under the skin [1, 4, 21]. Fujistu has a system that scans the palm with near-infrared light in order to verify the identity of an individual. Figure 6.4 shows a picture of the system; it is a contactless scan system. This system has been deployed worldwide, and there are high expectations for this system to be integrated into all kinds of application like ATMS, kiosks, time and attendance system, and other industry-specific applications [3].

Vein recognition has built-in security characteristics that make it difficult to spoof. But if vein recognition grows in popularity, there will be a greater incentive to attack these systems, and it is only a matter of time before it will be spoofed.

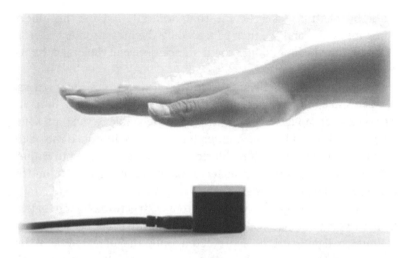

Figure 6.4. Vein recognition sensor by Fujistu [3].

Palmprint recognition would be an obvious way for another layer of security to vein recognition systems. A key factor that can make or break a biometric system is usability. A system is not going to be implemented if it is too complicated or too intrusive. If a user is scanning their palm for vein recognition, it would be no more difficult to take another image of that palm and send it to a palm recognition system. Research has proved that fusing vein and palm recognition has improved accuracy [4].

6.4.1.2 Hand geometry and palm

Hand geometry is another form of biometrics that could be combined with palm recognition. Hand geometry measures the size and shape to identify a person. This system is growing in popularity in systems that need to identify an individual, but does not require a one-to-one match [10].

6.4.2 *3D Palm Recognition*

There are several ways to capture 3D information from a palm. One way is to use laser triangulation devices; companies like Konica Minolta make devices that can take these images. These devices work by emitting laser beams that are reflected off the object being measured and are then captured by the measurement device. Triangulation is done to find the distance between the object being measured and the sensor.

These devices have been used for other forms of 3D biometrics. 3D face and ear biometrics have been researched, but palm biometrics is still not capable of using the current technology. Currently, the technology is not advanced enough for palm recognition. If the palm is scanned at high enough resolution, it will take too long to gather the data. So using the current technology is not a good option for collecting 3D palm information.

Another way to gather 3D data is to use structured light imaging. Structure light images are taken with regular 2D cameras, but a uniform light pattern is projected onto the object. When the uniform light pattern hits the object, it is distorted. By measuring the distortion caused by the object, it is possible to calculate its depth. There has been research in this area already.

It has been shown to have many advantages [22]. This system is less vulnerable to spoofing because it has 3D information. This experiment was conducted using a contact scanner with pegs to orient the fingers.

Another way to get 3D information from an object is a multiview photometric stereo [23]. This method uses two cameras to make a 3D model of an object (Fig. 6.5). This technique is considered a low-cost and low-accuracy method [22]. The palm is an almost 2D feature; this method has little to add to a contact palm recognition system because the palm flushes when placed against the sensor.

The multiview photometric stereo method could be useful for making a contactless palm recognition system. Using two or more cameras would allow the palm to be identified even if the hand is not orientated correctly. This could allow for a more ruggedized system that would compensate for someone who did not display their hand properly. For example, using multiview photometrics could compensate for someone who had their hand partially clinched or not aligned with camera.

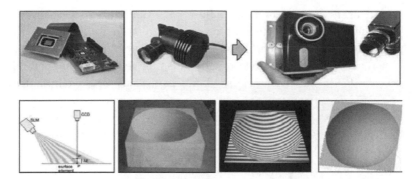

Figure 6.5. On the top row is the components and assembled structured light camera. On the bottom row is a picture describing the system, an regular picture of an object, an image of the previous object with structured light projected on it and a model of the object made using the projected light image [31].

Figure 6.6. Laser triangulation device [32].

6.4.3 *Touchless Palm Recognition*

A key factor that can make or break any biometric system is usability. If the system is too complicated for people to use, or if the system causes people to be uncomfortable, then the system will not be widely used. One way to make palm recognition more user-friendly and safe is to use contactless data acquisition method.

A major concern when implementing a biometric system is the fact that when many people touch the same sensor it can spread disease [16]. Using contactless data acquisition would eliminate these risks.

Contactless palmprint system would also be more user-friendly and inclusive. Contact palmprint systems often require users to position their hand in between pegs [11]. This process could be confusing for some people and could result in a false rejection from the system. People with injured fingers or arthritis could have difficulty maneuvering their hands into a palm recognition system, making it impossible for them to enroll.

If a contactless palmprint system was ruggedized enough, it would allow for people to be scanned even if they did not know that they were being scanned. This kind of biometrics is called noncooperative, and it is very useful for finding criminals who would not willingly scan their palm.

The obvious downside to contactless palm recognition is that it requires additional processing to extract the region of interest from the palm. The system has to compensate for rotation of the palm and varying distance to the sensor. As computers and programs continue to improve, this will become a reality.

6.5 Conclusion

In conclusion, palm recognition is an emerging area of biometrics that has several facets. Three different methods of palm recognition were discussed, including principal line, minutiae, and texture recognition. A system overview briefly explained how palm recognition works on a system level. Finally, predictions about the future of palm recognition were made. These areas include multimodal biometrics, 3D palm recognition, and touchless palm recognition.

References

1. Jain, A. K., Flynn, P., and Ross, A. A. (2007) *Handbook of Biometrics*. Springer, New York City.

2. Yang, F. and Ma, B. (2006) A New Mixed-Mode Biometrics Information Fusion Based-on Fingerprint, Hand geometry and Palm-print, 1, s.l. : IEEE Computer Society, January 2006, *Fourth International Conference on Image and Graphics*, Vol. 89, pp. 689–693.

3. Fujistu. *PalmSecure Palm Veig Authentication Technology,* Foothill Ranch, CA: s.n., 2010.

4. Wang, J.-G., Yau, W.-Y., Suwandy, A., and Sung, E. (2007) Fusion of Palmprint and Palm Vein Images for Person Recognition Based on "Laplacianpalm" Feature, *IEEE*.

5. Choras, R. S. and Michal, C. (2006) Hand Shape Geometry and Palmprint Features for the Personal Identification, *Proceedings of the Sixth International Conference on Intelligent.*

6. National Science and Technology Council (2006) *Palm Print Recognition.*

7. Tan, Z., Yang, J., Shang, Z., Shi G., and Chang, S. (2009) Minutiae-Based Offline Palmprint Identification System. *Global Congress on Intelligent Systems*, 466–471.

8. Wu, X., Zhang, D., and Wang, K. (2006) Palm Line Extraction and Matching for Personal Authentication. *IEEE Transactions on Systems, Man, and Cybernetics*, 978–987.

9. Chen, J., Zhang, C., and Rong, F. (2001) Palmprint Recognition Using Crease. *IEEE*, 234–237.

10. Zhang, D. D. (2004) *Palmprint Authentication.* Norwell, Massachusetts: Kluwer Academic Publisher Group.

11. Zhang, D., Kong, W.-K., You, J., and Wong, M. *On-Line Palmprint Identification.*

12. Lu, G., Zhang, D., and Want, K. (2003) Palmprint Recognition Using Eigenpalms Features. 2003, *Pattern Recognition Letters*, 1463–1467.

13. Wu, X., Zhang, D., and Wang, K. (2003) Fisherpalms based palmprint recognition. s.l.: www.computerscienceweb.com, 2003, *Pattern Recognition Letters,* 2829–2838.

14. Maylor, K. H., Leung, A. C. M. Fong, and Hui, S. C. (2007) Palmprint Verification for Controlling Access to Shared Computing Resources.*IEEE Computer Society,* 40–47.

15. Crossmatch Technologies. [Online] [Cited: 8 30, 2010.] http://www.crossmatch.com/l-scan-500p.php.

16. Ong, M. G. K., Tee, C., and Jin, A. T. B. (2008) Touch-less Palm Print Biometric System, *International Conference on Computer Vision Theory and Applications*, 423–430.

17. Parashar, S., Vardhan, A., Patvardhan, C., and Kalra, P. K. (2008) Design and Implementation of a Robust Palm Biometrics Recognition and Verification System, *Sixth Indian Conference on Computer Vision, Graphics & Image Processing*, 543–550.

18. Wu, X.-Q., Wang, K.-Q., and Zhang, D. (2002) Wavelet Based Palmprint Recognition. Bejing : IEEE. *First International Conference on Machine Learning and Cybernetics*. 1253–1257.

19. Choras, M., Kozik, R., and Zelek, A. A. Novel Shape-Texture Approach to Palmprint Detection and Identification. s.l. : IEEE Computer Society, 2008, *Eighth International Conference on Intelligent Systems Design and Applications*, 638–643.

20. Hui, Y. and Duo, L. Personal Identification Based on Multi-Modal Hand-Print Features. Chongqing, China: IEEE, 2008. *World Congress on Intelligent Control and Automation*. 7649–7652.

21. Fan, K.-C., Lin, C.-L., and Lee, W.-L. (2003) Biometric Verification Using Thermal Images of Palm-dorsa Vein-patterns., *16th IPPR Conference on Computer Vision, Graphics and Image Processing*, 188–195.

22. Zhang, D., Lu, G., Li, W., and Zhang, L. (2009) Palmprint Recognition Using 3-D Information.*IEEE Transactions on Systems, Man, and Cybernetics*, 505–519.

23. Hernandez, C., Vogiatzis, G., and Cipolla, R. (2008) Multiview Photometric Stereo.*IEEE Transactions on Pattern Analysis and Machine Intelligence*, 548–554.

24. Bong, D. B. L., Tingang, R. N., and Joseph, A. (2010) Palm Print Verification System., *Proceedings of the World Congress on Engineering*.

25. Fratric, I. and Ribaric, S. (2008) Colour-Based Palmprint Verification – An Experiment. *IEEE*, 890–895.

26. Hao, Y., Sun, Z., Tan T., and Ren, C. (2008) Multispectral palm image fusion for accurate contact-free palmprint. *IEEE*, 281–284.

27. Rajawat, A., Hanmandlu, M., and Pani, S. (2009) Fuzzy Modeling Based Palm Print Recognition System, *International Conference on Emerging Trends in Electronic and Photonic Devices & Systems*, 189–192.

28. Yang, J., Zhang, D., Yang, J. Y., and Niu, B. (2007) *Globally Maximizing, Locally Minimizing: Unsupervised Discriminant Projection with Applications to Face and Palm Biometrics, IEEE Transactions on Pattern Analysis and Machine Intelligence*, 650–664.

29. Kong, W. K., Zhang, D., and Li, W. (2003) *The Journal of the Pattern Recognition Society*, 2339–2347.

30. Song, Y.-G., Jang, W.-S., Kang, H.I., Lee, B.-H., Kang, H.-S., Cho, J.-H., and Kwon, K. S. Verification of live palm-print using sub-images reconstruction. s.l.: IEEE, 2007. *International Conference on Convergence Information Technology, 2432.*

31. *ViALUX. Lasers+Photonics. [Online] http://www.vialux.de/.*

32. *Minolta, K., Konica Minolta Homepage. [Online] http://www. konicaminolta.com.*

Chapter 7

Multimodal Biometrics

Zhi Zhou and Eliza Yingzi Du

Department of Electrical and Computer Engineering, Indiana University-Purdue University Indianapolis, 723 W. Michigan St. SL160, Indianapolis, 46202 Indiana, USA
zhizhou@iupui.edu and yidu@iupui.edu

Usually, a unimodal biometric has its own limitations. For instance, face recognition does not perform well with pose variations and is sensitive to illumination and shadows, fingerprint recognition cannot be applied for identification at a distance, and voice recognition can be affected by age, flu, or throat infection. In order to increase population coverage, extend the range of environmental conditions, improve resilience to spoofing, and achieve higher recognition accuracy, multimodal biometrics was introduced. Multimodal biometrics use more than one means of physiological or behavioral characteristics to identify and verify a person. In this chapter, the advantages and limitations of each kind of biometrics technologies are discussed. Traditional multimodal integration measures are reviewed and analyzed, including integration in multiple traits, integration in multiple snapshots of the same trait, and integration in multiple representations and matching algorithms of the same trait. The score fusion methods and applications in multimodal biometrics are discussed in the chapter as well.

Biometrics: From Fiction to Practice
Edited by Eliza Yingzi Du
Copyright © 2013 Pan Stanford Publishing Pte. Ltd.
ISBN 978-981-4310-88-8 (Hardcover), 978-981-4364-13-3 (eBook)
www.panstanford.com

7.1 Introduction

The biometrics systems have significant advantages over traditional identification methods. The identified person should physically be at the identification point, since biometric features cannot be shared and are difficult to imitate. However, for a unimodal biometrics, it usually has some limitations. Figure 7.1 shows some examples of biometrics.

Voice and face signals are easy to obtain, but the recognition accuracy is not high [35, 50]. Since the voice of a person changes with age, flu, or throat infection, voice recognition is not accurate all the time for human verification. Face images can be captured without user cooperation; however, face recognition cannot always

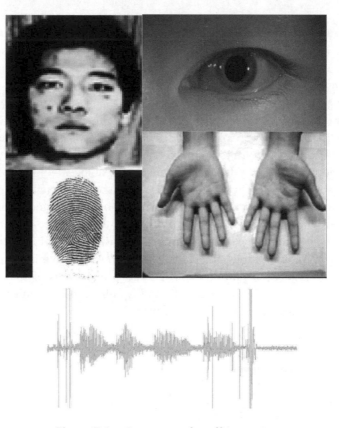

Figure 7.1. Some examples of biometrics.

Table 7.1. The pros and cons of various biometric systems

	Accuracy	Reliability	Stable	Identification (ID)	ID in distance	User co-op	Large population
Fingerprint	High	High	Yes	Yes	No	Yes	Yes
Face	Medium	Medium	No	Somewhat	Somewhat	Somewhat	No
Iris	Very high	Very high	Yes	Yes	Somewhat	Somewhat	Yes
Voice	Low	Low	No	No	–	No	No
Hand geometry	Low	Low	Yes	No	–	No	No
Ear shape	Medium	Medium	Yes	No	–	Yes	No
Signature	Low	Low	No	No	–	Yes	No

perform well with pose variations and is sensitive to illumination, shadows, etc.

Fingerprint and iris recognitions are very accurate and reliable, and they can be used for large databases. However, fingerprint recognition cannot be applied for identification at a distance, and it needs to keep the capture surface clean [29]. Moreover, it has been estimated that 5% of the people do not have legible fingerprints. For iris recognition to achieve high accuracy, it needs to be performed in near-infrared (NIR) spectrum, which requires additional NIR illuminators; this makes it very challenging to perform remote iris recognition in real-life scenarios [7, 10].

Other biometrics, e.g., palmprint, gait, ear shape, and signature, also have their own limitations. Table 7.1 summarizes the advantages and disadvantages of various kinds of biometrics technologies [11, 12].

In order to permit choice of biometric modality for authentication and increase population coverage by reducing the failure to enroll rate, multimodal biometrics have been introduced to enhance the performance. Multimodal biometrics combines multiple biometrics to do positive human identification in commercial applications since 1998. By using more than one means of biometric identification, the multimodal biometric identifier can obtain high recognition accuracy. In addition, using multimodal biometrics, we can extend the range of environmental conditions under which authentication can be performed, thus improving resilience to spoofing (Fig. 7.2).

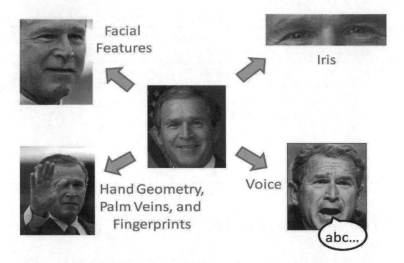

Figure 7.2. Multimodal biometrics.

7.2 Integration

There are several ways to integrate multimodal biometrics [1, 2, 4, 6, 9, 13, 14, 16–19, 21–27, 31, 33, 34, 37–40, 42–49, 52–55], and the most common one is to combine multiple traits, such as fingerprint and face, iris and face, fingerprint and voice, etc. With the same trait, more than one instance of the same biometric can be used for the identification and/or recognition, e.g., visible and NIR images of the face or iris, multiple samples of the voice, or multiple impressions of the same finger. Moreover, different approaches for feature extraction and matching of the single trait, such as iris or fingerprints, can be fused together to improve the recognition performance.

7.2.1 *Multiple Traits*

Figure 7.3 shows the process of integration in multiple traits. For different modalities, feature extraction and matching will be applied to generate matching scores. The final decision is based on the fused score.

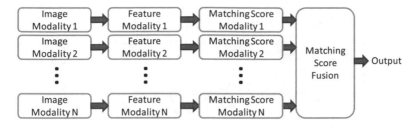

Figure 7.3. Integration in multiple traits.

Over the past decade, many multiple traits integration methods were designed. Frischholz and Dieckmann used facial features, lip movement, and voice recognition to achieve better accuracy of the recognition system. They claimed that the system reduced the false acceptance rate (FAR) significantly below 1% with 150 persons [19]. Kyong *et al.* compared the accuracy of face recognition and ear shape recognition with the combination of face and ear shape recognition. Their result shows that the rank one of the multimodal biometric is 90.9% versus 71.6% for the ear and 70.5% for the face using the 197 image training sets [26]. Figure 7.4 shows the process of the multimodal face and fingerprint recognition system.

7.2.2 *Multiple Snapshots of the Same Trait*

Unlike integration in multiple traits, we can also combine multiple snapshots of the same trait to perform multimodal biometrics systems. Figure 7.5 shows the process of integration in multiple

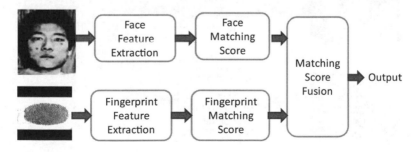

Figure 7.4. Face and fingerprints recognition system.

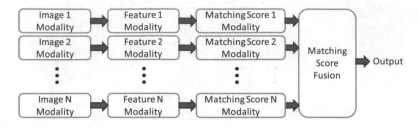

Figure 7.5. Integration in multiple snapshots of the same trait.

snapshots of the same trait. For each snapshot of the same modality, feature extraction and matching are applied.

Singh *et al.* integrated visible and infrared face images to enhance the performance of face recognition systems [44]. Figure 7.6 shows the process of integration of visible and infrared iris recognition systems.

7.2.3 *Multiple Representations and Matching Algorithms of the Same Trait*

This section involves combining different approaches to feature extraction and matching of single biometric. Figure 7.7 shows the integration in multiple representation and matching algorithms of the same trait.

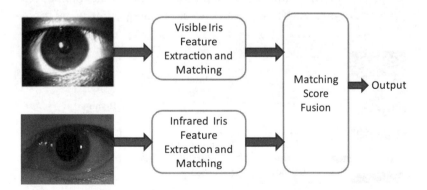

Figure 7.6. Visible and infrared iris recognition system.

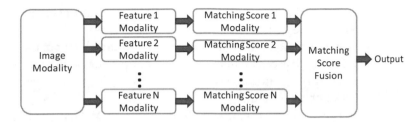

Figure 7.7. Integration in multiple representation and matching algorithms of the same trait.

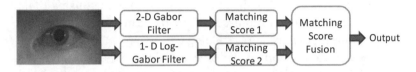

Figure 7.8. Enhanced iris recognition systems.

Kang and Park extracted vein and geometry patterns from a single finger image [23]. Their proposed multimodal biometric system improves the accuracy by 9.688% compared with the previous finger geometry recognition approach. Also, for the iris image, we can extract the iris features by 2D Gabor filter [7] and 1D Log-Gabor filter [3, 41] separately, and combine the matching scores to improve the recognition accuracy (Fig. 7.8).

7.2.4 *Score Fusion Methods*

In order to fuse different matching scores together to generate the final matching score, several score fusion methods were developed:

- Simple-sum method: Different normalized matching scores are simply added without weighting or other considerations. The simple-sum method can smooth the data using the average value, but if there are some images with bad quality, the system will have a lower false rejection rate (FRR).
- Min-score method: The fused score is obtained by taking the minimum value of different normalized matching scores. In

this way, the FAR of the system will be lower; however, the FRR will be higher.

- Max-score method: Contrary to the min-score method, the fused score is calculated by the maximum value of different normalized matching scores. The system will have lower FRR but higher FAR.
- Gaussian mixture model method (GMM): GMM has been tested and found to be one of the best methods to estimate the density using finite mixture models converging to the true density when a sufficient number of training samples are available. Nandakumar *et al.* [8] proposed using GMM for likelihood ratio-based biometric score fusion. However, this method requires training data.
- Principal component analysis (PCA) method [32, 36, 50, 51]: PCA, also called the eigenface method, is considered as a classic approach. Its principle is to find an orthogonal coordinate system such that data is approximated best and the correlation between different axes is minimized.
- Linear discriminate analysis (LDA) method [15, 28]: LDA searches the directions for maximum discrimination of classes. The within-class and between-class matrices are defined in order to achieve this goal.
- Support vector machine (SVM) method [13, 39]: The SVM method, as a nonprobabilistic binary linear classifier, is used to classify and analyze data by taking a set of input data and predicting. Like the GMM method, the SVM method also requires training data.

7.3 Applications

In corporate and public systems, consumer electronics, and sales application, multimodal biometrics systems are increasingly applied in human identification, board security, and identification cards. By using more than one means of biometrics, multimodal biometrics can achieve higher recognition accuracy. Depending on the level of security, the system can decide how many biometric identifiers should be required at one time.

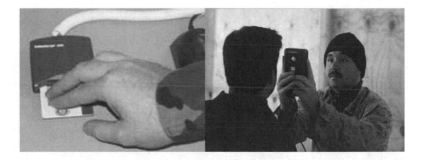

Figure 7.9. BAT system [30].

7.3.1 *Human Identification*

Biometrics Automated Toolset, which is called BAT, is used to help catch criminals throughout Afghanistan and Iraq. Each person in this system has a profile including name, iris images, front facial pictures, and fingerprints. With this multimodal biometric system, Iraqi detention facilities, military and police academies, and entry control can simplify the process of catching offenders (Fig. 7.9).

7.3.2 *Board Security*

As the world's safest airport, the Japanese capital's international airport began using the multimodal biometrics system since 2004 for check-in. As part of its "e-airport" program, it allows passengers especially business people to check in with face and iris recognition. Travelers can check in at the security gate at immigration and at boarding without stopping. The Narita airport hopes that its e-airport system can improve efficiency.

The "Clear" program, as the largest registered traveler program operating at U.S. airports, uses iris and fingerprints to allow users expedited access through airport security checkpoints.

The U.S. Citizenship and Immigration Services used fingerprint and face recognition to verify the identities of some 100,000 frequent visitors to the United States. In the near future, iris scans will be included.

Currently, about 20 countries are using biometrics to authenticate the citizenship of travelers. Frequent fliers to the United States

Figure 7.10. Multimodal biometrics system in Narita airport [20].

can enroll in the Registered Traveler Program, which is a biometric verification system using a combination of iris and fingerprint recognition, thus expediting the security check process at airports (Fig. 7.10).

7.3.3 *Identification Cards*

In the last decade, some countries, such as Australia, the United Kingdom, and Germany, have been issued identification cards and passports embedded with multimodal biometrics information to improve security and convenience of border control. The Brazilian government has also started adopting multimodal biometrics recognition systems on citizens' ID cards (Fig. 7.11).

7.4 Summary

Biometrics uses physical, biological, and behavioral traits to automatically identify and verify a person. However, different kinds of biometrics technologies have their own advantages and disadvantages. In order to permit choice of biometric modality for authentication, increase population coverage by reducing the failure to enroll rate, enhance the recognition performance, and improve resilience to spoofing, multimodal biometrics have been introduced.

Figure 7.11.   Multimodal biometrics in an ID card [5].

Multimodal biometrics combines multiple biometrics to do positive human identification in commercial applications since 1998. By using more than one means of biometric identification, the multimodal biometric identifier can obtain high recognition accuracy. There are several ways to integrate multimodal biometrics, and in this chapter we introduced three common measures: integration in multiple traits (such as fingerprint and face, iris and face, and fingerprint and voice), integration in multiple snapshots of the same trait (such as visible and NIR images of the face or iris, multiple samples of the voice, or multiple impressions of the same finger), and integration in multiple representations and matching algorithms of the same trait (such as different extraction methods in fingerprints recognition and different extraction methods in iris recognition). In addition, several traditional score fusion methods were reviewed in this chapter, including simple-sum, min-score, max-score, GMM, PCA, LDA, and SVM.

In the end, the applications of multimodal biometrics systems were discussed as well. Multimodal biometric systems are increasingly applied in human identification, board security, identification cards, etc. Iraqi detention facilities, military and police academies, and entry control can simplify the process of catching criminals using the BAT system. Airports in Japan and the United States use multimodal biometrics to allow users expedited access through airport security checkpoints. Also, some countries have been issued identification cards and passports embedded with multimodal biometrics information to improve security and convenience of border control.

References

1. Aleksic, P. S. and Katsaggelos, A. K. (2006). Audio-Visual Biometrics, *Proceedings of the IEEE*, 94(11), 2025–2044.

2. Alonso-Fernandez, aF., Fierrez, J., Ramos, D., and Gonzalez-Rodriguez, J. (2010). Quality-based conditional processing in multi-biometrics: Application to sensor interoperability, *Systems, Man and Cybernetics, Part A: Systems and Humans, IEEE Transactions* 40(6), 1168–1179.

3. Belcher, C. and Yingzi, D. (2008). A selective feature information approach for iris image-quality measure, *Information Forensics and Security, IEEE Transactions* 3(3), 572–577.

4. Beresford, A. R. and Bacon, J. (2006). Intelligent transportation systems, *Pervasive Computing, IEEE* 5(4), 63–67.

5. CNET (2010), Senators push Obama for biometric National ID card, http://news.cnet.com/8301-13578_3-20000758-38.html

6. Conti, V., Militello, C., Sorbello, F., and Vitabile, S. A Frequency-based approach for features fusion in fingerprint and iris multimodal biometric identification systems, *Systems, Man, and Cybernetics, Part C: Applications and Reviews, IEEE Transactions on* 40(4), 384–395.

7. Daugman, J. (2004). How iris recognition works, *Circuits and Systems for Video Technology, IEEE Transactions* 14(1), 21–30.

8. Derakhshani, R., Ross, A., and Crihalmeanu, S. (2006). A new biometric modality based on conjunctival vasculature, *Proceedings of Artificial Neural Networks in Engineering (ANNIE)*.

9. Dong-Su, K. and Kwang-Seok, H. (2008). Multimodal biometric authentication using teeth image and voice in mobile environment, *Consumer Electronics, IEEE Transactions on* 54(4), 1790–1797.

10. Du, Y. (2006). Review of iris recognition: Cameras, systems, and their applications, *Sensor Review* 26(1), 66–69.

11. Du, Y. (2006), Biometrics: Technologies and trend, in *Encyclopedia of Optical Engineering*, Marcel Deker, New York.

12. Du, Y. (2008), Biometrics, in *Handbook of Digital Human Modeling*, Lawrence Erlbaurm, Mahwah, NJ.

13. Ejarque, P. and Hernando, J. (2009). Score bi-Gaussian equalisation for multimodal person verification, *Signal Processing, IET* 3(4), 322–332.

14. Erzin, E., Yemez, Y., Tekalp, A. M., Ercil, A., Erdogan, H., and Abut, H. (2006). Multimodal person recognition for human-vehicle interaction, *Multimedia, IEEE* 13(2), 18–31.

15. Etemad, K. and Chellappa, R. (1997). Discriminant analysis for recognition of human face images, Springer, 125–142.

16. Faundez-Zanuy, M. (2005). Data fusion in biometrics, *Aerospace and Electronic Systems Magazine, IEEE* 20(1), 34–38.

17. Faundez-Zanuy, M., Fierrez-Aguilar, J., Ortega-Garcia, J., and Gonzalez-Rodriguez, J. (2006). Multimodal biometric databases: An overview, *Aerospace and Electronic Systems Magazine, IEEE* 21(8), 29–37.

18. Fox, N. A., Gross, R., Cohn, J. F., and Reilly, R. B. (2007). Robust biometric person identification using automatic classifier fusion of speech, mouth, and face experts, *Multimedia, IEEE Transactions* 9(4), 701–714.

19. Frischholz, R. W. and Dieckmann, U. (2000). BioID: A multimodal biometric identification system, *Computer* 33(2), 64–68.

20. GE (2006), Narita International Airport chooses GE Security Homeland protection CTX 9000 DSi explosives detection systems, http://www.sourcesecurity.com/news/articles/co-737-ga.990.html

21. Jiang, R. M., Sadka, A. H., and Crookes, D. Multimodal biometric human recognition for perceptual human–computer interaction, *Systems, Man, and Cybernetics, Part C: Applications and Reviews, IEEE Transactions* 40(6), 676–681.

22. Jie, L., Yu, F. R., Chung-Horng, L., and Tang, H. (2009). Optimal combined intrusion detection and biometric-based continuous authentication in high security mobile ad hoc networks, *Wireless Communications, IEEE Transactions* 8(2), 806–815.

23. Kang, B. J. and Park, K. R. Multimodal biometric method based on vein and geometry of a single finger, *Computer Vision, IET* 4(3), 209–217.

24. Kanhangad, V., Kumar, A., and Zhang, D. (2008). Comments on "An Adaptive Multimodal Biometric Management Algorithm," *Systems, Man, and Cybernetics, Part C: Applications and Reviews, IEEE Transactions* 38(6), 841–843.

25. Kumar, A., Kanhangad, V., and Zhang, D. (2005). A New Framework for adaptive multimodal biometrics management, *Information Forensics and Security, IEEE Transactions* 5(1), 92–102.

26. Kyong, C., Bowyer, K. W., Sarkar, S., and Victor, B. (2003). Comparison and combination of ear and face images in appearance-based biometrics, *Pattern Analysis and Machine Intelligence, IEEE Transactions* 25(9), 1160–1165.

27. Li, Z. J. J., Ferrer, M. A., Travieso, C. M., and Alonso, J. B. (2006). Biometric based on ridges of palm skin over the head of the second metacarpal bone, *Electronics Letters* 42(7), 391–393.

28. Lu, J., Plataniotis, K., and Venetsanopoulos, A. (2003). Face recognition using LDA-based algorithms,*IEEE Transactions on Neural Networks* 14(1), 195–200.

29. Maltoni, D., Maio, D., Jain, A., and Prabhakar, S. (2009). *Handbook of Fingerprint Recognition*, Springer-Verlag, New York.

30. Matthew, S. and Holly, O. (2007), BAT System Helps Catch Bad Guys, http://www.spacedaily.com/reports/BAT_System_Helps_Catch_Bad_Guys_999.html

31. Monwar, M. M. and Gavrilova, M. L. (2009). Multimodal biometric system using rank-level fusion approach, *Systems, Man, and Cybernetics, Part B: Cybernetics, IEEE Transactions* 39(4), 867–878.

32. Moon, H. and Phillips, P. (2001). Computational and performance aspects of PCA-based face-recognition algorithms,*Perception-London* 30(3), 303–322.

33. Ortega-Garcia, J., *et al.* (2003). MCYT baseline corpus: A bimodal biometric database, *Vision, Image and Signal Processing, IEE Proceedings*, 150(6), 395–401.

34. Ortega-Garcia, J., *et al.* The Multiscenario Multienvironment BioSecure Multimodal Database (BMDB), *Pattern Analysis and Machine Intelligence, IEEE Transactions* 32(6), 1097–1111.

35. Pearce, D. and Hirsch, H. (2000). The Aurora experimental framework for the performance evaluation of speech recognition systems under noisy conditions, 29–32.

36. Pentland, A., Moghaddam, B., and Starner, T. (1994), View-based and modular eigenspaces for face recognition, *IEEE Computer Society Conference on Computer Vision and Pattern Recognition*, 84–91.

37. Poh, N. and Bengio, S. (2005). How do correlation and variance of base-experts affect fusion in biometric authentication tasks? *Signal Processing, IEEE Transactions* 53(11), 4384–4396.

38. Poh, N., Kittler, J., and Bourlai, T. Quality-Based Score normalization with device qualitative information for multimodal biometric fusion, *Systems, Man and Cybernetics, Part A: Systems and Humans, IEEE Transactions* 40(3), 539–554.

39. Poh, N., Windridge, D., Mottl, V., Tatarchuk, A., and Eliseyev, A. addressing missing values in kernel-based multimodal biometric fusion using neutral point substitution, *Information Forensics and Security, IEEE Transactions* 5(3), 461–469.

40. Poh, N., *et al.* (2009). Benchmarking quality-dependent and cost-sensitive score-level multimodal biometric fusion algorithms, *Information Forensics and Security, IEEE Transactions* 4(4), 849–866.

41. Pozdin, V. and Du, Y. (2007), Performance analysis and parameter optimization for iris recognition using Log-Gabor wavelet, *Proceedings of SPIE* 6491, 649112.

42. Ribaric, S. and Fratric, I. (2005). A biometric identification system based on eigenpalm and eigenfinger features, *Pattern Analysis and Machine Intelligence, IEEE Transactions* 27(11), 1698–1709.

43. Ribaric, S., Ribaric, D., and Pavesic, N. (2003). Multimodal biometric user-identification system for network-based applications, *Vision, Image and Signal Processing, IEE Proceedings* 150(6), 409–416.

44. Singh, R., Vatsa, M., and Noore, A. (2008). Integrated multilevel image fusion and match score fusion of visible and infrared face images for robust face recognition, *Pattern Recognition* 41(3), 880–893.

45. Snelick, R., Uludag, U., Mink, A., Indovina, M., and Jain, A. (2005). Large-scale evaluation of multimodal biometric authentication using state-of-the-art systems, *Pattern Analysis and Machine Intelligence, IEEE Transactions* 27(3), 450–455.

46. Taekyoung, K. and Hyeonjoon, M. (2008). Biometric Authentication for Border Control Applications, *Knowledge and Data Engineering, IEEE Transactions* 20(8), 1091–1096.

47. Toh, K. Λ. and Wei-Yun, Y. (2004). Combination of hyperbolic functions for multimodal biometrics data fusion, *Systems, Man, and Cybernetics, Part B: Cybernetics, IEEE Transactions* 34(2), 1196–1209.

48. Toh, K. A., Wei-Yun, Y., and Xudong, J. (2004). A reduced multivariate polynomial model for multimodal biometrics and classifiers fusion, *Circuits and Systems for Video Technology, IEEE Transactions* 14(2), 224–233.

49. Toh, K. A., Xudong, J., and Wei-Yun, Y. (2004). Exploiting global and local decisions for multimodal biometrics verification, *Signal Processing, IEEE Transactions* 52(10), 3059–3072.

50. Turk, M. and Pentland, A. (1991). Eigenfaces for Recognition, *Journal of Cognitive Neuroscience* 3(1), 71–86.

51. Turk, M. A. and Pentland, A. P. (1991). Face recognition using eigenfaces,*IEEE Computer Society Conference on Computer Vision and Pattern Recognition*, 586–591.

52. Vatsa, M., Singh, R. and Noore, A. (2009). Unification of Evidence-Theoretic Fusion Algorithms: A Case Study in Level-2 and Level-3 Fingerprint Features, *Systems, Man and Cybernetics, Part A: Systems and Humans, IEEE Transactions* 39(1), 47–56.

53. Veeramachaneni, K., Osadciw, L. A., and Varshney, P. K. (2005). An adaptive multimodal biometric management algorithm, *Systems, Man, and Cybernetics, Part C: Applications and Reviews, IEEE Transactions* 35(3), 344–356.

54. Wahab, A., Chai, Q., Chin Keong, T., and Takeda, K. (2009). Driving Profile Modeling and Recognition Based on Soft Computing Approach, *Neural Networks, IEEE Transactions* 20(4), 563–582.

55. Wang, Z. F., Han, Q., Li, Q., Niu, X. M., and Busch, C. (2009). Complex common vector for multimodal biometric recognition, *Electronics Letters*, 45(10), 495–496.

Chapter 8

Biometrics on Smart Card

Tai-Pang Chen,[a] Wei-Yun Yau,[a] and Xudong Jiang[b]

[a] *Institute for Infocomm Research, A*STAR, Singapore*
[b] *Nanyang Technological University, Singapore*
tpchen@i2r.a-star.edu.sg

8.1 Introduction

Biometrics is being more and more widely used in ID cards. One of the most popularly used biometrics ID card is smart card. In particular, research into fingerprint authentication using digitized images has been on track for decades, but recent advances in computer hardware, fingerprint sensor technology, smart card, and computational power have finally enabled applications to be affordably deployed on a large scale. Some computer notebooks and personal digital assistances (PDAs) have built-in fingerprint sensor for users to gain security access. Since the introduction of e-passport by the International Civil Aviation Organization (ICAO), enhanced authentication solution employing smart card and biometrics aroused attention in many countries and the IT industry more than ever before. Certain countries, especially in Asia, use fingerprint authentication with e-passport or e-ID cards

Biometrics: From Fiction to Practice
Edited by Eliza Yingzi Du
Copyright © 2013 Pan Stanford Publishing Pte. Ltd.
ISBN 978-981-4310-88-8 (Hardcover), 978-981-4364-13-3 (eBook)
www.panstanford.com

at immigration checkpoints to accelerate identity verification time for citizens to cross the border using an automatic gantry. However, most of the existing solutions are using an authentication technique called off-card biometric comparison, which is a biometric comparison performed outside the smart card by biometric verification system against the stored biometric reference data in the user's smart card. In other words, the smart card is used as a secured storage device to retain the user's information and biometric data. The major advantages of such technique are (1) easy of implementation and (2) low-cost smart card usage. However, the major disadvantage is that the biometric reference data, which is the user's biometric data collected and encoded during the enrolment process, is exposed from the smart card to the outside world during verification as the biometric comparison is executed at the biometric verification system, which unusually is a PC or an embedded device. Such external communication poses security threats. Hence, to protect biometric reference data, cryptographic protection using secure messaging in smart card is required. If the keys of crypto-operation are compromised or the cryptomechanism is hacked, user's information and biometric reference data will be lost and revealed. To overcome the potential security loophole of off-card biometric comparison, on-card biometric comparison can be used. On-card biometric comparison is the process by which the smart card performs biometric comparison and decision making on the smart card, where the biometric reference data is retained inside the card. Hence, on-card biometric comparison provides stronger security protection for biometric authentication that attracts more attention from the governments and the IT industry. In 2006, the subcommittee 17 (SC17) under the Joint Technical Committee of International Organization for Standardization (ISO) and International Electrotechnical Commission (IEC) formed a new Work Group 11 (WG11) to define the functional blocks and components for the use of smart cards in applications, where the comparison of biometric identifiers is to be performed on-card. As of January 2010, WG11 has drafted a document "Information technology — Identification cards — On-card biometric comparison," [1] and this document is in the Final Committee Draft stage (all technical contents are settled; only editorial amendments are allowed until the publication of this document as International Standards). In this paper, an introduction on implementation of on-card fingerprint comparison using ISO/IEC 24787 will be presented. A simple local and global structure (LGS) fingerprint matching technique will be introduced and the methodology of using the work-sharing mechanism specified in ISO/IEC 24787 will be mentioned. The data structures of smart card and the security policies, which are application dependent, will not be addressed in the paper

8.2 Fingerprint Matching Algorithm

The primary algorithm considered here will be the minutiae-based fingerprint matching algorithm. The advantages of this approach are fast matching time, long history of implementation, and good accuracy for generic applications. The comparison process of enrolment template $\mathbf{m}_i$ against the query template $\mathbf{m}'_j$ can be formulated as the following equation [2]:

$$\underset{\Delta x, \Delta y, \Delta \theta, P}{\textbf{Maximize}} \sum_{i=1}^{m} match(Tr_{\Delta x, \Delta y, \Delta \theta}(\mathbf{m}_{Search(i)}), \mathbf{m}_i) \qquad (8.1)$$

where $match(\cdot)$ is the matching function to match minutia $\mathbf{m}_i$ against $\mathbf{m}'_j$ with a predefined threshold, $Tr(\cdot)$ is the geometric transformation that maps a minutiae $\mathbf{m}_i$ into $\mathbf{m}'_j$ using Δx, Δy and $\Delta \theta$ which is the x-offset, the y-offset and the difference in orientation respectively of the enrolment template against the query template, and the $search(\cdot)$ function is to find the index of minutia in $\mathbf{m}'_j$ which can pair up with the minutia in $\mathbf{m}_i$. The objective of Eq (8.1) is to search for the maximum number of matched minutiae in the enrolment template against the query template. In fact, the $search(\cdot)$ function and the $Tr(\cdot)$ function can be considered as the alignment process of $\mathbf{m}_i$ against $\mathbf{m}'_j$. The alignment process involves exhaustive search process to find the best correspondences in $\mathbf{m}_i$ and $\mathbf{m}'_j$ for the subsequent $match(\cdot)$ function to compute the overall matching score. In general, the process of minutiae matching is to maximize the number of matched minutiae points between the enrolment template and the query template while keeping the matching error to minimum among the matched local substructures of minutiae due to distortion caused by the elastic deformation of finger skin. In the past, numerous researchers have studied the minutiae matching problem. Geometric hashing [3] is the method to compare the similarity of two sets of points. Chung *et al.* [4] proposed to use this method to perform fingerprint matching in the fingerprint database. This method requires rotating the query template to generate different hashes to compare with the enrolment template so as to search for the optimal matching score. Such computationally intensive algorithm is not suitable for implementation on smart card. To overcome the computational problem, Pan *et al.* [5] proposed a memoryefficient algorithm of using multiscale geometric hashing technique to perform on-card matching which lowers the requirements; but this method still requires a 1K RAM and a 32-bit processor which are only suitable for expensive high-end smart card to execute such demanding collation algorithm. Krivec *et al.* [6] proposed a hybrid fingerprint matcher, which combines minutiae matcher and homogeneity structure matcher, to perform authentication on the smart card. However, this hybrid approach cannot increase the accuracy significantly compared to minutiae matcher alone, but incurs extra processing time to perform host-side matching. Besides solely using minutiae information, Rikin *et al.* [7] proposed using minutia ridge shape for fingerprint matching. The ridge shape information is used during minutiae matching to improve the matching accuracy. In their experiment, they showed that the accuracy was comparable to the conventional matching, but the process had a greater matching speed. For Javacard implementation, Moon *et al.* [8] proposed a method using collaborative fingerprint authentication with a trusted host. In order to speed up the matching process, the template is aligned on the host side by fetching the alignment information of the enrolment template from the Javacard. The authors suggested using the mean minutiae position and the mean ridge direction of the enrolment template as the alignment information. Such information may not be ideal for alignment especially for partial print and noisy fingerprint. References [9] and [10] are other implementations of on-card fingerprint matching, but the performance in terms of speed and accuracy is generally not at the satisfactory level.

To implement the overall minutiae matching process with acceptable matching time, a native implementation on smart card with sufficient processing power is required. If the smart card does not have sufficient processing power, the alternative way of solving the problem is to compute the alignment process outside the smart card by work-sharing mechanism, but the computation of final *match*(·) function is still retained inside the smart card. In this case, the requirement of the smart card's computation power can be lowered To compute the alignment process, various methods, including the leastsquare method [11], the brute force search [12] as well as the LGS method [13] are proposed in the literature. To avoid security threat, it is recommended that the Cartesian coordinate $(x_i y_i)$, the ridge angle θ_r and the minutia type (t_i) specified in the ISO/IEC 19794-2 Fingerprint Minutiae Specification [14] as mandated features inside the enrolment template are not revealed to any external device. Hence, the LGS method is one of the techniques that can be used for on-card fingerprint comparison with external alignment because it can separate the template into an open portion and a secured portion. The LGS method will be used as an example in this paper for the implementation of on-card fingerprint comparison using work-sharing technique.

8.3 An Overview of Local and Global Structure

Jiang *et al.* [13] proposed the LGS technique based on the local and global structures. The local structure, which contains the relative distance, relative direction, relative radial angle and relative ridge counts between minutia neighbors, is used to find the common minutiae base and the orientation difference for template alignment in order to construct the global structure for the subsequent matching process. The global structure, which is in polar coordinate representation, is used to compute the final matching score. The global structure is computed from the absolute information of minutiae such as coordinates, ridge directions and types. Each minutiae point can be described as a feature vector that is given by

$$\mathbf{M}_k = (x_k \ y_k \ \theta_k \ t_k), \tag{8.2}$$

where x_k and y_k are the coordinates of the given minutia, θ_k is the local ridge direction, t_k is the minutiae type (bifurcation or ridge end) and k is the index of the minutia. We can construct the minutiae template that consists of all detected minutiae $\mathbf{M}_k$, $k = 1, 2,$ ... N, where N is number of detected minutiae in the template. This secured portion of template, which is specified as finger minutiae data in ISO/IEC 19794-2 as mandated features, shall be used only for internal smart card fingerprint matching process. The smart card should never send out this template to any external device

Figure 8.1 illustrates a minutia and its nearest neighbors. The white arrow indicates the direction of the minutiae. Consider minutia m_i, where i is the index of minutiae. Three neighbors surrounding m_i can be found in the figure. The relative information of minutia m_i and its three neighbors nm_1, nm_2 and nm_3 can be calculated and encoded as the following local feature vector (LFV$_i$).

$$\begin{pmatrix} d_i^j \\ r_i^j \\ \varphi_i^j \\ \phi_i^j \end{pmatrix} = \begin{pmatrix} \sqrt{(x_i - x_j)^2 + (y_i - y_j)^2} \\ \text{Ridge count between minutiae} \\ \theta_j - \theta_i \\ \tan^{-1}\left(\frac{y_j - y_i}{x_j - x_i}\right) - \theta_j \end{pmatrix} \qquad (8.3)$$

$$\text{LFV}_i = [d_i^1 r_i^1 \varphi_i^1 \phi_i^1 d_i^2 r_i^2 \varphi_i^2 \phi_i^2 d_i^3 r_i^3 \varphi_i^3 \phi_i^3]^T \qquad (8.4)$$

LFV$_i$ contains the relative distance, relative ridge counts, relative ridge direction and the difference between the slope (dashed line in Fig. 8.1) and ridge direction of the nearest neighbor. All relative features can be calculated using Eqs. (8.3) and (8.4)

The local feature template (LFT) can be constructed by combining all LFVs together. Three nearest neighbors were used in our implementation. Of course, it is possible to use more nearest neighbors but the computation time will be longer as well as have larger template size of the LFT.

LFT contains only the relative information with limited number of nearest neighbors. Hence, such information cannot be easily used to reverseengineer the information in $\mathbf{M}_k$ as specified in Eq. (8.2) because

- The indexes of the nearest minutiae are not revealed
- It is difficult to guess the connectivity of the local structure as the order of the indexes can be scrambled

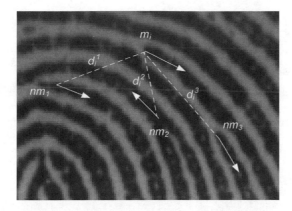

Figure 8.1. A minutia and its three nearest neighbors.

- Each nearest neighbor may or may not connect to another local structure

The LFT can be encoded as an open portion of auxiliary data as specified in ISO/IEC 24787 during the enrolment process. The open portion can be sent out to the biometric verification terminal to compute the alignment process with the query template. Minutiae M_k can be encoded as a secured portion of reference data according to ISO/IEC 19794-2 Finger Minutiae Speciation and stored in the smart card as secured portion which shall never be sent out to the biometric verification terminal or any other external device.

8.4 Work Sharing Mechanism for On-Card Comparison

Figure 8.2 shows the architecture of work-sharing for on-card fingerprint comparison which is tailored for fingerprint comparison using the LGS technique. Work-sharing on-card comparison (WOC) is one type of on-card comparisons, which computes certain processes, such as template alignment, outside the smart card. This type of comparison is designed for a smart card that does not have sufficient computing power to execute the entire matching process of biometric data. In this case, certain computations that are computationally intensive, such as template alignment, are sent

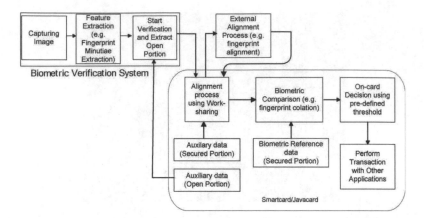

Figure 8.2. Architecture of work-sharing for on-card fingerprint comparison.

to the biometric verification system to perform the calculation. The result of the computation, such as aligned template, is sent back to the smart card so that the final determination of the matching score is calculated on the card. It is recommended that the communication between the smart card and the biometric verification system is protected using secure messaging mechanism.

Figure 8.3 shows the sequence diagram of the WOC mechanism. WOC consists of two major components: a biometric verification system (a terminal with a PC, a fingerprint sensor and a smart card reader) and a smart card. The biometric verification system captures the fingerprint image using the fingerprint sensor and encodes the query minutiae template (LFT′ and $\mathbf{M}'_k$) from the fingerprint image. During enrolment, LFT and $\mathbf{M}_k$ are stored in the smart card During verification, the smart card will send the LFT^{enroll} (open portion) to the biometric verification system for the alignment process. The details of the computation of external alignment process will be discussed later.

ISO/IEC 7816-4 [15] specifies the Application Protocol Data Unit (APDU) commands and definitions of response bytes for the smart card reader to communicate with the smart card to perform specific card operations. The overall WOC, which is using runtime work-sharing mechanism as specified in ISO/IEC 24787, can be divided into two portions: off-card alignment and on-card comparison. To

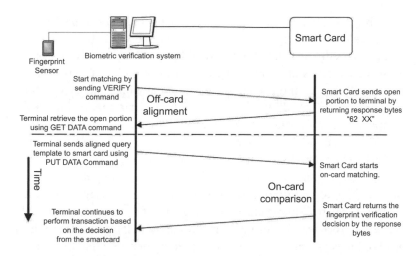

Figure 8.3.   Sequence diagram of work-sharing on-card comparison.

start fingerprint verification, a VERIFY command is sent to the smart card to initiate the fingerprint comparison process. Upon receiving the VERIFY command, the smart card sends a work-sharing response byte "62 XX" to the terminal to request work-sharing where XX is the size of the open template. After the biometric verification system receives the response byte "62 XX" a GET DATA command "00 CB 00 00 XX" is issued to the card to retrieve the open portion of the template (LFT^{enroll}). The alignment process involves exhaustive search procedures in order to find the best minutiae base for translational and rotational alignment of the input template for subsequent on-card comparison. The off-card alignment takes place right after the retrieval of the open portion (LFT^{enroll}). The terminal usually has a more powerful processor to perform exhaustive search to find the best reference base for alignment. Once the alignment process is completed, the terminal will send the aligned template and alignment information to the smart card using the PUT DATA command "00 DB 00 00 YY" where YY is the size of the data packet that contains the aligned template with other matching-related information. The smart card uses the alignment information to align the enrolment template and eventually perform the on-card comparison. As both templates have been aligned, the smart card can perform direct comparison to compute the matching score. The matching score will be compared with the predefined threshold to decide the final security status. If positive security status is found, the smart card will return response bytes "90 00" to indicate a successful matching. Otherwise, the response bytes "6X XX" will be returned to indicate a matching error (imposter found). The details of VERIFY command can be found in ISO/IEC 7816-11 and ISO/IEC 24787, while GET DATA and PUT DATA can be found in ISO/IEC 7816-4 and ISO/IEC 24787.

The overall smart card transaction is protected by secure messaging (cryptographic protection). Even though the open portion contains relative information that cannot be reverseengineered easily to recover the original minutiae template, cryptographic protection is recommended as an extra layer of protection to further enhance the overall security. The communication can use the weaker cryptoengine found in most intermediate or low-end smart cards.

8.5 Off-Card Alignment

Searching a pair of optimal bases for template alignment is very important for on-card fingerprint comparison. Unlike fingerprint matching in PC where the PC has the luxury to try multiple bases for alignment until a good matching score is found, the smart card cannot afford to perform multiple global matching as the computational resources are limited. Hence, searching a pair of optimal base is particularly important.

Let the open portion, LFT^{enroll}, be the LFT from the smart card that is generated during enrollment process and LFT^{query} be the template of local structure that is generated at the time of verification. The smart card sends LFT^{enroll} to the terminal for reference base finding. The terminal constructs the LFT^{input} and the global information as well form the minutiae detection engine. The terminal will then search for the matched pairs (MP) of the local structures by using Eqs. (8.5) and (8.6). Equation (8.6) is to compute the weighted error of LFV and Eq. (8.5) compares the matching error with threshold T_M. Only for those pairs with matching error less than T_M will be appended in the MP. Each entry of MP consists of one

LFV_i^{enroll} and one LFV_j^{query} which are matched LFV from enrollment template and input template respectively.

$$MP_k = \begin{cases} (\mathbf{mi}_i, \mathbf{mi}_j), & \text{if } (match(\mathbf{LFV}_i^{enroll}, \mathbf{LFV}_j^{input}) < T_m) \\ 0, & \text{otherwise} \end{cases} \quad (8.5)$$

$$match(a, b) = w_1 \cdot |d_a - d_b'| + w_2 \cdot |r_a - r_b'| + w_3 \cdot |\varphi_a - \varphi_b| + w_4' \cdot |\phi_a - \phi_b'| \quad (8.6)$$

where k is the index of MP, i and j are the indexes of enrollment template and input template respectively, mi_i and mi'_j are indexes of matched enrolment template and query template respectively, and w_1, w_2 w_3 and w_4 are weights to calculate the weighted error. Multiple MPs can be found during the comparison process. The best MP for alignment can be chosen by selecting the local structure with the lowest weighted error and the area of the structure is sufficiently large. Once all MP**s** are found, the 10 MPs with the lowest weighted error will be selected. The MP with largest area among the other nine MP**s** is selected as the reference base The size of the local structure can be estimated by adding the distance d_j in the LFV^{query}. The LFV with largest area usually is more unique and thus has a higher chance to be the best reference minutiae for alignment and comparison.

8.6 On-Card Comparison

Since the reference pairs of minutiae are determined, the alignment of the query template can be computed at the terminal side. Equations (8.7) and (8.8) compute the alignment template of the query template and the enrolment template respectively.

$$AT^{query} = \begin{cases} r_k' = \sqrt{(x_k' - x_b')^2 + (y_k' - y_b')^2} \\ \theta_k' = \tan^{-1}\left(\frac{y_k' - y_b'}{x_k' - x_b'}\right) \\ \varphi_k' \end{cases} \quad (8.7)$$

$$AT^{enroll} - \begin{cases} r_i = \sqrt{(x_l - x_b)^2 + (y_l - y_b)^2} \\ \theta_l = \tan^{-1}\left(\frac{y_l - y_b}{x_l - x_b}\right) - O_b \\ \varphi_k - O_b \end{cases} \quad (8.8)$$

where $(x_b \ y_b)$ and $(x'_b \ y'_b)$ are the Cartesian coordinates of the base minutiae of enrolment template and query template and O_b is the orientation difference between two templates. The alignment process is to convert the Cartesian coordinate to the Polar coordinate to perform global matching. Three types of information are calculated: the distance between the reference base and minutia r'_k the slope of base and minutia θ'_k and the ridge direction φ'_k. O_b is not known at the terminal as there is no Cartesian coordinates of enrolment template in the terminal to calculate the orientation difference between templates Once the off-card alignment process for query template is completed, the computed AT^{query} and Cartesian coordinates of the matched LFV^{query} structure and matched minutiae index of LFV^{enroll} (alignment information) will be sent to the smart card for the on-card alignment of enrolment template and template comparison. The orientation angle adjustment O_b is computed upon receiving the alignment information from the terminal as well as the AT^{enroll} is calculated by Eq. (8.8) inside the smart card. Finally, the comparison process of AT^{query} and AT^{input} takes place inside the card to calculate the matching score using Eqs. (8.9) and (8.10).

$$Score = \frac{\sum_{k=l}^{N_{enroll}} match(k)}{(N_{enroll} + N_{query})/2} * 100 \qquad (8.9)$$

$$match(i) = \begin{cases} 1, \min(\varpi_1|r_i - r_j| + \varpi_2|\theta_i - \theta_j| + \varpi_3|\varphi_i - \rho_j|) \\ < Th_{polar}, \forall_j = 1 \ldots N_{query}, 0, otherwise \end{cases}$$
$$(8.10)$$

where N_{enrol} and N_{query} are the total number of minutiae of enrolment template and query template respectively, *Score* is the overall matching score, ϖ_1 to ϖ_3 are the weights to calculate the weighted error with the constraint that the total sum of ϖ_1 to ϖ_3 should equal to 1, and Th_{polar} is the threshold to match minutiae and min(.) is the minimum function to find the minimum weighted error. Once the score is computed, the score can be compared to the predefined security threshold of the required security as specified in ISO/IEC24787 to determine the security status.

8.7 Performance Comparison

An experiment was performed using the FVC 2000 DB2a database. This database has 100 fingers and each finger has 8 images. The equal error rate (EER) of using the new scheme is approximately 5% of using one set of reference bases for alignment and matching. Compared with the implementation from Jiang [16] with EER = 2.5%, the performance of our implementation is lower. However, the algorithm from Jiang was implemented using FPU on a PC platform running at 2.4 GHz and using multiple reference bases for alignment; but our implementation used 16-bit integer calculation on a 16-bit Sharp Javacard platform running at 25 MHz. The Javacard executes the on-card matching applet using Java Virtual Machine (JVM) which is slower than the native implementation. As the existing smart card and Javacard do not support the work-sharing mechanism proposed in ISO/IEC 24787, extra Java functions were implemented to simulate the work-sharing mechanism in the Javacard incurring extra processing time. The average matching time on the Sharp Javacard is approximately 2 sec.

8.8 Conclusion

An approach for on-card fingerprint comparison with work-sharing mechanism is presented. A modified LGS algorithm is proposed to split the comparison process into two separate sections: off-card alignment and on-card matching. The enrolment template is separated into two portions: open portion and secured portion. Open potion consists of relative information that can only be used to find the optimal set of reference bases for subsequent alignment. It is difficult to use relative information to reverse engineer the original minutiae template. The secured portion of biometric reference data which consists of the Cartesian coordinates, ridges directions and types of minutiae, as specified in ISO/IEC 19794-2 will never be sent out to any external device and only be used for on-card comparison. A new method of estimating the optimal bases using the minimum weighed error and largest local structure area is suggested. Finally, the method to compute the on-card alignment of enrolment template and the on-card template comparison are also introduced. The EER of a sample implementation is approximately 5% using a Javacard running at 25 MHz with average matching time of 2 s. Hence, using work-sharing scheme, it is possible to implement the on-card biometric comparison with low-cost smart card which has limited processing power. In the suggested implementation, the scheme of computing the reference bases and the on-card computation of matching score can still be further improved which will further enhance the performance of the on-card comparison.

References

1. ISO/IEC 24787 (2009) *Information technology—Identification cards—On-Card biometric comparison* (International Organization for Standardization).
2. Maltoni, D., Maio, D., Jain, A. K. and Prabhakar S. (2003) *Handbook of Fingerprint Recognition* (1st Ed.), Springer
3. Wolfson, H. J., Rigoutsos, I. (1997) Geometric hashing: An overview, *IEEE Computational Science & Engineering* 4(4), 10–21.
4. Chung Y, Kim K, Kim M, Pan S., Park N. (2005) A hardware implementation for fingerprint retrieval, *Knowledge-Based Intelligent Information and Engineering Systems LNCS*, pp. 374–380
5. Pan, S. B, Gil Y. H, Moon D, Chung Y., Park C. H. (2003) A memory-efficient fingerprint verification algorithm using a multi-resolution accumulator array, *ETRI Journal*, 25(3), 179–186.
6. Krivec V., Birchbauer J. A., Marius W., Bischof H. (2003) A hybrid fingerprint matcher in memory constrained environments, *Proceedings of the 3rd International Symposium on Image and Signal Processing and Analysis*, pp. 617–620
7. Rikin A. S., Li D., Isshiki T., Kunied A. H. (2005) A fingerprint matching using minutia ridge shape for low cost match-on-card systems, *IEICE Transactions Fundamentals* E88-A(5), 1305–1312
8. Moon Y. S., Ho H. C., Ng K. L., Wan S. F., Wong S. T. (2000) Collaborative fingerprint authentication by smart card and a trusted host, *Canadian Conference on Electrical and Computer Engineering* 1, 108–112.
9. Allah M. M. A (2005) A fast and memory efficient approach for fingerprint authentication system, *IEEE Conference on Advanced Video and Signal Based Surveillance* pp. 259–263.

10. Mimura M., Ishida S., Seto Y. (2002) Fingerprint verification system on smart card, *International Conference on Consumer Electronics*, pp. 182–183.

11. Chang, S. H., Cheng, F. H. Hsu, W. H., Wu, G. Z. (1997) Fast algorithm for point pattern-matching: Invariant to translation, rotation and scale changes, *Pattern Recognition* 30(2), 331–320.

12. Huvanandana, S., Kim, C., Hwang, J. N. (2000) Reliable and fast fingerprint identification for security application, *Proceedings International Conference on Image Processing*, vol. 2, pp. 503–506.

13. Jiang, X., Yau, W. Y. (2000) Fingerprint minutiae matching based on the local and global structures, *Proceedings International Conference Pattern Recognition* 2, 1042–1045.

14. ISO/IEC 19794-2 (2005) *Information technology: Biometric data interchange formats Part 2: Finger minutiae data* (International Organization for Standardization).

15. ISO/IEC 7816 (2004) *Identification cards: Integrated Circuit Cards Part 4: Organization, security and commands for interchange* (International Organization for Standardization).

Chapter 9

Smart Clothes for Biometrics and Beyond

Kee-Sam Jeong,[a] Sun. K. Yoo,[b] Joohyeon Lee,[c] and Gilsoo Cho[c]

[a]*Department of Medical Information Systems, Yongin Songdam College, Yongin, Kyeongki 449-710, Korea*
[b]*Department of Medical Engineering, and*
[c]*Department of Clothing and Textiles, Yonsei University, Seoul 120-749, Korea*
ksjeong@ysc.ac.kr

9.1 Introduction

Technology generally goes through a period of birth, growth, and then maturity. When a technology reaches that stage and finds its place in laymen's everyday lives, it can have an enormous cultural impact. In particular, the late 20th century growth of informational technology and the synergies that it created with a variety of other industries transformed the daily lifestyle to previously unexpected levels. The birth of smart clothing must be understood under this context.

Smart clothing can be generally defined as clothing that has combined electronic technology with functional fabrics in order to enhance human performance or help individuals cope better with their surroundings—but not at the price of user's discomfort. Therefore smart clothing should either have the electronic devices

Biometrics: From Fiction to Practice
Edited by Eliza Yingzi Du
Copyright © 2013 Pan Stanford Publishing Pte. Ltd.
ISBN 978-981-4310-88-8 (Hardcover), 978-981-4364-13-3 (eBook)
www.panstanford.com

Figure 9.1. Different forms of smart clothes (Yonsei university).

embedded or provide a platform that is convenient to use. Each and every fiber can form an electric circuit or act as a sensor or an actuator thereby effectively culminating into a complete system. The use of microprocessors and semiconductor components can overcome traditional barriers and grant smart clothing the power of computing. In the environment of ubiquitous computing as Mark Weiser envisioned, smart clothes will take on the role of invisible computers [1].

In the future that we will live through, we will communicate not only with computers but with our surroundings and objects. Ubiquitous technology fundamentally aims to create an environment where human beings can communicate with objects and where objects can exchange information with other objects. In order for this to become reality, a system enabling mutual recognition among the pervasive objects is crucial. In the case where one of the objects is a human being, the machine needs to be able to identify the individual while simultaneously recognizing his present "conditions" in order to be able to provide adequate services. Conditions in this context go beyond the individual's physical attributes to encompass a comprehensive set of information including health conditions as well as emotional well being. The smart clothing of the future will be able to retrieve and communicate information that is called for in the ubiquitous environment. Furthermore the services provided for by the ubiquitous environment will be made available to humans through the convenience of smart clothing. But before that can happen, technology that will enable men to communicate with his surroundings needs to be developed. The technology, however, should veer away from interfaces that are dictated by machines as are the cases with keyboards and mice, and become centered on the user, or the human being. The services rendered, too, must go beyond transmission of simple information and reach the realms of services centered on health and emotional services.

The need for such technology has prompted many nations to encourage research on smart clothing related areas since the 1990s. Table 9.1 shows research that has been completed or is currently in progress around the world. The European Union is most proactive in its support for research. As can be seen from Table 9.1, the European Commission has already completed or is in progress with many healthcare related projects. America's Wearable Motherboard project is another prime example of how smart clothing has garnered international interest. Similar government-sponsored projects have been carried out in many other nations.

Many companies are also manufacturing smart clothing related products independent of government support. Electronics firms, clothing firms, and sports goods firms are cooperating with a variety of industries to research and develop products of the future. What was once a figment of one's imagination—namely, a world of seamless communication between the ubiquitous environment and men—is increasingly becoming a reality. This chapter will examine the various technologies that are necessary to enable smart clothes to become a medium for communication between the environment and men. Specifically, we will look at the future of smart clothing as the retriever of information from the body and it surroundings; clothing as a monitoring platform; and the role of smart clothing in the expanded sphere of biometrics services.

Table 9.1.   Cases of smart clothing projects around the world

Country	Projects
EU (EC Projects)	**MyHeart**(http://www.hitech-projects.com/euprojects/myheart/)
	- Fighting cardiovascular diseases by preventive lifestyle & early diagnosis (2004–2007)
	BIOTEX(http://www.biotex-eu.com/)
	- Bio-Sensing Textiles to Support Health Management (2005–2008)
	PROETEX(http://www.proetex.org)
	- Protection e-Textiles: MicroNanostructured fibre systems for Emergency-Disaster Wear (2006–2010)
	STELLA(http://www.stella-project.eu/)
	- Stretchable Electronics for Large Area Applications (2006–2010)
	OFSETH(http://www.ofseth.org/)
	- Optical Fibre Sensors Embedded into technical Textile for Healthcare (2006–2009)
	CONTEXT(http://www.context-project.org/)
	- Contactless sensors for body monitoring integrated in textiles (2006–2008)
	MERMOTH
	- Medical Remote Monitoring of Clothes(2003–2006)
	SYSTEX(http://www.systex.org/)
	- Coordination action for enhancing the breakthrough of intelligent textile systems (e-textiles and wearable microsystems)(2008–2011)
U.S.A.	**Wearable Motherboard**^{TM} (http://www.smartshirt.gatech.edu/)
	- Smart Shirt(1996–1998)
Hong Kong	**Nanotechnology Centre** for Functional and Intelligent Textiles and Apparel
	Smart Textile Development: Shape Memory Fabrics/Garment
Korea	**Smart Clothing**(http://www.smartclothing.org/)
	- Technology Development of Smartwear for Future Daily Life

9.2 Smart Textile Sensors

Smart textile sensors refer to fabrics or textiles that can react to the external environment or recognize a stimulus. Zhang and Tao [1–4] grouped smart textiles into three categories according to the extent of intelligence: *passive smart textiles*, *active smart textiles*, and *very smart textiles*. Passive smart textiles are first generation smart textiles whose capabilities are limited to merely recognizing an external stimulus or its environment. Active smart textiles have equal sensing capabilities but are also able to react to the stimulus. In other words they possess both sensing and actuator functions.

Very smart textiles go steps further from active smart textiles and are able to adapt to changes in the environment. This is made possible by the existence of a microprocessor in addition to its basic sensor and an actuator. Ultimately, these third-generation smart textiles are capable of perceiving and reacting to a given condition and offer services accordingly.

Though smart textiles research has seen remarkable progress in the last decade, a sensor with the true physical properties of textiles is still quite rare. Most sensors are produced using the inherent characteristics of the substance. For example, if a textile exists whose length or color reacts to changes in temperature, it could be used as a textile sensor. The sensors that are used in thermometers and manometers in the electronics industry are produced by making use of the piezoelectric effect and thermoelectric effect. Ideally, smart textiles would utilize existing sensing materials. Sensors used in the electric industry, however, are usually too stiff and either too big or harmful to the human body to be used directly in making clothes. They must therefore be processed in the following ways to become practical for use. First and ideally, sensor materials will be processed in the form of textiles or films. This will guarantee a level of flexibility. If spinning is possible with the sensor material, weaving in the form of a fabric may be possible. Processing in the form of a film will also allow for it to be applied directly to smart clothes by way of adhesion to the fabric. As of now, plenty of research using the electrospinning method to manufacture smart textile sensor is underway [5, 6]. The second method of processing textile sensors takes advantage of the fabric's three-dimensional structure. The three-layer construction of fabrics that are most widely used in the sports clothing industry is similar to the architecture of an electronic parts sensor or a transistor. By inserting a sensor material or a switching material in the middle layer and forming electrodes in the remaining two layers it can function as either a sensor or an input apparatus. Knitted fabrics of highly elastic structure allow for the production of sensors by taking advantage of the structural changes that occur when the fabrics are extended or contracted. The last method has to do with utilizing a very small sensor that is usually used in electronics products. This may be the most practical alternative. A small sensor can be directly embedded or attached to the fabric using adhesives. In clothing, subsidiary materials such as buttons, beads, and rivets can be used. If sensors used in the electronics industry is of the size and shape of these subsidiary materials, they could most probably be used in the clothing industry as well.

9.2.1 *Biosignals*

Medical equipments are designed to the convenience of the medical personnel for diagnoses purposes rather than patient—and naturally so. Medical equipments can measure biosignals with great precision, but at the same time must control the patient's movement and to a certain extent the environment. Therefore, using medical equipments to monitor an individual's biosignals in everyday life for an extended period of time is obviously impractical. Smart clothing can offer a solution to this problem. The service rendered would be able to measure biosignals constantly while the user is comfortable enough with the sensor so as to be unconscious of it. The following are the general signals, based on which smart clothing can offer a variety of services.

- Vital signs   :   Body temperature, pulse, respiration, blood pressure
- Movement   :   Physical activity, gesture, shock, etc.
- Biopotential   :   ECG, EMG, EEG, GSR, etc.
- Environment   :   Temperature, Humidity, luminance, GPS, etc.

The most widely used "vital signs" in the medical field are body temperature, blood pressure, pulse rate, and respiration rate. Vital signs provide the basic information on the person's overall physiological and pathological conditions. They reflect the human body's homeostasis, and are therefore closely related to the autonomic nervous system (ANS). For most ANS human body control mechanisms, the sympathetic nervous system (SNS) and the parasympathetic nervous system (PNS) react antagonistically to each other. When an imbalance is spotted in the human body the mechanism is put to use to compensate for the loss. Some of the factors that cause bodily imbalances include pathological conditions, physical activity and mental stress. Therefore, signals related to vital signs can offer important information in inferring an individual's physical and psychological conditions.

Movement signals can also provide a variety of information in analyzing a user's actions in various contexts that include but are not limited to walking, running, working and sleeping etc. [7]. For example, converting a day's activity level in to calorie amounts could be useful in determining the appropriate level of exercise in maintaining one's health [8]. In the case of elder men, if his or her daily activity level has decreased precipitously one might suspect early development of a sickness. Moreover the user could make conscious gestures to control or input data on the digital device [9].

Biopotential has been used to predict specific diseases with accordance to certain signals and mechanisms. Electrocardiogram (ECG) is the primary signal used to diagnose heart diseases such as cardiac arrhythmia. Analyzing heart rate variability (HRV) by using ECG allows for close analysis of activities of the ANS and knowledge of the respiration cycle [10]. While electroencephalogram (EEG) can be used to diagnose brain disease, it can also reveal the user's current psychological conditions [11]. Electromyogram (EMG) test can reveal the extent of muscular tension, evaluate the effects of rehabilitation and diagnose diabetic neuropathy.

The environment variable is an important variable for context awareness purposes. Climactic changes can affect not only physical activity but also one's psychological and emotional conditions. Information on the user's whereabouts gives clues on the user's current activities. For example, whether the user is at home, at school or at work is an important piece of information in deciding what type of service the user will find necessary.

To attain the variety of signals as described above, sensors as specified in Table 9.2 are required.

9.2.2 *Textile Electrode*

In order to measure biopotential like the ECG, EEG, and EMG, electrodes are necessary. Disposable electrodes, which are the most widely used electrodes in hospitals, are attached to the human skin using adhesives. Disposable electrodes use electrolyte gel to reduce

Table 9.2. Sensors and biosignals

Sensors	Biosignals
Electrode	ECG, EMG, EEG, GSR, Respiration, Body Composition, etc.
Temperature Sensor	Body & Skin Temperature, Room Temperature, etc.
Pressure Sensor	Blood Pressure, Pulse, Respiration, Gesture, ...
Accelerometer	Movement & Activity, Gesture, ...
Optical Sensor	SpO_2, Pulse, Luminance, Color, ...
Etc.	Humidity, GAX, GPS, ...

contact resistance between the skin and the electrode. For this reason, conventional disposable electrodes have also been called "wet electrodes." The adhesive material and the electrolyte gel are generally uncomfortable for the user, and extended exposure to the material can cause rashes. Therefore extended use of disposable electrodes are not appropriate for the purpose of monitoring biosignals in everyday life [12]. Rather, forming electrodes with cloth made of conductive fiber or materials made of flexible conductive rubber are a more conducive way of measuring biosignals via smart clothes. These types of electrodes do not use electrolyte gel and are therefore dubbed "dry electrodes"—as opposed to wet electrodes [13–15]. Dry electrodes tend to exhibit higher contact resistance, which itself is subject to high variability depending on the level of movement; however, stimulation to the skin is minimal and the material used is similar to that of normal clothing and therefore more comfortable for the user to use. Electrodes require conductive materials that have a large surface area. The ideal textile electrode should be characterized with high flexibility, high moisture permeability, and high washability, i.e., all qualities of textiles. Figure 9.2 shows electrodes that are currently in use in smart clothing products.

In the beginning, conductive rubber was widely used as raw material for electrodes. It was both cheap and easy to manufacture. Compared to fabrics, however, conductive rubber is neither as flexible nor permeable. In the most ideal situation, conductive textiles that possess properties of a typical textile will be processed and used. As of now, metal yarn boasts the highest conductivity among textiles. In the current market, a variety of products made

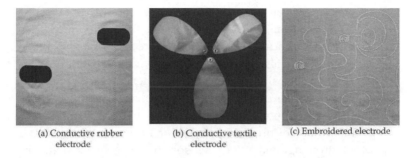

| (a) Conductive rubber electrode | (b) Conductive textile electrode | (c) Embroidered electrode |

Figure 9.2. Electrodes that used in smart clothing products.

of metal filaments, the thickness of 1/60 times of a normal hair, are available. Metal yarns can be used to make threads by twisting metal fiber or used in the form of blended yarns, which are a blend of metal and regular textiles. These types of products are extremely tender and are virtually indistinguishable from regular textiles. There are three methods of utilizing metal yarns as electrodes. The first is to weave or knit the metal yarn and to attach the necessary quantities to the clothing. This has the least influence on the design of the clothing and can be applied even to completed clothes. Consequently it is the most widely used method. The second method involves equipments like Jaquard loom, which makes possible the embedding of electrode on a specific part of the metal yarn during the weaving process. The resulting electrode is seamless and easy to mass produce; another method takes advantage of embroidery. Embroidery does away with the weaving process and is particularly suitable when producing a small amount or when aesthetic effect is called for.

Apart from metal yarns, yarns with electroless plating or textiles coated with conductive material or other metals can be used.

9.2.3 *Textile-Based Piezo Sensor*

Pressure sensors generally make use of the piezoelectric effect or the piezoresistive effect of specific materials. The signals generated from the pressure sensor can measure pressure but can also be converted to a physical quantity such as speed, shock or vibration depending on the sensor or the way it was processed. A pressure sensor can be used on a human body to measure blood pressure, pulse rate, respiration, or physical activity. Blood pressure is an important health indicator but when measured continuously blood pressure signals can also be useful in observing the overall control processes of the cardiovascular system. There are two methods of continuous measurement. The first involves directly inserting a catheter with a pressure sensor into the artery while the second makes use of pressure sensors or optical sensors such as a photoplethysmography (PPG) sensor in order to estimate the relative changes in pressure levels from outside of the body [16]. Therefore, to use blood pressure signals in the context of smart clothing is quite impractical. Pulses can be measured by the wrist or the neck. Pulse contains information not only on the heart beat cycle, but also on its strength and is therefore useful for many purposes. A typical person will have a breathing cycle of 4 s, though that can vary depending on physical activity or the degree of stress levels. Respiration signals are detected by converting the change in chest volume during inspiration and expiration to changes in pressure or electrical impedance. Bodily movements can be detected in various places depending on the object of usage and can be used for various purposes. A pedometer can estimate the overall level of action and the level of calorie exhaustion. Movement recognition systems can sense movement and communicate that information with information systems. Recently there have been attempts to distinguish people by their manner of walking. This research is known as gait biometrics [17, 18]. As can be seen in the previous examples, the usage of pressure sensors in the smart clothing industry can be wide. Sensors that have been used in the electronics industry include the mechanical pressure sensor, the strain gauge, the semiconductor piezoresistive, and the piezoelectric sensor. In terms of form some of them are film shaped and therefore easier to use, while others are too big or too stiff to be directly used on clothing. Therefore the development of sensors with the appropriate designs that are suitable for the clothing industry is necessary. There has been abundant research on textile pressure sensors using the structure of materials. Some of those sensors are textile sensors [19], piezoresistive sensors [20], capacitive pressure sensors [21, 22], and flexible plastic optical fiber (POF) sensors [23]. Among

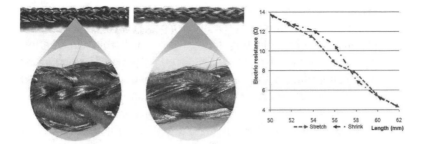

Figure 9.3. Textile piezoresistive sensor.

these sensors, the sensor closest to textiles is the method using the fabric structure. This sensor [24] is a braided product of elastic yarn such as polyester yarn or spandex and metal yarn. As can be seen in Fig. 9.3, when a yarn is elongated, electric contact among metal yarns increases thereby decreasing the amount of electric resistance between the two terminals. This is an example of how sensors can be made with just textile materials.

Apart from biosignals, a user may directly input data to the computer or a mobile device with textile pressure sensors. Primary examples of its commercial application include products of quantum tunneling composite (QTC) material [25]. QTCs react to increased pressure with lower electric resistance and are used as raw materials for switches in textile keypad products.

9.3 Smart Clothing as a Biomonitoring Platform

A number of cars are equipped with human body recognition systems that can automatically adjust the seat positions to accommodate for the driver's body type. For such systems to be in operation, a program that enables the machine to recognize the person needs to be put in place. For low-security-level tasks or general services, the machine must not pose undue restrictions on the user to the point that the latter is annoyed. In this respect, smart clothes are perhaps the best platform from which to recognize humans. Clothes are virtually inseparable from everyday life and as such are in the perfect position to offer relevant information pertaining to the user's movements. If an intelligent fiber existed that could recognize the surroundings and if it were possible to produce smart textiles and clothing with that fiber, a lot of valuable information would become readily available. This technology will be able garner details not only on an individual's habits (behavioral biometrics) but also offer information on the context of that individual's actions (context awareness computing). Regularly measuring one's vital signs will yield information on the individual's health conditions (healthcare information). There also exists research on signals such as EEG, ECG, GSR (galvanic skin response) which can be used to deduce information on one's emotional conditions. Smart clothing technology goes beyond merely recognizing signals and includes technology that can efficiently extract relevant information with its limited sensors. From that information, it must then offer the appropriate service. Naturally, smart clothing in the future will take the role of communication medium between intelligent machines and human beings.

The structure of such platforms can take two perspectives: one centered on clothing and the other on communications.

The approach centered on clothing takes on a physical composition as can be seen in Fig. 9.4. Listing the clothes in the order of proximity to the skin, underwear will come first, then the middle wear such as T-shirts and lastly, the outerwear. Underwear is in direct contact with the skin and is therefore suitable for measuring biopotential using electrodes. It is also relatively indifferent to changes in temperature and so is suitable for measuring body temperature. It can also measure minute changes in pressure and surface area of the skin caused by breathing, for example. Platforms

Figure 9.4. The layered system of smart clothing.

for digital devices such as MP3 players or cell phones can be formed in the outerwear. Pockets for digital devices, power supply components, or textile keypads for human interface can be secured in this third layer. Wireless equipments such as the cell phone will take on important roles as they transmit signals that have been detected by the smart clothing. The outer layer is in essence the gateway connecting the human to its surrounding environment. The middle layer, on the other hand, can take on the role of a gateway between the other two layers. It can hold sensors that are difficult to secure in the inner layer or include platforms for sensors and actuators. Should an outer layer not exist, the middle layer could take on a dual role as both the middle and the outer layer.

On the other hand, from a communications point of view, the sensors, actuators and digital devices embedded in clothing could form a network. The method of communication could be any of wireless, wired or hybrid of the two. The best known example of the wireless platform is the ubiquitous sensor network (USN). USNs are often formed under the basis of wireless communication networks such as the Zigbee. If a wireless sensor network is used, the clothing designer does not need to worry about wiring, which in turn makes production much easier. On the other hand, each node will require independent power sources which can cause inconveniences related to batteries. If a large battery is used so as to ensure stable service, the size could interfere with the design. The need to recharge or replace the batteries is also a disadvantage that must be addressed. If a wired network is formed, every node will have to be wired thereby limiting room for design. The most common material used for wiring is the metal yarn which is relatively stiff and inelastic compared to the typical textile used in clothing. Particular attention is necessary when the metal yarn is used in parts of the body with frequent movement. As can be seen in Fig. 9.5, more elastic textile wires have recently been developed and are being applied to products.

The hybrid method offers an adequate combination of the two methods. Under the hybrid method the platform would be wired, but where wiring is inconvenient the wireless method would be implemented.

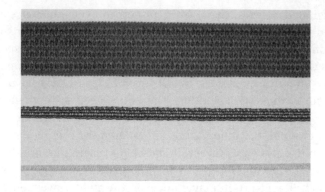

Figure 9.5. Textile wires with considerable elasticity (Silveray Co. Ltd., Korea).

9.4 Biometrics and Intelligent Services

The National Biometric Security Project (NSBP) classified the types of biometric technologies and applications in the following way in their publication of the Biometric Technology Application Manual (BTAM) [26, 27].

Types of biometric technologies:

- Dynamic signature analysis
- Facial imaging or recognition
- Fingerprint
- Hand geometry
- Iris recognition
- Keystroke analysis/keystroke dynamics
- Palmprint
- Retinal scan
- Skin spectroscopy/skin texture/skin contact
- Speaker verification
- Vascular biometrics
- Other biometric technologies

A functional classification of applications:

- Access control
- Identity management

- Transactions
- Other

The method of biometric information gathering is centered on machines, and therefore to make use of biometric technologies as defined by BTAM in the context of current smart clothing technology is difficult. The area of application is also quite different from that of smart clothing. As of now, readily available smart clothing technologies are limited to ECG and human gait recognition systems. In the recent decade, much research on distinguishing humans on the basis of ECG waves has taken place [28, 29]. Technology using ECG is not quite as reliable as existing biometrics recognition systems such as fingerprint identification, but is reasonably accurate when used against a limited group. Distinguishing members of a family is one example of how ECG may be useful. In a ubiquitous environment, service should be provided constantly albeit subtlety but in order for that to occur the u-object must first be able to recognize the individual to which it will be providing the service to. In the case of smart clothing, once it is worn ECGs can be constantly measured and can therefore provide useful information for recognition. Recognizing gait patterns is also possible with the use of smart clothing, though admittedly with limited capacity. Every person has his own style of walking which is why we can recognize different people at a distance. Gait biometrics [17, 18], however, require a complex system which must take into account different movements and spaces. Consequently, the technology that is available today is not yet sufficiently reliable and therefore limited in its capacity for various applications.

Therefore the application of biometrics in smart clothing needs to be approached in a different direction. The smart clothing of today is used in its own independent capacity, but in the future smart clothing will be connected with communication networks and become a medium through which to communicate with the surroundings. It will eventually be able to offer calm services to humans. But In order to provide such services, technology that enables sensors to identify and recognize the current condition of the user must be available. In other words, information pertaining not only to the body and physical activity but one that has taken into account the context is necessary. In this respect, smart clothing can potentially provide very useful information.

Take the information gathering process through ECG signal processing, for example. Hospitals use electrocardiographs to diagnose cardiovascular disease. Two methods of interpretation of the ECG in terms of disease diagnoses exist. First is the method of morphological analysis and rhythm analysis. Morphological analysis can diagnose aberrant electrical conduction by detecting abnormal waves that occasionally occur. Rhythm analysis on the other hand can detect arrhythmia caused by ectopic contraction. Generally abnormal waves or ectopic contractions cannot be observed in a matter of seconds or minutes. Instead data for an extended period of time is necessary. For accurate diagnoses of cardio related diseases, hospitals use Holter monitors to acquire ECG signals for 24 h. HRV analysis can detect minor changes in the intervals between normal heartbeats and is therefore useful in analyzing the activities of the automatic function. Even a typical person resting with no particular heart disease will show slight variations in his heartbeat intervals. This is the result of the automatic nervous system trying to maintain homeostasis and compensate for the constant imbalance within the human body. Physical stimulation such as exercising can accelerate the sympathetic tone and increase the heartbeat rate. At this point, by analyzing the change of the heartbeat rate, the intensity and the level of physical activity can be inferred. Mental stress will also accelerate the sympathetic tone and increase the rate of heartbeat or blood pressure. HRV analysis provides a standard index for the activities of the sympathetic and the parasympathetic systems. With this, it is possible to infer human emotions, the information of which can be very useful in the ubiquitous environment [30].

The application of the acquired information can be manifold. As opposed to ECG analysis in hospitals, limiting the purpose of ECG analysis in smart clothing for detecting emergency situations, and for limited medical and health reasons is probably more reasonable. If the extraction of information on human emotions is possible through HRV analysis its area of application could be expanded to the field of affective computing. Professor Picard of the Massachusetts Institute of Technology (MIT), Media Laboratory, asserted the following in her *Affective Computing* [31].

Computers are beginning to acquire the ability to express and recognize affect, and may soon be given the ability to have emotions. The essential role of emotion in both human cognition and perception, as demonstrated by recent neurological studies, indicates that affective computers should not only provide better performance in assisting humans, but also might enhance computers' abilities to make decisions.

Indeed the intelligent service that she is envisioning will mark an important place in the future of smart clothing and wearable computing.

9.5 Conclusions and Future Work

One of the common goals of biometrics and smart clothing is their constant search for ways to make the usage of the information and communication infrastructure easier and safer for us human beings. The main field of biometrics research was of identifying an individual in a large group and its primary area of application was in security. As mentioned before, if the purpose of biometrics takes on a broader meaning, it can include not only identification but also recognition. Furthermore, researchers must ponder what the necessary information is once an individual has been identified in a group. Figure 9.6 shows an extended sphere of biometrics.

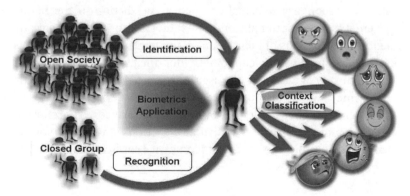

Figure 9.6.   The sphere of biometrics extended.

In the future society of information and communication, accurate identification of an individual will be important but reliable recognition of a constituent in a limited area will also be critical. In this case, if the ultimate purpose is to provide general services that entail little security concerns, smart clothing technology will have a large part to play. Furthermore, recognizing an individual's current conditions will also be very important. For example, let us say that an ATM machine is equipped with a fingerprint identification system. The current biometrics system allows the individual to access the security system as long as the prints match. In other words, the individual's emotional state—whether he is calm or extremely agitated—is not of any interest. If the machine could determine the psychological state of the individual, the security system could react in a different manner.

Let us talk about a more general example and assume that a person or a pet that one loves is right beside the individual. The first thing that the lover or the pet will recognize is the person's very existence. From there, based on my appearances or actions what can they recognize and how will that recognition affect the person? If the person is sad or angry, they may offer some consolation. If the person looks unhealthy, the lover may suggest the individual to see a doctor.

Then what does it mean to say that a machine recognizes a person? And if that were to be possible what services can the machine render for the human being? Behavioral biometrics can offer secondary information such as prediction of the bodily movements or emotional conditions in addition to the already mentioned functions of identification and verification. For example, keystroke dynamics can lead to both identification of the individual and to the recognition of the user's emotional state. Recognizing one's emotions means that the computer or the machine (or the ubiquitous environment) can offer new services. Therefore, if constant monitoring of an individual's actions and physiological changes is possible, the sphere of biometrics services could expand to the following fields.

- The first area of application that comes to mind is services related to security. If a vehicle can recognize that the driver is either dozing off or not paying enough attention to road conditions, accidents could be prevented. If a user is extremely agitated, the machine could even suggest the user to refrain from its usage. For occupations that require high level of concentration such as a pilot, constant examination of the operator's physical and emotional status will be necessary.

- The second area is health-related services. As mentioned earlier in the case of ECG applications, vital signs and automatic nervous system activities are important indices for early recognition of many diseases. Identifying diseases and signs of possible exacerbation of a chronic illness at an early stage could be of great help in maintaining good health. Confusion in the body's control mechanism could be prevented by fixing the stress level. Providing detailed data on the body while exercising would help athletes make the most out of their workouts.

- The third field is in the area of emotions. Communicating a person's emotions with a computer has increasingly become a reality in recent years. With time it will become possible for a computer to go beyond its traditional role of computation and exchange emotions with a person. This ability will most probably be applied first to the cell phone, toy, and game industries.

- Lastly, biometrics services could be applied to special operations. For military serviceman or firefighters, measurement of human physiological conditions could be a vital tool in saving lives.

In truth, research in the services listed above has already begun in the field of ubiquitous technology or wearable computing. Though the two fields have different approaches, they share the same goal which is to provide human centered services. The same could be said about biometrics technology for it too attempts to unlock the door to an environment of better human control, via human centered technology. The development of scientific technology of the 20th century has increasingly made sciences more and more specialized. And the more science became specialized, technology became more and more advanced but at the price of limited communication with other fields. The pursuit of depth has come to face a technological limit in the 20th century. A single technology cannot solve all the problems in the world and therefore interdisciplinary cooperation with other fields has become inevitable. Such fusion deepens the depth of technology while also expanding its area of possible application. As the coming together of the electronic industry and the textile industry has resulted in the birth of a new industry of smart clothing so too will the combination of biometrics and smart clothing technology lead to their expansions to previously uncharted fields of study.

References

1. Weiser, M. (1994) The world is not a desktop, *Interactions of the ACM* 1, 7–8.

2. Zhang, X., Tao, X. (2001) Smart textiles: Passive smart, *Textile Asia* June, 45–49.

3. Zhang, X., Tao, X. (2001) Smart textiles: Active smart, *Textile Asia* July, 49–52.

4. Zhang, X., Tao, X. (2001) Smart textiles: Very smart, *Textile Asia* August, 35–37.

5. Wang, X., Drew, C., Lee, S.-H., Senecal, K. J., Kumar, J., Samuelson, L. A. (2002) Electrospinning technology: A novel approach to sensor application, *Macromolecular Science, Part A* 39(10), 1251–1258.

6. Wang, X., Kim, Y. G., Drew, C., Ku, B. C., Kumar, J., Samuelson, L. A. (2004) Electrostatic assembly of conjugated polymer thin layers on electrospun nanofibrous membranes for biosensors, *Nano Letters* 4(2), 331–334.

7. Villalonga, C., Roggen, D., Lombriser, C., Zappi, P., Tröster, G. (2009) Bringing quality of context into wearable human activity recognition systems, *LNCS* 5786, 164–173.

8. Buttussi, F., Chittaro, L. (2008) MOPET: A context-aware and user-adaptive wearable system for fitness training, *Artificial Intelligence in Medicine* 42(2), 153–163.

9. Moeslund, T.B., Nørgaard, L. (2003) A brief overview of hand gestures used in wearable human computer interfaces, Technical Report CVMT 03-02, Computer Vision and Media Technology Lab., Aalborg University, Denmark.

10. Task Force of the European Society of Cardiology and the North American Society of Pacing and Electrophysiology (1996) Heart rate variability: Standards of measurement, physiological interpretation and clinical use, *Circulation* 93(5), pp. 1043–1065.

11. Horlings, R., Datcu, D., Rothkrantz, L. (2008) Emotion recognition using brain activity, *Proceedings 9th International Conference Computer Systems and Technologies and Workshop* for Ph.D. Students in Computing, ACM New York, NY, USA.

12. Van Langenhove, L., Hertleer, C. (2004) Smart clothing: A new life, International *Journal of Clothing Science and Technology* 16(1/2), 63–72.

13. Hoffmann, K. P., Ruff, R. (2007) Flexible dry surface-electrodes for ECG long-term monitoring, Proceedings 29th ann. Int. Conf. IEEE EMBS, 1, pp. 5739–5742.

14. Puurtinen, M. M., Komulainen, S. M., Kauppinen, P. K., Malmivuo, J. A., Hyttinen, J. A. (2006) Measurement of noise and impedance of dry and wet textile electrodes, and textile electrodes with hydrogel, Proceedings 29th ann. Int. Conf. IEEE EMBS, 1, pp. 6012–6015.

15. Paradiso, R., Loriga, G., Taccini, N., Gemignani, A., Ghelarducci B. (2005) WEALTHY—a wearable healthcare system: New frontier on e-textile, *Journal of Telecommunication and Information Technology* 4, 105–113.

16. Parati, G., Casadei, R., Groppelli, A., Di Rienzo, M., Mancia, G. (1989) Comparison of finger and intra-arterial blood pressure monitoring at rest and during laboratory testing, *Hypertension* 13, 647–655.

17. Ailisto, H. J., Lindholm, M., Mäntyjärvi, J., Vildjiounaite, E., Mäkelä (2005) S. M. Identifying people from gait pattern with accelerometers, *Proceedings SPIE* 5779, 7–14.

18. Gafurov, D., Helkala, K., Søndrol, T. (2006) Biometric gait authentication using accelerometer sensor, *Journal of Computers* 1(7), 51–59.

19. Sung, M., Baik, K., Cho, J., Jeong, K., Cho, G. (2007) Characteristics of low-cost textile-based motion sensor for monitoring joint flexion, 11th International Symposium on Wearable Computers Proceedings of the Doctoral Colloquium, ISWC, pp. 29–31.

20. Pacelli, M., Loriga, G., Taccini, N., Paradiso, R. (2006) Sensing fabrics for monitoring physiological and biomechanical variables:E-textile solutions, Proceedings 3rd IEEE-EMBS International Summer School and Symposium on Medical Devices and Biosensors, 1, pp. 1–4.

21. Meyer, J., Lukowicz, P., Troster, G. (2006) Textile pressure sensor for muscle activity and motion detection, 10th IEEE International Symposium on Wearable Computers *ISWC*, 69–72.

22. Sergio, M., Manaresi, N., Tartagni, M., Canegallo, R., Guerrieri, R. (2004) A textile based capacitive pressure sensor, *Sensor Letters* 2(2), 153–160.

23. Rothmaier, M., Luong, M. P., Clemens, F. (2008) Textile pressure sensor made of flexible plastic optical fibers, *Sensors 2008* 8, 4318–4329.

24. Sung, M., Jeong, K., Cho, G. (2009) Establishing a measurement system for human motions using a textile-based motion sensor, *LNCS* 5612, 784–792.

25. http://www.peratech.com/qtcmaterial.php

26. National Biometric Security Project (2008) *Biometric Technology Application Manual Volume 1: Biometric Basics* (http://nationalbiometric.org/btamvol1.pdf).

27. National Biometric Security Project (2008) *Biometric Technology Application Manual Volume 2: Applying Biometrics* (http://nationalbiometric.org/btamvol2.pdf).

28. Agrafioti, F., Hatzinakos, D. (2008) ECG biometric analysis in cardiac irregularity conditions, *Signal, Image and Video Processing*, pp. 1683–1703.

29. Irvine, J. M., Israel, S. A. (2009) A sequential procedure for individual identity verification using ECG, EURASIP, *Journal on Advances in Signal Processing* 2009, 1–13 (Article ID 243215).

30. Yoo, S. K., Lee, C., Lee, G., Lee, B., Jeong, K., Park, Y. (2006) Portable device for bi-emotional state identification using heart rate variability, *LNCS* 4239, 528–536.

31. Picard, R. W. (1995) Affective computing, M.I.T Media Laboratory Perceptual Computing Section Technical Report No. 321, (MIT Press, Cambridge, USA).

Chapter 10

Spoof and Vulnerability of Biometric Systems

Alexander D. Meadows

Department of Electrical and Computer Engineering,
Indiana University–Purdue University at Indianapolis,
799 W. Michigan Street, Indianapolis, Indiana 46202, USA
aldmeado@iupui.edu

In this chapter I will familiarize the reader with potential vulnerabilities of biometric systems and how malicious parties may exploit them. I also will introduce definitions and key thoughts regarding vulnerability and biometric security. Some duplication of material is to be expected between sections, so that the chapter may serve adequately as a reference.

10.1 Introduction

Security specialists suggest biometric systems with increasing frequency as a means of secure identity verification, often called authentication. Anyone who has lost his keys or his identity card can testify to the allure of biometrics as a key. Onc cannot leave home without his eyes, for instance. Biometric security systems are rightly perceived as the high-tech locks of the future. Beyond this

Biometrics: From Fiction to Practice
Edited by Eliza Yingzi Du
Copyright © 2013 Pan Stanford Publishing Pte. Ltd.
ISBN 978-981-4310-88-8 (Hardcover), 978-981-4364-13-3 (eBook)
www.panstanford.com

is a further perception that these locks are virtually impenetrable to unauthorized parties. This second belief is founded in the fallacy that biometric data is secret or difficult to obtain. The reality is quite the opposite.

Identification systems can be divided into two categories: knowledge based or possession based. Knowledge-based systems depend on possession of secret information, such as the PIN (personal identification number) for your debit card. Possession-based systems require custody of a physical item or property to substantiate identity [4]. For example, if I have the key to the house at 123 Partridge Lane, I must be an occupant. Most readers will see this last statement as excessively simple logic: many people may have a key to 123 Partridge Lane without being an occupant. Most people fail to realize is that biometrics falls into this possession-based system, rather than knowledge-based. Another interesting example of this system is found in the amusement park sign which reads, "You must be this tall to ride." This simple biometric system tests the users for possession of the physical property of height.

Whereas secret information such as a PIN usually requires coercion or cooperation to determine, it is trivial to acquire hundreds of pictures of a user—without knowing so much as the user's name. It is easy to conceive of innumerable scenarios where a user may be photographed without arousing suspicion or without his knowledge. An example may be to follow a known user to a public place and take pictures of the building or other parties while including the target in the field of the image. High-resolution cameras of today would provide an image of ample quality for reproductions to spoof most facial recognition systems. In the modern world of social networking sites such as Facebook, MySpace, Twitter, LinkedIn, and others, it is even more feasible to acquire biometric data anonymously.

The fact that biometric data is unchanging and irrevocable leads to a potential problem whenever biometric data is submitted for use in any system. Once registered with a system, it is virtually impossible to eliminate all records of such information. If the registered biometric is compromised, it will never again be secure for use in authentication. This is equivalent to having a front door lock which *cannot* be rekeyed in the event that the key is lost or

Figure 10.1. The public Facebook page of former President George W. Bush provides an image of sufficient quality for generation of false input for spoof of facial recognition systems.

stolen. Thus it should be only after the most careful consideration that biometric data is given to an entity for the purpose of authorization. This is especially true of biometric data which is more difficult to obtain clandestinely, such as hand geometry or retinal imaging.

A biometric system is often evaluated based on its false rejection rate (FRR) and its false acceptance rate (FAR) [1]. To describe these measurements we must first describe two overall classes of users. The legitimate class includes the set of users who should be allowed access. The imposter class includes the set of all users who should not be allowed access. When a legitimate is not allowed access, this is a False Rejection event. When an imposer is allowed access, this is a False Acceptance event. The FRR is a measurement of the number of False Rejection events divided by the number legitimate users. The FAR is formed as the ratio of the number of false acceptance events to the number of imposters. For the purposes of these calculations, it is important to consider that a legitimate user may also be an imposter.

For instance, Susan and Sarah are both legitimate users of a system. On a particular day, Sarah uses the system and is recognized as herself and allowed access. On the same day, Susan uses the system and is recognized as Sarah and allowed access. Even though Susan is a legitimate user, she is an imposter in the event described.

10.2 Background: Doddington's Taxonomy

In 1998, George Doddington and others proposed a classification for users of a biometric system into four categories based on parameters of their recognition by the system [1]. Use of this classification is widespread in biometric literature and serves as a compact description of user classes and exploitation goals. The classifications are as follows:

- **Sheep**—The majority of users fall into this category. These are legitimate users whose recognition exemplifies the goal of the system. They are sufficiently distinct that they are recognized correctly by the system and are not confused with other users.
- **Goat**—These are users whose features make them difficult for the system to recognize. These are legitimate users that are often rejected by the system. Presence of Goats in the database increases the FRR of the system. Goats are more dangerous in identification systems than in authentication systems.
- **Lamb**—These are legitimate users whose features lack specificity. The general nature of their parameters frequently causes the system to identify other users as Lambs. The presence of Lambs in the database increases the FAR of the system.
- **Wolf**—This final category of users may be legitimate or malicious. The Wolf has features which are matched by the system to other legitimate users. Wolves in the database increase the FAR of the system. Wolves are the most dangerous category of users in authentication systems. Because Wolves outside the database cannot be quantified, the FAR of the system is only a lower boundary.

10.3 Classification of Vulnerability

Vulnerability in a biometric system includes the set of all defects or limitations of a biometric system which increase the FAR or FRR of the system or which can be made to do so by a malicious party. An attempt to exploit a vulnerability is referred to as an attack. As with any security system, the general likelihood of an attack is proportional to the value of the information or material protected by the system and inversely proportional to the difficulty of exploiting the vulnerabilities and the severity of the consequence of failure.

$$\text{Likelihood} \propto \frac{F_1 \text{ (Value)}}{F_2 \text{ (Difficulty, Consequence)}} \quad (10.1)$$

In the strictest sense of this definition, legitimate users who fall into the latter three categories of taxonomy are considered vulnerabilities [6]. These types of users are called weak users because they contribute to system vulnerability. As will be discussed below, some areas of research focus on dealing specifically with the presence of weak users in the system.

10.3.1 *Internal and External Vulnerabilities*

Some vulnerabilities come from within the biometric system itself. The source of these internal vulnerabilities may be design dependent as with segmentation functions which make oversimplistic assumptions about biometric data content. The human elements in biometric systems also introduce internal vulnerabilities, both from the operators and the users.

External vulnerabilities are exploited from outside the system. The most widely recognized type of external vulnerability is spoofing. Spoofing is the act of exploiting vulnerabilities of a biometric sensor, usually through prerecorded or previously manufactured false biometric data. Hacking is another example of an attack on an external vulnerability. Hacking refers to the use of computers and other technology to force a system to perform according to the wishes of the hacker. This can include modifying the electronics of a sensor, running a brute-force password cracking program, or snooping for open and unsecured network ports on control computers. For the most part, when hacking is discussed in biometric systems, it refers to computer-based methods which attempt to gain access to the computer which controls the biometric system for the purpose of altering either the data in the system or the programs themselves. Hacking is such a nebulous concept that its specifics lie far outside the scope of this work. Therefore, we will only address where hacking may be employed against the system. The specific areas and how they might be affected will be discussed below.

10.4 Biometric System Architecture Vulnerabilities

It is convenient to consider the vulnerabilities associated with the individual sections of a complete biometric system iteratively. Figure 10.2 is a block diagram of the general architecture of a biometric system. Most real biometric systems can be considered as an implementation of some or all of the parts of this diagram. The division between elements of the diagram can be more conceptual than actual in some real systems. Some systems have external, distributed databases contained in portable memory hardware sometimes referred to as tokens [2]. These tokens are submitted at the sensor as part of the identity claim. Some systems may have a remotely located sensor, which may be hundreds of feet or thousands of miles away.

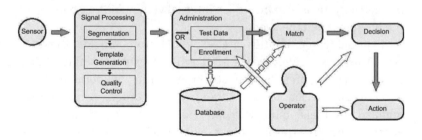

Figure 10.2. Biometric system architecture showing fundamental sections. Gray arrows represent travel of data through the system. Dashed arrows indicate flow of user templates. White arrows indicate operator interactions.

10.4.1 *Sensor Level*

The sensor is the one part of the system which is necessarily exposed to uncontrolled inputs. There are many different types of sensors used for each type of biometric data to be acquired. Sensor technology is constantly evolving to address vulnerabilities, reduce cost, reduce size, or increase resolution. Some biometric scanners incorporate additional sensors for spoof detection as discussed below.

For authentication systems, the sensor can be spoof attacked by presenting false biometric data belonging to a legitimate user [1, 3]. This false data may be generated, as in the case of a silicon or gelatin finger print, or may take the form of a replay attack [1, 2]. In such an attack, legitimate data is recorded through eavesdropping of a legitimate user interaction. This eavesdropping need not be specifically audio biometric data.

In some cases, digital recording electronics may be attached to the sensor to record the output data from legitimate interactions. This data may be used either for a replay attack on the transmission lines, or may be analyzed to reconstruct the input biometric data [3]. The biometric data of a legitimate user may be acquired from a cooperative party, either from the user to be impersonated or from an operator of the system. Finally, the data may be acquired through hacking the data storage of the system or an alternative system which has the same data. The hardware of the sensor itself may also come under attack if sufficient access and time is available and the attacker has the necessary skills and equipment.

Identification systems are particularly vulnerable at this level, as the party seeking to avoid detection need only change or obscure his biometric data. In many cases, this requires only prosthetics as trivial as a fake mustache or cotton balls in the cheeks for facial recognition systems. For fingerprint systems, prominent minutiae used in identification may be physically damaged in such a way that they are no longer recognized by the system.

10.4.2 *Signal Processing*

The signal processing portion of the biometric system is responsible for segmentation, template generation and quality control [1].

These processes happen successively, usually internal to one device or computer system. The exception is in distributed biometric systems, such as biometric authentication over networks. In these systems, some or all of the subprocesses may be localized to the authenticating computer to minimize bandwidth requirements. In such cases, the transmission of data between subprocesses may come under a transmission attack as discussed below.

The segmentation function identifies the parts of the input signal from the sensor which contain biometric data and eliminates parts of the signal which are of no use. In some cases, this function can be attacked through the sensor. In an identification system, prosthetics can be employed that cause the segmentation routine to be unable to extract features from the input images and so no biometric candidates are produced. Knowledge of the segmentation routine is required for success. Since most segmentation applications are developed from published research, it may not be difficult to determine what will trick the system. Adler [1] suggests that a facial recognition system which assumes a face has two eyes may be attacked simply by covering one eye with a hand.

The feature extraction routine identifies and qualifies the specific traits of the segmented biometric data which are used by the system for discrimination. It may be replaced with a fake routine through hacking the system if sufficient details of the routine are known. The fake routine may fail to segment or always produce the same segmentation image, or introduce artifacts into the segmented image to lower data quality. This type of attack is primarily used for denial of service (DoS). In some systems the overall matching criteria may be lowered by repeated poor segmentation and so create additional Lambs in the database.

Some biometric systems employ quality control functions which analyze the segmented and extracted data to determine if data is of sufficient quality. These quality control routines may be hacked to pass images regardless of quality or to reject all images. Since quality checking is generally algorithm specific, knowledge of the algorithm as above can provide the means to create features which cause specific data to be passed or rejected. Because most legitimate biometric signals contain primarily low-frequency content, one metric for rejection of images is excessive high-frequency content.

Image-based recognition systems such as iris and facial recognition are often spoofed with printed images. The use of pixel-based printing technology causes these images to be rich in high-frequency signals related to the sharp boundary between pixels.

10.4.3 *Administration*

The administration section controls enrollment and test data routing. Hacking this part of the system may allow recording of biometric information, corruption of template storage, illegitimate enrollment, or DoS.

10.4.4 *Database*

The database of a biometric system is used to store a set of enrolled biometric templates for each user. For an authentication system, when an identity claim is issued, the records associated with the identity are retrieved for comparison with templates generated from current input. For identification systems, the templates from current input are compared to all the templates in the database to find the entries which are most similar.

In authentication systems, the database is a primary candidate for identity theft through hacking, particularly if user information is stored with biometric data. Legitimate user data may also be replaced with false data, either to deny that person access or to allow another to masquerade as that person. Deletion of stored biometric templates may facilitate re-enrollment. If other systems have been compromised, this can serve as a catalyst to activate a trojan horse or to allow a substituted segmentation or feature extraction program to create Lambs in the database. If an authentication system incorporates varying levels of access, biometric templates may be exchanged to provide a user with legitimate lower level access with a higher clearance. In identification systems, simply deleting data in the database may be sufficient to allow malicious parties to avoid detection.

In some token-based authentication systems such as biometric ID cards and biometric passports, biometric template data is stored in memory hardware contained in the token. This is an example of a distributed database comprised of the data storage in the tokens. This data may be encrypted or may be in plain text. This type of identity claim authentication is very fast because of the small database containing only the owner of the card. However, the database is exceptionally vulnerable to manipulation or theft by skilled parties. Many token-based implementations store data using noncontact data transmission schemes such as radio frequency identification (RFID) systems. The data on these systems is vulnerable to retrieval by malicious parties with the right hardware simply by walking within fifteen feet of the token.

10.4.5 *Matching*

The matching section of a biometric system is responsible for comparison of the template data from the current sensor input to templates stored in the database. After comparing each set of templates, a matching score is generated based on the degree of similarity. For authentication systems, there are usually only a small number of comparisons made. For instance, a user might make an identity claim at the sensor and present his face for recognition. A template is generated and passed to the matching routine. Enrollment images, of which there are perhaps three, are retrieved from the database. After comparison, a matching score is generated for each pairing of the current sensor image with each enrollment image, possibly 65, 80, and 71. In practice, the matching score may be a percentage difference, a tally of the number of pixel differences, or any arbitrary function. The final matching score may be an average of the three scores (72 in our example), the highest score (80), or the lowest score (65). The final matching score is passed to the decision section.

Attacks against the matching section may take the form of hacking, with the goal of replacing the matching scores before they are passed on. Another possibility would be to replace the matching program with one which generates only low scores, or only high scores or produces random scores. The goal of these attacks may be DoS or identification avoidance.

In some identification systems, the matching section also contributes to global thresholds in the decision section which may be based on how poorly each input matches to all candidates in the database. This applies primarily to systems employing Fisher discriminant strategies and is called the between-class scattering [1]. In such systems, it may be possible to lower global thresholds by hacking the matching section. In the example above, the matching threshold may be set initially to 70. If the matcher is replaced with a program that returns a serious of low matching scores for the first several attempts to enter, before passing a legitimate matching score, the decision system may lower the global threshold to 65. As the threshold is lowered, more lambs are created in the database.

10.4.6 *Decision*

The decision section of the biometric system is responsible for making a final determination as to the validity of an identity claim. In some biometric systems, the final decision of the system is monitored by a human operator in a process termed verification. This is the first location of human operator vulnerability. If the human operator can be identified, the verification process may be compromised through coercion or cooperation of the operator. After a series of DoS attacks, an operator may also be stricken with boredom or mistrust of the system. Under this condition, the operator may require relatively little assurance that the system has made a mistake and so override a valid decision.

10.4.7 *Action*

At the action section of a biometric system some effect is generated based on the result of system processing. In authentication systems, this may be the unlocking of a protected door. In an identification system, this may be the separation of a suspicious individual for further consideration. There are two vulnerabilities associated with this section of the system. In the case of a human operator, coercion or cooperation may be used to force an override of the system output. It may also be possible to bypass the action of the system. This is particularly true of self-contained systems, such as a biometric door lock. It does not matter how difficult it may be to compromise the biometric system if one can instead break a pane of glass and reach though to open the door.

10.4.8 *Transmission*

Wherever data is transmitted between segments of the biometric system, there is an opportunity for attack. Gray arrows in Fig. 10.2 represent transmission lines which are vulnerable to attack. Working from the input of the system, the first transmission is between the sensor and the signal processor. This line is carrying the result of digitally encoding the presented biometric data. In the case of facial or iris recognition, this is probably an image of the face or eye of the user. In the case of voice recognition, this is an audio file, such as a wave or mpeg. An attack here would consist of either a replay of previously recorded legitimate data for an authentication system or substitution of false data to avoid identification.

A similar attack might be used on the next transmission line: between the signal processing and administration segments. In this case, the data being transmitted is likely a biometric template image. A replay attack of pre-recorded or manufactured templates may be employed when the administration section is running its *test data* routine. Alternatively, substituted biometric data can be provided during the *enrollment* routine of authorization systems to be stored in the database under the guise of a legitimate user. This attack would create a vulnerability for later use.

Transmission to and from the database of the biometric system (dashed white arrows) may allow theft of template data as it is stored or retrieved, or substitution of template data when the breach of an authentication system is attempted. Because the storage architecture in the database need not be known, it may be easier to attack transmission of templates from the database than the database itself. These same attacks also apply to transmission from the administration section to the matching section.

Transmission between the matching and decision sections is most likely the matching score or scores for the current input. If this data is not encrypted and the transmission line is accessible, it may be one of the most vulnerable points of transmission due to the relatively simple nature of the data.

The final transmission location is between the decision section and the action section. This may be simply a logic-level (DC voltage) enable signal for an electronic door lock. Such a system would be quite vulnerable if not properly hardened against attack.

10.5 Analysis of Vulnerabilities: Attack Trees

Biometric systems can be quite complex. Even a single section of the system may be threatened with multiple types of attacks and each attack may be accomplished along multiple avenues. To understand the relative threat levels throughout the system, the hierarchy of an attack is often diagrammed in a directed graph called an attack tree [1]. At the top of the tree is a specific attack. At the next level down are all the requirements of that attack. At each successive level, the conditions that must be met for each preceding item are detailed. The conditional nature of requirements can be represented in the diagram by the use of AND and OR in the branch connections. In some cases, each node of the tree is assigned a relative score for threat, difficulty, opportunity and resource requirement. Each threat to the system can be addressed individually and collectively to determine protection strategies. It is not necessary to prevent all conditions for an attack from being met. If an attack requires conditions A, B, and C; then when condition C can be unilaterally mitigated it will become inconsequential whether conditions A and B are met.

Through analysis of attack trees, common attack requirements can be identified. Figure 10.3 depicts a possible attack tree for a voice recognition system. Even though there are multiple avenues for attack, nearly half of the tree can be mitigated by addressing the "Gain Unobserved Access to Sensor" node. This could be accomplished by adding security personnel at the sensor or by installing additional, redundant security cameras. Some of the nodes are marked with special conditions that contribute to the difficulty of these attack branches. A survey of the diagram shows that the most likely attack (i.e., the least costly in material, skills, and opportunity) involves spoofing the biometric sensor with recorded data acquired with a directional microphone. Based on this cursory

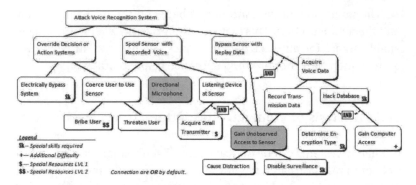

Figure 10.3. A possible voice recognition system attack tree with primary concerns highlighted.

analysis, the system administrators would do well to address the two highlighted nodes first. One possible approach would be to introduce noise around the sensor to obscure spoken words in recordings. The noise would then be subtracted from the sensor in real time. The remaining conditions which are less likely to occur or which have prohibitively high resource cost (monetarily or computationally expensive, for instance) can be addressed last or not at all, depending on the security goals of the system implementation.

10.6 Spoof vs. Common Biometric Technologies

Thanks in part to Hollywood movies; most people consider spoofing as the primary means of defeating a biometric system. Spoofing generally implies the use of falsified data or prosthetic devices which are applied to the sensor of the biometric system. Consequently, many modern sensors incorporate some means of identifying attempted spoofs. Spoofing may be independent of any specific biometric system, such as with criminals leaving fake fingerprints at crime scenes as a red herring for investigators.

As antispoof technology matures, so does spoof technology. As each new means of detecting a spoof is implemented, spoofers are forced to develop more advanced and elaborate spoofs. Following is a brief discussion of the spoof technologies employed against the most widespread biometric systems. In most cases, the application of spoofing requires that the sensor is not itself under surveillance from a human operator. Spoofing is almost exclusively applied to authentication systems where it is necessary to mimic a legitimate user. For identification systems, the equivalent behavior may be thought of as disguising, such as when a spy dons the uniform of a subdued guard so that he may wander the halls of building without arousing suspicion. Personnel watching on security cameras are looking for spies or others who do not belong, but pay no attention to other guards.

10.6.1 *Fingerprint*

The earliest record of fingerprint spoofing is from 1920 when Alert Wehde, a photographer and engraver, used contrast powder and a camera to capture images of latent fingerprints [3]. He then used the negative of the film to etch the print into a copper plate. With grease applied to the plate, he could leave false latent prints. The techniques of today are not significantly different from this. Tsutomu Matsumushi is a Japanese professor who is well-known for making silicon and gelatin fingers using a similar process: a latent print is photographed with a digital camera (sometimes after being enhanced with contrast powder or cyanoacrylate (superglue) fumes [5]. The image is printed on transparency paper and used to image photosensitized copper-clad printed circuit board blanks. After etching, the relief of the remaining copper forms a mold for casting 3-D prints using silicon or gelatin. Some inkjet printers create enough relief to fool simple fingerprint sensors [3].

One of the first suggestions that fingerprints might be spoofed was in the 1907 story *The Red Thumb Mark* by R. Austin Freeman. In the story a young man's fingerprint is found in a drop of blood inside a safe from which diamonds have been stolen. Only the fictional detective Dr. John Thorndyke believes in the boy's innocence and vows to discover how the fingerprint was spoofed.

Early advances in antispoofing of fingerprints involve detecting body temperature. This is often defeated by warming the fake finger with a bag of hot water. Some sensors detect the flow of blood in the finger or the pulse of the heart. More complex fake fingers include a tube that fluid is pumped through to simulate these signals. Current research into antispoof technology is in examining fingerprint patterns below the surface of the skin, electrical conductivity of the skin, and detection of perspiration [3, 5].

10.6.2 *Voice*

Just as the forty thieves in *The Thousand and One Nights* used the command "Open sesame!" to open the door to their treasure cave, voice recognition can be a useful biometric for authentication systems. Because we use voice communications in almost every aspect of our lives, a great deal of infrastructure already exists for the implementation of voice recognition systems. Authentication systems can be implemented over the phone network, for instance. Identification systems can listen for specific word use in public places, such as listening for someone saying "bomb" or "hijack" in airports. This type of biometric identification is not particularly hard to defeat. Since speech is voluntary, people wishing not to be identified need only stay silent. Authentication systems allow access in response to successful speech patterns. In a simplistic system, such as the treasure cave above, a specific word or passphrase will open the door. Ali Baba, upon hearing the password was able to open the cave door. More complex systems in use today actually detect minor variations in the waveform produced by human speech. Such systems can be spoofed with a replay attack using commonly available digital recorders. The 1992 movie *Sneakers* employed this spoof after a memorable effort to record a legitimate user saying fragments of the passphrase: "My voice is my passport, verify me." To thwart such attempts, many systems employ call and response architectures which ask the user to say randomly selected words from a database, rather than using a fixed passphrase [5].

10.6.3 *Facial*

Early 2-D facial recognition systems were easily fooled by presentation of a photograph of an enrolled user or even an image on a laptop computer screen [3]. Evolution of these systems inspects the presented image for blinking eyes or changing facial expressions.

These systems are still bypassed by video shown on a laptop screen. Call and response-type systems may be employed which require the user to smile or frown or look in certain directions in response to a random sequence of requests in an attempt to verify that data is being received in real time. This type of system may be countered with the use of synthetic face generation software which can morph the presented face image in response to user commands. The most modern implementations of facial recognition are 3-D. These systems use either multiple cameras or a projected grid pattern on the face to generate 3-D image data [3]. Some of these systems can be fooled with latex masks of a legitimate user. Perhaps the most effective protection against spoof for 2-D and 3-D systems is the use of facial thermograph images which show the characteristic variations in temperature of the face due to the distribution of veins and arteries [3].

10.6.4 *Iris*

Iris recognition systems can be duped in a similar manner to facial recognition systems. Early sensors were fooled by high resolution iris images, or with iris images printed on contact lenses [5]. Hollywood has imagined more gruesome spoofs for iris scanners. In the 2002 movie *Minority Report*, Tom Cruise's character presents a human eye to an iris scanner, while Wesley Snipes' character does the same in 1993's *Demolition Man*. Liveliness detection is employed in most systems to eliminate these inputs. The most common system detects involuntary microscopic contractions of the pupil. It may be possible to fool these systems with a sufficiently high resolution video device. Just as with the inputs to facial recognition systems, looking at the input signal in the frequency domain can reveal high frequency components from image pixilation that does not occur with legitimate inputs [5].

10.7 Reasons for Exploitation and Attacks

Exploitation of vulnerabilities may occur for many reasons. These reasons may depend on the implementation type of biometric system (identification or authentication) or may depend on the entity responsible for the system. Four of the more common reasons are discussed below.

10.7.1 *Gain False Access*

The most commonly considered purpose in exploiting vulnerabilities is to gain access illegitimately. This reason applies to authentication systems, such as biometric locks or entry checkpoints. Access may also refer to masquerading as a legitimate user for banking purposes or information security. This is the type of attack common to innumerable heist movies. High-tech criminals want to steal the Klopman diamond or a savvy spy wants to see what the enemy army is planning. Whenever something is kept locked up or information is kept secret, it is almost certain that someone else desires to possess it or learn it.

10.7.2 *Avoid Identification*

A more dangerous reason for exploitation may be to avoid identification. This purpose applies to identification systems using databases such as terrorist image databases and fingerprint databases. Facial recognition systems are frequently paired with surveillance cameras at large events, such as the Super Bowl or the Olympic Games to search the crowds of incoming spectators for known criminals and terrorists in real time. Anyone wishing to go unrecognized must defeat the system.

10.7.3 *Denial of Service*

DoS attacks intend to undermine operator trust in a system. Such attacks often target the matching, feature extraction or quality control segments of the system. The goal of DoS is to generate mistrust of the system or increase boredom of system operators. This type of attack is similar to the story of *The Boy Who Cried Wolf*, in which a child repeatedly raises the false alarm of a wolf attack and is later consumed when his cries of "wolf!" are no longer believed by townsfolk. The DoS attack may precede attempts of a malicious party to gain access to an authentication system through less secure authentication means or allow them to be ignored when highlighted by identification systems. This type of attack may also be employed merely to harass an organization, such as with an activist group targeting a laboratory which employs animal testing.

10.7.4 *Identity Theft*

The threat of identity theft hinges on the fact that biometrics are irrevocable by nature. Once you lose control of your fingerprints, you cannot trade them in on a new set. This threat is particularly dangerous because different systems may use the same set of biometric data but may have completely different approaches to security. A supermarket or even a bank may use a fingerprint as a quick means to authorize a monetary transaction. The same fingerprint may be used by an internet café to access a user's virtual desktop. These institutions may have vastly different security concerns. The internet café may regard the fingerprint as a convenience for identification and since the café is a relatively public place, people are unlikely to leave personal information on their virtual desktop. As such, the importance of keeping the biometric fingerprint data secure is of little concern, particularly to immature youth likely to work at a minimum-wage institution. This internet café may have multiple vulnerabilities from operators to computer systems making it a prime target for identity theft, with the eventual goal of spoofing the more secure financial systems.

10.8 Approaches to Safeguard Against Vulnerability

Protecting a biometric system from attack is a field of continuing research. There are many avenues of discussion, both philosophical and specific. In most cases, secrecy is one of the best policies of security. If it cannot be determined how templates are stored, it is difficult to extract them—this is especially important since biometric data itself is not secret.

Often, the solution to one vulnerability creates another vulnerability. This is most apparent with the addition of a human operator. Though the operators may watch the input in an attempt to guarantee no spoofing occurs, they are also vulnerable to boredom, coercion or even cooperation with attacks.

Another approach to security is to combine as many systems as possible into contiguous units. If the database, matcher and decision sections are all contained in one unit, it is difficult or impossible to attack transmission of data between them. Some specific approaches to minimize vulnerability are discussed below.

10.8.1 *Spoof Detection*

Spoof detection seeks primarily to determine that the current input sample is from a live person. This sort of determination is called liveliness testing. There are only three fundamental ways that liveliness testing can be accomplished [3].

The most difficult and least-used method is to analyze the biometric signal which is already being gathered. This is usually impractical because the biometric being gathered does not usually include liveliness information. For instance, the shape and distribution of minutiae in fingerprints is in not affected by life status.

The second and more practical method of liveliness testing involves taking multiple samples of biometric data. An analysis of sequential data can show liveliness signs for some biometrics. This method is commonly applied to facial recognition to look for blinking eyes and changing expression. This method also works well for iris recognition systems where successive images will show microscopic contractions and dilations of the pupil in live subjects. In some cases this method is applied with addition of external stimulus, such as asking users to look in different direction, to smile or to frown, or looking for the contraction reflex of the pupil in response to a bright light.

The final method of liveliness testing is to employ additional sensors to acquire signals which can be correlated to life. This method is frequently used in fingerprint biometric systems. These sensors often measure body temperature in the "finger" presented or detect motion of blood within the "finger." Some systems look for a pulse or measure the skin resistance. One problem faced by this type of system is that many of the liveliness signals may not be consistent between users or even for the same user. Skin temperature may be lower in users with poor circulation or who have just come in from the cold. Skin temperature may be higher with illness or exertion.

10.8.2 *Watermarking*

Watermarking is a method that addresses replay vulnerabilities. The method is to encode additional information in the biometric sensor data, such as adding a date and time stamp to a fingerprint image before processing it [2]. Later, in signal processing the date and time are extracted from the signal and used to exclude expired input signals. For successful watermarking, it is desirable to encode or encrypt the time stamp of the watermark. As with any form of security technology it is desirable to keep the means of security a secret. This method is an example of cryptographic steganography, which is the process of hiding secret information in the form of another obvious message, sometimes called the cover text. One advantage of steganography is that the information does not draw attention like encrypted data.

One interesting method of watermark storage is to replace the least significant bit of each pixel of an image to create a data space in which to store the watermark information. This method can be employed most easily on non-compressed image formats such as bitmaps and TIFFs. If image compression is used, the watermarking must be applied after compression or the compression algorithm may corrupt the stored information.

This method creates a change in pixel intensity of an insignificant (and imperceptible) amount. For an 8-bit, gray-scale image, where the color value of each pixel is stored as a number from 0 to 255, the difference between two adjacent colors in the color space is 1/256th or about 0.39%. This very small change in intensity provides a great deal of storage space. In a 100×100 pixel image, there are 10,000 pixels. Taking every 8 pixels to encode one ASCII character, there are $10,000/8 = 1250$ characters available in this small image. For reference, the first two paragraphs of this section contain 1248 characters including punctuation and spaces. Figure 10.4 shows an example of watermarking a 100×100 pixel image with the first two paragraphs of this section. Image C is formed by subtraction of image

Figure 10.4. An example of watermarking. (A) Original image, (B) watermarked image, (C) difference between A and B (intensity scaled), (D) watermark data (intensity scaled).

B from image A. Black pixels represent a reduction in value, white pixels represent an increase in value, and gray pixels represent no change. The images in Fig. 10.4C,D were scaled to make the data visible—both images would appear black if not scaled.

If fewer characters are required, more data can be stored. For instance, if only 26 letters and 6 punctuation marks are needed, only 5 bits are required per character and the message length can be increased to 2000 characters. The watermark information can easily be encrypted before storage in the image and would be invisible when an image was viewed.

Watermarking only addresses replay attacks which bypass the location of the original watermarking. Most systems would apply primary watermarking at the sensor location. For example, a system which uses the fingerprint biometric for authentication may encode the date, time, and identity of the user into the image at the sensor when the finger is presented. Perhaps Bob enrolls his fingerprints with the security system on Monday, and the images are encoded with {Bob Smith, Monday}. On Tuesday, Bob attempts to enter the system and his fingerprint is scanned and encoded {Bob Smith, Tuesday} at the sensor and sent to the system. The system looks at the image and extracts "Tuesday" from the watermark, finds that this matches the current day, and allows access. Unknown to Bob, Andy has hacked the sensor and records the image marked {Bob Smith, Tuesday}. On Saturday, when no one is around, Andy presents the image to the system, bypassing the sensor. The system extracts "Tuesday" from the watermark but does not allow access since the date does not match "Saturday." An actual system would record the date and time much more precisely and would probably include either encryption of the data or a one-way hashed checksum of the data to prevent a savvy misanthrope from adjusting the stored date and time.

10.8.3 *Human Verification*

Despite the great computational power available in biometrics systems, the human element still forms one of the most reliable means of verification. Human operators can quickly address false rejection situations or verify that spoofing is not occurring. As mentioned before, human operators also may be bribed, coerced, or bored. This problem can be mitigated to some extent by careful training and periodic monitoring of personnel.

10.8.4 *Multimodal Biometrics*

If a single lock does not seem sufficient to secure an apartment door, one can use additional locks. This approach to security is the basis behind the use of multimodal biometric systems. In such a system a user must present multiple forms of biometrics to be authorized. This may constitute multiple biometric technologies such as facial recognition and an iris scan or a thumb print and a voice command. Alternatively, it may encompass several different biometric signals of the same type, such as the irises of both eyes or fingerprints from multiple fingers and thumbs. This type of system addresses some vulnerabilities in the front part of the biometric system, but may not affect later parts of the system at all. Some systems can have greater vulnerabilities in the matching and decision sections if the matching score calculation gives undue preference to one type of biometric over another, or if a poor matching score for one biometric is eclipsed by a nearly perfect match.

10.8.5 *Passive and Active Biometrics*

In keeping with the idea that secret information is more secure, one of the best methods of increasing security is the use of passive and active biometrics. This is an interesting subset of multimodal biometrics. Some biometric technologies by their nature can be gathered without the knowledge of the user. The most notable candidates for these passive biometrics are facial recognition, iris recognition, gait recognition, and to a lesser extent, voice recognition. The approach to this type of system would be to set up an obvious active biometric scanner, perhaps for fingerprint or hand geometry while at the same time, an inconspicuous camera captures video for passive facial or iris recognition. A malicious onlooker might recognize the fingerprinting sensor, but attempted spoof attacks would fail against the unknown facial recognition system.

10.8.6 *Mitigation of Weak Users*

As mentioned previously, so-called weak users are a significant source of vulnerabilities in biometric systems. These are the users who contribute to FAR and FRR due to their unusual matching characteristics [6]. Two types of weak users can be addressed using similarity and difference scores. Similarity scores are a measure of how closely inputs resemble each other. Difference scores are a measure of the dissimilarity of two inputs. For a given user, it is not difficult to determine a similarity score among all the enrollment templates for that user. It is also not difficult to determine a difference score among that user's enrollment templates and all other enrollment templates in the database. By careful analysis of these two scores, users can be classified as either Goats or Lambs. Because Wolves may be internal or external, it is hard to predict their presence. When Goats and Lambs are identified, additional biometric or other security methods are required. Users who are classified as Sheep may be able to give a single fingerprint to enter a facility, whereas users who are known to be weak require a second or third enrolled finger to be presented. This is a unimodal implementation. An alternative is available for multimodal systems. A weak user in one biometric type is often strong in another biometric type. If multiple biometric modes are available, preference can be given to one mode over another for some users. For instance if someone's facial features are difficult for the system to classify, they may instead verify their identity with the use of a palm scanner.

This system improves security for those users who can be correctly classified as Lambs and Goats but does not address Wolves [6].

10.8.7 *Biometric Encryption*

Encryption technology is well known and constantly evolving. In biometric systems, encryption is most commonly used to enhance the security of stored templates and transmitted information. Encryption of matching scores can prevent their substitution during transmission [1]. Encryption can be used in the sensor section of the system to minimize the risk of replay attacks. Templates in the database can be stored as encrypted files. Obviously, it is important to keep the encryption key secret.

10.8.8 *Revocable Biometrics*

Perhaps the most interesting and modern method of protection is the idea of revocable biometrics. In this system, the raw biometric data of the user is not recorded. Instead, the biometric signal is distorted in a known way—think funhouse mirror. This distorted signal is used as a proxy biometric for the user [1]. Enrolled templates are handled normally and candidate biometric signals are distorted in the same way before comparisons are made. In the event that a person's stored biometric identity is compromised, he can be re-enrolled using a different distortion, or a different seed value for pseudorandom distortion. As with other methods of security, the distortion algorithm and pseudorandom number seeds must be kept secret.

10.9 Conclusions

Since the origin of the species, what one man has, another man wants. Whenever material or information must be protected, a security system must be employed. From a simple lock box to a time-controlled bank vault to the biometric systems of today, these security systems have grown in subtlety and complexity. As the systems become more complex, those who would bypass them must become more devious; as the technology to protect advances, so too does the technology to manipulate. The cycle continues interminably. Who can say what future technology will bring to biometric security? Perhaps DNA testing will be available within a few seconds of collection as in the 1997 movie *Gattaca*. Perhaps high-tech criminals will employ subdermal implants that allow them to change the shape and thermograph of their face on the fly. Perhaps complex brain activity maps will provide a new source of biometric identification. With each new biometric technology development, it is as important to understand the vulnerabilities as it is to consider the possibilities. As security scientists of the future implement new technologies, they will continue to apply the methods and considerations discussed in this chapter.

References

1. Jain, A. K., Flynn, P., and Ross, A. A. (2008) Biometric system security, in *Handbook of Biometrics* (Adler, A., Ed.), Springer Science, Business Media, LLC., New York, pp. 381–402.

2. Xiao, Q. (2005) *Security Issues in Biometric Authentication,* IEEE, West Point, NY, 0-7803-9290-6/05.

3. Faúndez-Zanuy, M. (2004) *On the Vulnerabilitiy of Biometric Security Systems. IEEE A&E Systems Magazine,* June.

4. Sabena, F., Dehghantanha, A., Seddon, A. P. (2010) *A Review of Vulnerabilities in Identity Managment using Biometrics,* IEEE, 978-0-7695-3940-9/10.

5. Jain, A. K., Flynn, P., and Ross, A. (2008) Spoof detection schemes, in *Handbook of Biometrics* (Nixon, K. A., Aimale, V., Rowe, R. K., Eds.), Springer Science, Business Media, LLC., New York, 2008, pp. 403–423.

6. Ross, A., Rattani, A., and Tistarelli, M. (2009) *Exploiting the "Doddington Zoo" Effect in Biometric Fusion,* IEEE, 978-1-4244-5020-6/09.

Chapter 11

Challenges in Biometrics: Accessibility, Usability, and the Legal Framework

Ing. Mario Savastano

Institute of Bio-structures and Bio-images, National Research Council of Italy,
Via Pansini 5, 80131 Napoli, Italy
mario.savastano@unina.it

11.1 Introduction

Nobody can deny that the introduction of the biometric technologies has represented a significant step ahead in the field of security. Anyway, beyond all the technological triumphalism, the experience gained through the on-field applications has clearly shown that the aspects connected to the legal, social, and ethical fields play a fundamental role in biometrics.

The analysis of such aspects, which we will call for simplicity "cross-jurisdictional," requires a good knowledge of many different disciplines and a "mirabilis" ability to integrate the expertise.[a]

On the other hand, the unexpected failure of several initiatives in the area of biometrics has highlighted how an inadequate contemplation of the cross-jurisdictional aspects may be fatal for a project.

---

[a]The study of biometrics should include competences, at least, in computer science, mathematics, medicine, law, and psychology.

Biometrics: From Fiction to Practice
Edited by Eliza Yingzi Du
Copyright © 2013 Pan Stanford Publishing Pte Ltd.
ISBN 978-981-4310-88-8 (Hardcover), 978-981-4364-13-3 (eBook)
www.panstanford.com

This chapter deals generically with these kind of aspects focusing on legal issues, accessibility, usability, and ethical issues. It does not pretend to make a detailed analysis but, rather, aims at underlining some less debated features that are rarely considered in the several documents and books written on these topics [1–3].

The chapter draws inspiration from the activities of ISO/IEC JTC1 SC 37 "Biometrics" WG 6 on "Cross-Jurisdictional and Societal Aspects" that I have had the honor to convene.

The long and passionate discussions over a cup of coffee (or a glass of red wine after the working hours) with other distinguished experts coming from all over the world have given me the privilege of looking at the world of biometrics from a real multigeographic point of view, and this chapter aims at reflecting such multicultural perspectives.

11.2 A Real Challenge for Biometrics

Even if the mathematical algorithms—on which biometrics is based—are increasing ever more in accuracy and the devices capturing the biometric characteristics are much more sophisticated than in the past, the cross-jurisdictional aspects of biometrics are playing a fundamental role in mitigating the triumphalism—in good or bad faith—of its advocates.

The point is that even the most robust mathematical algorithms or the most sophisticated technological alchemies cannot completely manage the fragility and mutability of the human beings involved in a biometric process. On the other hand, it is a common opinion that as the use of biometrics is becoming popular, the social, ethical, and legal aspects of biometrics are gaining a growing importance.

In other words, it is all the more clear that the success of a biometric implementation depends as much on the technology aspects as, in a preeminent way, on the possibility to find a valid compromise with a large number of heterogeneous factors that represent the object of the present chapter, which is organized as follows.

Section 11.3 describes the evolution of the attention paid to the cross-jurisdictional issues of biometrics. Section 11.4 analyzes some legal aspects with particular reference to the sphere of privacy. Section 11.5 describes some aspects of accessibility [4] and usability [5] of biometrics, while Section 11.6 discusses the medical aspects of biometrics [6]. Section 11.7 reports some observations about the ethical implications of biometrics, whereas Section 11.8 highlights the activity of standardization of biometrics with particular reference to the work carried out in the ISO/IEC JTC1 SC 37 "Biometrics" WG 6 on "Cross-Jurisdictional and Societal aspects." Finally, Section 11.9 draws the conclusions.

11.3 "Early" Biometrics

The development of a biometric project can be compared to the construction of a building. As this requires solid fundaments, a biometric project needs an initial robust analysis of several heterogeneous factors such as the compliance with the legal framework, its accessibility, and its usability [7].

Unfortunately, in the early years of biometrics, these very important aspects were partially or, on some occasions, totally underestimated, since all the efforts of vendors to convince potential buyers were directed to highlighting the technological aspects.

This was absolutely logical because many firms had invested large capitals in biometrics and were eager to be compensated for their strong financial efforts, by highlighting the more attractive peculiarities of biometric innovations.

In this scenario dominated by technological challenges, there was practically no possibility to address the cross-jurisdictional aspects of biometrics, such as accessibility or legal issues, and the amazing capabilities of the new technologies, often corroborated to approximate test campaigns, seemed to be the only mantra to chant in order to convince customers to buy biometric systems.

On the other hand, this paradoxical and unrealistic scenario of technological perfection, in the collective imaginary, was amplified by several mass media channels, such as science-fiction movies [8].

Hollywood's products such as *Mission Impossible* or *Minority Report* have shown biometrics as an amazing and stainless technology and, at the same time, have exported an image of its user (generally young, pleasant, and smart) that, along with the time, has shown to be very distant from the reality.

This "super user"[b] of the early biometrics had perfect finger-prints, did not know the term "eye cataract," had a perfect sight and hearing, was able to understand soon the instructions, did not tremble in front of a sensor—in other words, he or she was in the so-called golden window of biometrics.

Unfortunately, most likely, several triumphalistic tests carried out to evaluate the performance of various biometric technologies have been based just on super users who, obviously, being much better than other categories of users, were able to give to the biometric systems the possibility to exhibit the best performance.

This experience has inexorably forced the biometric community to forget the super users and to start much more realistic and meaningful test campaigns to take into account a series of "awkward" factors such as the age, ethnicity, or skills of the users.

A rather clear example of the "biometric inebriation" boosted by rather false expectations may be proved by the sudden diffusion and disappearance in the airports of biometric systems based on face recognition in the aftermath of 9/11.

Also on the basis of, maybe, too enthusiastic advertising campaigns, the biometric technology based on face recognition was presented to the public as an adequate countermeasure to the severe threats that characterized the transportation sector, with specific reference to airports.

Vendors claimed to be able to detect suspects on the basis of comparing passengers' faces with the blacklisted ones, but the reality clearly highlighted that, using the mathematical algorithms and technology available at the time, it was difficult, if not impossible, to manage the large amount of false positives.

In practice, after this unrealistic phase, biometric technologies slightly turned to what they are nowadays considered: not a panacea

---

[b]It is also interesting to note that music has contributed to amplifying this concept of "super user" since the promotion of biometrics through advertising spots has generally involved the use of soundtracks, sometimes aggressive, based on rock, disco, or house music.

but only one of the many rings of the long, controversial, and complex chain of security.

Along the years, the consideration that biometric technologies had to be necessarily tied to a series of factors connected to the user has become an important prerequisite for every project.

11.4 Privacy

If a speaker has to give a presentation on biometrics to a "critical" audience and, perhaps, his or her emotional difficulties are flirting with a severe jet lag, this speaker may start the "exhibition" with a statement very hard to contradict: "The relationship between privacy and biometrics is particularly difficult."

Most likely, none among the audience will pose any objection to such a truthful issue and then the speaker will able to break the ice easily. If, afterward, the speaker definitively wants to fascinate the audience, he will probably offer a slide on the "fuzzy boundaries between privacy and biometrics."[c]

Apart from this humorous example, it is absolutely true that the relationships between privacy and biometrics represent an important argument of discussion [9, 10]. The biometric community is often heard complaining about the severity of some data protection authorities that go along with a public concern that is often based only on a scarce knowledge of the argument. On the other hand, privacy advocates warn against a too ready acceptance of biometrics, because of its potential for excessive intrusion in the life of those subjected to i, and therefore they claim that often privacy, data protection, profiling, and ethical factors mix together creating a fatal and poisonous cocktail.

A large number of scientific and academic meetings and conferences tailored on biometrics and privacy are organized every year. Those attending these events are often divided in two groups: legal experts, who obviously have often a scarce knowledge of the

---

[c]In the context of the conferences, the term "fuzzy" has often the same effects that James Bond produced on women and enemies: love and respect. Those who know what is "fuzziness" will love this term, and nonexperts will not dare to pose questions.

technical aspects of biometrics, and technicians, who habitually have no idea of legal issues.

They may debate for days, have legendary dinners together, and seal genuine proposals of collaboration in front to a glass of good Chianti, but at the end of the event, every team probably remains with its beliefs and quite often will confess to being absolutely glad to have avoided the boring studies of the other.

This does not mean that these get-togethers are not useful, but the wall between privacy and biometrics generally remains very high and difficult to climb. The good news is that the wall is crumbling, and the bad one is that there are other walls, much higher.

In practice, even if, traditionally, "privacy" occupies the first position among the human factors connected to biometrics, such leader position is probably due only to historical motivations, since privacy issues of biometrics have started to be studied from a long time.

Even if the relations between biometrics and privacy remain an important topic, nowadays other delicate points, as will be shown in Section 11.5, are rapidly becoming more crucial and, probably, much more difficult to approach.

11.4.1 *The Fragmentation of the Privacy Issues*

Typing together the words "biometrics" and "privacy" in an Internet search may give a considerable number of results. This is a clear sign of the popularity gained by the binomial and, at the same time, of the difficulties in writing something new on an argument that has been much debated on.

An interesting property privacy, often underestimated, is its temporal "mobility," or, in other words, its continuous modeling of some rules according the evolution of society.

Furthermore, privacy also depends on the geopolitical context in the sense that every country has its peculiarity in writing and applying the normative context.

A first important consequence of the temporal mobility is that a habit that, from the privacy point of view, can be considered inappropriate at a certain time may become acceptable later.

With reference to the generic context of security, a good example of changes in the consideration of privacy may be provided by the introduction, in 2008, of a new technology in airports.

The proposal of installing in the airports the so-called whole-body scanners gave rise to a passionate discussion in the EU Parliament about possible infringements of privacy. In the aftermath of a missed terroristic attack in December 2009, the only possibility that the whole-body scanners could have contributed to detect the threat, attenuated the concerns for privacy to the point that several European countries decided to immediately start implementing such technology.

This "event-driven" metabolization of privacy, along the years, has been particularly evident in the context of biometrics where many applications have started to be accepted on the basis of public opinion because the applications proved to be useful as well as always more compliant with privacy requirements.[d]

Only in March 2001, a European Data Protection Authority defined, in a specific context, the use of fingerprints as "a non proportional sacrifice of the individuals liberty sphere" [11] and in the following years has softened this position allowing their use for several applications.

This "time variance" of privacy is probably the main reason why many experts are optimistic about a possible good cohabitation with biometrics, provided that this technology has a tangible effect both in increasing security and in providing generic benefits to its users.

The location variance of privacy, addressing the evidence that its perception is different in the various countries of the world, represents one of the most demanding tasks of the work carried out in the Working Group 6 "Cross-Jurisdictional and Societal Aspects" of the ISO/IEC JTC1 SC 37 "Biometrics."

Even if it might be correct to affirm that, at a global level, there is a generic common understanding of the concept of privacy, the application of specific rules, the level of real influence of such rules, and the measures to adopt in case of their infringement may vary noticeably from country to country.

---

[d]Along with the years, the research on the PET (privacy-enhancing technologies) has assumed a great importance.

Anyway, with particular reference to biometrics, and to some geographic context, the principle of proportionality should be considered reasonably common and relevant.

11.4.2 *Some Considerations on the Proportionality Principle Applied in the Context of the Biometric Technologies*

With particular reference to the EU member states, experience has clearly shown that the principle of proportionality is often a decisive factor in the legal review of biometric systems by the Data Protection Authorities (DPA) [12].

The proportionality principle, as clearly defined in the context of the EU Fidis[e] initiative, refers to a general principle of law that requires a fair balance and reasonable relationship between the means requested or used, including the severity and the duration of the means, and the objective sought.

The proportionality principle[f] has its origin mainly in public law, where it lays down some fundamental rules for justifying state interference with fundamental rights and freedoms of individuals, as developed in case law and legal doctrine [13].

Within the framework of the European Data Protection Directive (officially Directive 95/46/EC on the protection of individuals with regard to the processing of personal data and on the free movement of such data), the principle of proportionality implies that data collected may not include more than what is required to fulfill the purpose for which they were collected. According to this principle, personal data must be adequate, relevant, and not excessive in relation to the purposes for which they are collected and further processed.

These definitions may be also interpreted in the sense that the principle of proportionality is satisfied when benefits exceed their costs by a considerable margin. Again, in basic terms, with particular reference to biometrics, the definitions may be interpreted in the

---

[e]FIDIS (Future of IDentity in the Information Society) is a network of excellence (NOE), which has received research funding from the EU's 6th Framework Programme (www.fidis.net).
[f]Mainly in the European context.

sense that, in certain national jurisdictions, the implementation of a biometric project may require a valid "justification," which should not be only of economic kind.

But, let's take an example: the owner of a company decides to install a biometric system to increase the security of the company's time and attendance system. This decision may be caused by the need to avoid illicit exchange of badges among employees or simply to modernize the system.

Assuming that the biometric system of the present case is not addressing specifically the safety of the employees (we will analyze such a case later on), in several countries this straight application of a biometric system is currently not allowed. The point raised by privacy advocates is that the possible financial damage that the employer suffers cannot be considered a valid justification for the use of a system that, under some circumstances, may be considered prejudicial to the dignity of the employees.

From the practical point of view, this means that, in several national jurisdictions, the use of a biometric system only for time and attendance purposes is not allowed. An interesting document of the Italian Data Protection Authority on the prohibition of using biometrics for time and attendance, in a specific case, is reported in [14].

At the same time, if the access of the employees is linked to a condition in which the badge exchange may lead to a risky situation, from the safety point of view, the proportionality principle is satisfied and, most likely, the use of the biometric system will be allowed.

For example, three Italian grain mills (located where one would not think about high-security access systems immediately) were allowed by the Italian Data Protection Authority to use a biometric system for entering in some areas because it was demonstrated that inappropriate access by nonexpert employees could lead to a risk for public safety (possible fires and explosions).[g]

---

[g]Flour explosions are a much larger risk in areas where large amounts of flour are handled. Although a small dust cloud of flour might ignite in a home kitchen, the damage would probably not be severe. In a grain elevator or flour mill, however, the potential for a very large cloud of flour or grain dust is much higher. For this reason, care is taken in these facilities to prevent dust clouds, and potential sources

11.5 Accessibility and Usability in Biometrics

Accessibility and usability are two terms that are commonly heard in the discussions concerning biometrics.

Accessibility is a general term used to describe the degree to which a product, device, service, or environment is available to as many people as possible [15], and despite a popular argument in the entire ICT context, its implications in biometrics are particularly relevant for the utmost importance assumed by the body itself in the transactions.

Classical categories of users who may face accessibility problems in using biometric devices are people who are visually or hearing-impaired or wheelchair-bound, or those who may have difficulty using a product or system that does not take their needs into appropriate consideration.

The real dimension of the accessibility problem in biometrics is not yet clear, because technologies evolve and their impact on the impaired population evolves in parallel.

To overcome the problems connected to accessibility, more biometric modalities can be combined to produce a system that would allow more flexible use. For example, biometric systems built for both fingerprint and face recognition could allow the use of only the facial image for verification when users have problems enrolling their fingerprints, and vice versa [16].

In practice, up to now, there are quite a few applications based on multimodalities, and several indicators (mainly of economic kind) suggest that it will not be easy to see a massive diffusion of such approach to overcome the problem of disabilities in biometrics.

Accessibility should not to be confused with usability that is used to describe the extent to which a product (e.g., device, service, and environment) can be used by particular users to achieve specific goals with effectiveness, efficiency, and satisfaction in a specified context of use (ISO 13407:1999).

Careful attention to usability issues helps ensure that systems and products are easy to learn, effective to use, and enjoyable from the users' perspective.

---

of open flame are usually protected (http://www.wisegeek.com/what-causes-flour-to-explode.htm, accessed June 2011).

11.5.1 *The Elderly Dilemma*

It is a common opinion that in today's society the elderly generation is becoming increasingly isolated and excluded from large parts of the daily life because of the difficulties they face in approaching a technological world that is extremely complex and probably too articulated for them.

To understand this type of "digital divide," several studies have analyzed the use of the Internet and have come to the common result that, over a certain age, the number of connected users decreases dramatically.

If it is documented that elderly people encounter difficulties in using the Internet, it is also reasonably evident that they may find it difficult to use biometrics, due both to physical and cognitive difficulties.

Continuing the ideal parallel between the use of the Internet and that of biometrics, there is probably also another consideration to make. In using the Internet for accessing a service or gaining a generic benefit, the users make an "option," while, at least in some particular contexts, the use of biometrics may assume the role of an "obligation" and therefore a compromised "biometricity" may have more consequences for the elderly who have faced a number of problems in using biometrics.

For example, fingerprints of the elderly cannot be acquired in a satisfactory way because of an increased dryness of the skin and less significant papillary reliefs. Those who undergo cataract operations require a re-enrollment in the systems based on iris recognition, and in general a considerable number of small or large deteriorations of the nervous, muscular, and bone systems may seriously interfere with an appropriate use of a biometric system.

In the future, it will certainly be possible for biometric designers to create systems that are ever more accessible or usable. Nevertheless, it is unfortunately true that at a certain point in human life and at least on the basis of current technologies, every user may become "biometrically disabled." Even in the future, there will probably be nothing to do apart from excluding the elderly from biometric procedures, as currently happens for several applications where an age limit for the users of a biometric system is fixed.

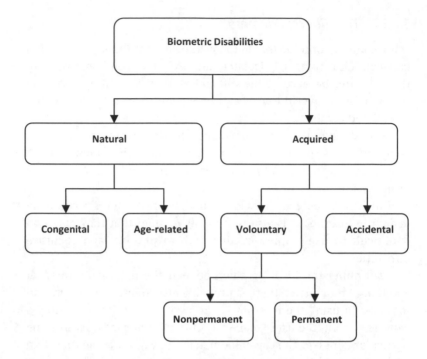

Figure 11.1. Tentative block diagram of biometric disabilities.

11.5.2 *Biometric Disabilities*

The sphere of disabilities in biometrics may be ideally divided into two wide areas, natural and acquired. A tentative block diagram for biometric disabilities is presented in Fig. 11.1.

Natural biometric disabilities are due to congenital characteristics of individuals (such as the lack of a part of the body that should be used for a biometric process) or to aging, as highlighted in the previous paragraph.

Acquired biometric disabilities are generally "accidental" and due to an event (trauma or illness) that makes it impossible to use a biometric system or represents a serious impediment in doing so.

On the other hand, "voluntarily" acquired biometric disabilities are intentional alterations of a specific part of the body that may be permanent or nonpermanent.

The nonpermanent kind generally involve biometric technology based on face recognition and may be caused by the use of particular kinds of make-up or ornaments, or even by men's facial hair styles.

Permanent voluntary modifications are particularly relevant and are described separately.

11.5.3 *Voluntary Permanent Modifications*

The intense use of biometric technologies in investigative and judicial contexts is one of the probable causes of the highly sensitive problem of voluntary alterations of biometric characteristics in order to avoid possible identification.

This phenomenon is of particular interest in the area of fingerprint recognition since the alterations may get to the point of making a subject totally invisible to some biometric systems. Also, in these instances, the legislative background is still not ready at the international level.

A very interesting case was reported in December 2009 concerning a woman who managed to enter into a country illegally by having plastic surgery to alter her fingerprints, thus fooling immigration controls.

Actually, there is probably a lack of legal coverage to prevent a subject to undergo such a kind of surgical operation. It would be interesting to analyze the counts of indictment used in this case since, most likely, this has represented one of the first cases in which the body has been considered to be necessarily not to be subjected to voluntary alteration if used in the identification context.

11.6 Medical Aspects of Biometrics

All experts in biometrics agree that, since the cooperation of the users is an absolutely essential factor for the success of a biometric project, particular attention should be devoted to all those factors that can compromise such cooperation.

Analyzing those factors, the medical implications of biometrics seem apparently scarcely important. Indeed, they are potentially very relevant, mainly from the psychological point of view.

Already in 2002, the Biovision project [17] identified safety of use of the equipment among factors that make systems unacceptable and highlighted that only low popular knowledge about biometrics and a relatively modest diffusion of biometrics in everyone's common life were the causes of a low interest for the medical problems associated with it.

At the same time, the project launched the warning that the ever wider popularity of biometrics could increase the curiosity about or even a volunteer speculation on medical implications and therefore enable users to raise a series of questions about the effects on their own health or on the privacy violations of some biometric techniques.

Two types of medical implications have been identified: direct medical implications (DMI) and indirect medical implications (IMI). The former refer to the potential risks of damage associated with the use of biometric devices, and the latter relate to the ethical risk of biometric data being used to reveal private medical information. Both types of implications can be seen as fuzzy quantifications of risks, but DMI refer to physical, measurable potential damaging effects, whereas IMI are about the possibility of extracting medical information.

11.6.1 *Direct Medical Implications*

In some circumstances, the interaction of a part of the body with a biometric sensor may give rise to some concerns from the point of view of a potential health risk.

For example, if the biometric system includes a sensor that requires a contact with a part of the body (e.g., a hand), some users may fear to be contaminated by germs or bacteria. The real risk may be minimal, especially when compared to similar everyday actions (touching doorknobs, public telephones, etc.), but the perceived risk may have a negative impact on public acceptance. Regular cleaning of the surface of the sensor or even decontamination through ultraviolet light can minimize concerns.

A second potential risk relates to the biometric sensors that use particular irradiations, such as near-infrared (NIR) light, to assist acquisition.

In general terms, biometric sensors are deployed with a certification of compliance with safety standards, but quite often these data are not made easily available to users.

Furthermore, for precaution, it would be advisable to intensify studies on the possible effects of NIR light in extreme working conditions such as very long exposure times or irradiation of already damaged skin tissues.

11.6.2 *Indirect Medical Implications*

Indirect medical implications refer to the possibility of biometric data revealing sensitive health information, leading to social and ethical concerns.

References to the indirect medical implications may be found in discussions on the overlapping between iris recognition and iridology [18] or, more recently, in the concerns raised by the possibility that biometric systems based on face recognition could reveal medical conditions.

11.7 Some Ethical Factors of Biometrics

Using parts of the body as authentication tokens imposes a particular care from the ethical point of view. Several documents and initiatives have addressed these issues, and in particular this section deals with the work actually carried out at the Italian National Committee for Bioethics (CNB, Comitato Nazionale di Bioetica, http://www.palazzochigi.it/bioetica/).

Some of the considerations reported here may be found in a document on biometrics published in 2010 by this committee [19].

11.7.1 *The Human Body as Password: Biometric Characteristics in "Good Shape"*

As anticipated in Section 11.5.2, the use of biometric technologies may entail new specific code of conducts. An interesting point is the necessity for the users of a biometric system to maintain their own biometric characteristics as similarly as possible to those stored in the enrolling phase.

This concerns, for example, face appearance that not only should be as neutral as possible to facilitate a biometric recognition but also as free as possible from alterations that could compromise the biometric process such us make-up, ornaments, piercings, or tattoos.[h]

Such necessity is quite innovative since, up to now, even if within certain limits, every individual has had the freedom to dispose of his or her own appearance.

The necessity of maintaining a "standard" look is particularly important in the light of other alterations that may be caused by social and ethnic or also religious tendencies, which often originated in the mists of time.

Another important factor that will probably become popular in using biometric systems will probably be the always more necessary care with the part of the body to be used for the transactions. The biometric characteristics will have to be maintained "in good shape," and the concept of a very specific preservation of some parts of the body, most likely, has no precedents in the context of the relationship between individuals and society.

Most likely, quite soon, a relevant part of the population will become accustomed to the fact that a certain service or benefit may be lost if "physical" identity credentials — such as fingertips — are unreliable, just as it happens nowadays in the case of damaged paper ID documents.

11.7.2 *Biometrics in Preventing Human Trafficking*

A common discussion on the ethical aspects of biometric technologies almost always highlights the concerns that these technologies may create.

In reality, there are several facts that show how biometric technologies may promote ethical factors, for example the role they play in preventing human trafficking.

---

[h]Special norms and explanatory rules are actually proposed by the governments or standardization organizations for the expression of the face to be adopted in using biometrics.

Poverty and lack of economic opportunity make especially women and children potential victims of traffickers associated with international criminal organizations. The figures related to human trafficking are scary: it is estimated that millions of people are trafficked worldwide annually.

Many actions have been suggested to prevent human trafficking, but there is a common understanding that stricter visa regulations and border controls, especially for young women and children, represent valid countermeasures, and in this sense biometric technologies represent the most efficient and flexible innovation of the last years in strengthening border control.

It is difficult to estimate how much biometrics is supporting the fight to human trafficking, because a good portion of its effect is caused by the deterrence to try to cross the border illegally.

For sure, biometrics is unanimously considered, more than any previous generation of authentication technology, a solution particularly efficient in identifying fake travel documents and passports.

11.8 The Standardization Activity

Created in June 2002, subcommittee 37 of ISO/IEC JTC1 held its first full meeting in Orlando, Florida, in December 2002.

On the basis of adopted resolutions, six study groups were created, and in the course of the Rome meeting, held following year, the study groups became the six working groups on which the activity of SC 37 is currently based.

A list of the SC 37 working groups is given below:

1. JTC 1/SC 37/WG 1 — Harmonized biometric vocabulary
2. JTC 1/SC 37/WG 2 — Biometric technical interfaces
3. JTC 1/SC 37/WG 3 — Biometric data interchange formats
4. JTC 1/SC 37/WG 4 — Biometric functional architecture and related profiles
5. JTC 1/SC 37/WG 5 — Biometric testing and reporting
6. JTC 1/SC 37/WG 6 — Cross-jurisdictional and societal aspects of biometrics

11.8.1 The ISO/IEC JTC1 SC 37 "Biometrics" WG 6 on Cross-Jurisdictional and Societal Issues

The sphere of activity of ISO/IEC JTC1 SC 37 "Biometrics" WG 6 on Cross-Jurisdictional and Societal Issues includes several aspects of biometrics that are not completely linked, if not detached, to the technological context and that cover many of the issues discussed in this chapter.

One of the points of strength of WG 6 is its ability to facilitate the gathering of experts around a table from all over the world, thereby making, most likely, WG 6 the only context in biometrics whose documents are shared at such a wide geographical level.

The activity of WG 6 is reflected in one international standard published in 2008:

— ISO/IEC TR 24714-1:2008 (Information technology — Biometrics — Jurisdictional and societal considerations for commercial applications — Part 1: General guidance), which gives guidelines for the stages in the life cycle of a system's biometric and associated elements.

Furthermore, WG 6 is currently working on the following items:

— ISO/IEC TR 29144: Information technology — Biometrics — The use of biometric technology in commercial identity management applications and processes
— ISO/IEC TR 29194: Guidance on the inclusive design and operation of biometric systems
— ISO/IEC WD 24779: Pictograms, icons and symbols for use with biometric systems

In early 2011, a new project dealing with the delicate relationships between biometrics and children started.

11.9 Conclusions

This chapter, without pretending to describe in detail the aspects characterizing cross-jurisdictional issues of biometrics, tried to gather a number of factors that could be relevant in a future characterized by a massive diffusion of biometric technologies.

A great deal of the arguments touched upon in this chapter reflect the activities carried out by ISO/IEC JTC1 SC 37 WG 6 on Cross-Jurisdictional and Societal Aspects of Biometrics. My sincere gratitude goes to all the kind colleagues from several parts of the world who, in the course of recent years, have made outstanding contributions to the development of international standards in the area of biometrics.

References

1. Ashbourn, J. (2000) *Biometrics: Advanced Identity Verification: The Complete Guide*, Springer.
2. Wayman, W. Jain, A., Maltoni, D., Maio, D. (Eds.), (2005) *Biometric Systems: Technology, Design and Performance Evaluation*, Springer.
3. Woodward, J., Orlans, N. M., Higgins, P. (2003) *Biometrics: Identity Assurance in the Information Age*, McGraw-Hill.
4. http://www.tiresias.org/accessible_ict/what.htm
5. National Institute of Standards & Technology, *Usability & Biometrics, Ensuring Successful Biometric Systems*, http://zing.ncsl.nist.gov/biousa/docs/Usability_and_Biometrics_final2.pdf
6. *Biometrics at the Frontiers: Assessing the Impact on Society*, EC-DG JRC-IPTS, http://ec.europa.eu/justice_home/doc_centre/freetravel/doc/biometrics_eur21585_en.pdf
7. Savastano, M.,*Non-Technical Aspects of Biometrics*, http://www.biometrics.org/bc2004/Presentations/Conference/1%20Monday%20September%2020/Mon_Ballroom%20B/2%20Biometrics%20and%20Privacy%20Talk/Savastano_Presentation.pdf
8. http://pagesperso-orange.fr/fingerchip/biometrics/movies.htm
9. www.privacy.gov.au/materials/types/speeches/view/6324
10. *Large-scale Biometrics Deployment in Europe: Identifying Challenges and Threats*, JRC Scientific and Technical Report, 2008, http://www.a-sit.at/pdfs/biometrics_report.pdf
11. Garante Italiano per la Protezione dei Dati Personali, *"Videosorveglianza — raccolta di impronte digitali associata ad immagini per l'accesso a*

banche", http://www.garanteprivacy.it/garante/doc.jsp?ID=30947 (in Italian) BANCHE

12. Lie, Y. (2009) The principle of proportionality in biometrics: Case studies from Norway, *Computer Law & Security Review* 25, 237–250.

13. http://www.fidis.net/resources/deliverables/hightechid/int-d37001/doc/18/

14. http://www.garanteprivacy.it/garante/doc.jsp?ID=1664257 (in Italian) LENZI

15. http://en.wikipedia.org/wiki/Accessibility

16. http://www.tiresias.org/research/guidelines/biometric_systems.htm

17. http://ftp.cwi.nl/CWIreports/PNA/PNA-E0303.pdf CONTROLLARE SE BVN

18. http://www.cl.cam.ac.uk/~jgd1000/iridology.html

19. *L'identificazione del corpo umano, profili bioetici della biometria,* http://www.governo.it/bioetica/pareri_abstract/biometria_20101126.pdf (in Italian)

Chapter 12

Cancellable Biometrics

Yan Sui,[a] Xukai Zou,[a] and Yingzi Du[b]

[a] Department of Computer and Information Science,
[b] Department of Electrical and Computer Engineer, Indiana University - Purdue University Indianapolis, 723 W. Michigan Str. Indianapolis, 46202 Indiana, USA
ysui@cs.iupui.edu

In "conventional" biometric systems, there are many situations where it is important to consider security and privacy issues. For example, biometric-related information is not secretly stored or transmitted, which implies that compromise of biometric information would lead to unauthorized access and information misuse, and the enrolled biometric data are not revocable, which implies that compromise of biometric data will result in permanent lost of biometric traits. Since the biometric data are permanently associated with a user and the biometric resources of a user are limited, the legitimate user would not be able to regenerate another set of valid biometric identifiers. The security and privacy of biometric data have gained tremendous interest among researchers; however, serious criticisms against the biometric technology have not been addressed satisfactorily. Thus, we devote a considerable amount of time to discuss the security and privacy of biometric data as well as the existing solutions to the problems in this chapter.

Biometrics: From Fiction to Practice
Edited by Eliza Yingzi Du
Copyright © 2013 Pan Stanford Publishing Pte Ltd.
ISBN 978-981-4310-88-8 (Hardcover), 978-981-4364-13-3 (eBook)
www.panstanford.com

12.1 Introduction

Biometrics has been used for emerging applications and is becoming an important ally of security, intelligence, and law enforcement. However, a survey of "American public security" reported that 88% of the respondents are concerned about possible misuse of their personal information, and 54% of them are very concerned [64]. Users' concern and psychological resistance against centralized control of biometric data motivate the research to enhance the security and privacy in biometrics. Actually, there are indeed several security- and privacy-related shortcomings when using biometrics. From the security point of view, potential targets to be attacked in a biometric system are the stored biometric features and the original biometric patterns. Compromise of the stored biometric features would lead to several vulnerabilities [24–25], e.g., the original biometric traits could be reconstructed from the compromised features as shown in Refs. [1, 19, 43] and a physical spoof can be created from the biometric traits and then presented to the biometric collection devices such as sensors or cameras to gain unauthorized access, the stolen biometric features can be replayed to the matcher to gain unauthorized access, etc. Compromise of the original biometric patterns would lead to other vulnerabilities, e.g., the biometric traits of a legitimate enroller can be spoofed from the biometric patterns to circumvent the system as shown in Refs. [12, 18, 34], compromised biometrics data can be injected into the transmission channel of the biometric system to gain unauthorized access, etc. More attacks can be performed over a biometric system so that the system is disabled, e.g., the feature extraction process can be overridden or bypassed, genuine biometric features can be corrupted so that legitimate users cannot pass authentication, legitimate features can be replaced by the impostor's features to gain unauthorized access, and with the worst case the final matching decision can be overridden by the attacker [23–24]. In the privacy point of view, the main weakness of a biometric system is the concern that if biometric features are compromised or biometric data are revealed, there is no way to assign a new set of biometric features to the legitimate user. Compromised biometric data would be misused for unintended purposes, such as database cross-matching, which may infringe upon a user's right to privacy [25]. More security and privacy issues are analyzed in Refs. [24–25, 33, 39, 45, 60]. Due to these facts and concerns, storing biometric features or storing them with an unprotected form in a central database should be avoided [50].

To overcome the security- and privacy-related shortcomings of biometric systems, many schemes have been proposed in the literature, including the concept "cancellable biometrics" proposed by Ratha *et al.* [40] and "cancellable templates" presented in Ref. [4]. The biometrics is cancellable in the sense that compromise of the stored transformed features would not lead to compromise of the original biometric trait, and a new transformed template could be derived from the same biometric data and replace the old one. Essentially, Ratha's cancellable biometrics performs a distortion of the original biometric signals or extracted features before matching. The variability of the distortion parameters provides the cancellable nature of the scheme. The definition of cancellable biometrics proposed by Toeh *et al.* is "the intentional and systematically repeatable distortion of biometric features in order to protect sensitive user-specific data" in Ref. [57].

Here, we define cancellable biometrics as a way of incorporation of protection mechanisms or replacement features with biometrics, which enables the revocability of "old" biometric identifiers and the regeneration of "new" identifiers using the same biometric data. Cancellable biometrics is one of the solutions to overcome the security and privacy shortcomings of biometric systems. In order to realize ideal cancelable biometrics, designing the proper protection mechanisms and replacement features is very important. The main design criteria are as follows [24, 57]:

- Security: It must be computationally hard [49] to obtain the original biometric data from the compromised biometric identifiers or helper data. This property prevents an adversary from creating a physical spoof of the biometric trait from a stolen biometric identifier.
- Revocability: It should be feasible to revoke a compromised biometric identifier and reissue a new one derived from the same original biometric data.

- Performance: The introduction of biometric protection mechanisms and replacement features should not degrade the recognition performance of the whole biometric system.
- Diversity: There are two levels of diversities. For the application-level diversity, the system must allow generation of different identifiers from the same biometric data so that different applications could use different protection mechanisms and replacement feature sets, and database cross-matching is forbidden, which ensures user's privacy. For the user-level diversity, the protection mechanism and replacement feature set should be user-dependent, so that compromise of a biometric identifier from a single user would not make influences to others. However, it is sometimes difficult to design such a single user-dependent mechanism for each user enrolled in the system at the same time satisfying all design specifications [50].

There are other important design criteria that need to be considered, one of which is the scalability of the system. Since the number of enrolled users of a biometric system may vary over time, the system design has to be flexible enough to accommodate user dynamic change.

A naive protection mechanism of biometric features is the encryption of biometric templates. However, a complicated key management problem is introduced by this solution. Furthermore, compromise of the key materials would reveal the biometric data to some extent. Another protection mechanism is to store a hashed biometric template. However, due to the variability of the biometric data and the imperfect data acquisition process, conventional hash algorithms, such as MD-5, are extremely difference sensitive and would give completely different outputs even if the inputs are very close to each other, so the authentication that happened in the hashed domain would not work. Due to the same reason, one cannot store a biometric template in an encrypted form and then perform matching in the encrypted domain. While it is possible to decrypt the biometric templates and perform matching between the query and decrypted templates, such an approach would expose biometric templates during every query and not provide secrecy, thus making them vulnerable to some attacks. Hence, directly applying standard cryptographic techniques is not a good solution or at least a complete solution for securing biometric systems.

The content of this chapter is as follows. Section 12.2 introduces the approaches for generating cancellable biometrics. Applications of biometrics and their security- and privacy-related issues are shown in Section 12.3. Future research areas on biometrics security and privacy and a brief conclusion are presented in Section 12.4.

12.2 Approaches

Many approaches for generating cancellable biometrics have been proposed in the literature. The basic idea of the existing cancellable biometric schemes is to apply a transformation function to the original biometric features, and only the resulted transformed biometric features are stored in the database as a unique biometric identifier for the enroller. Typically, the parameters of a transformation function are derived from some auxiliary information, and the characteristics of the transformation function directly affect the security, revocability, as well as other properties of biometric systems. Depending on the characteristics of the transformation function, the proposed cancellable biometric schemes in the literature can be broadly classified into two categories, namely, noninvertible feature transformation approach and biometric salting [24]. In the noninvertible feature transformation approach, the transformation function is typically chosen as a one-way function [49] and directly applied to the original biometric features. In biometric salting, the auxiliary information, such as key, password, or user-dependent information is bound to the original biometric features to derive a distorted form of the biometric features. The distortion in the salting biometrics is usually invertible, so that the security of such scheme is mainly based on the secrecy of the binding information, which is quite different from the noninvertible feature transformation approach, whose security depends mainly on the one-way property of the transformation function.

12.2.1 *Noninvertible Feature Transformation Approach*

Some of the existing cancellable biometric schemes fall into this category. One instance in this domain was proposed by Ratha *et al.* in 2001 [40]. In the proposed method, distortion methods are applied in either the signal domain or the feature domain. Some easy examples of the signal-level distortion include morphing as shown in Fig. 12.1 and block permutation as in Fig. 12.2. It is reported that the transformed images will not be matched to the original images or other transformed images using different parameters [40].

An example of the transformation in the feature domain is a set of random, repeatable perturbations of feature points, which can be done within the same physical space as the original or by increasing the range of the axes [40].

In 2005, Tulyakov *et al.* proposed a method that hashes the fingerprint minutiae information and performs fingerprint minutiae matching in a new domain [58]. The hashing functions designed in this approach are one-way functions, and given the hash values, it is computationally hard to reconstruct the original template. With only transformation and storage of the hashed biometric templates,

Figure 12.1. Signal level morphing of fingerprint biometrics. See also Color Insert.

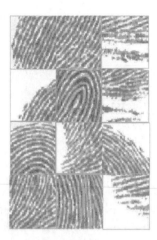

Figure 12.2. Signal level block permutation of fingerprint biometrics. See also Color Insert.

even if the hashed templates are compromised, users will be able to be re-enrolled using the new hash functions. Security, revocability, as well as diversity requirements are all satisfied. From the obtained fingerprints, minutia locations can be found; then hashes of minutia subsets are constructed, which are transmitted and stored in the database. During the verification stage, the same hash functions are applied to the test fingerprints and the retrieval hash values on the new fingerprints minutia are compared to those stored in the database to identify a user.

There are also other noninvertible feature transformation approaches working on fingerprint data, e.g., Ang *et al.* presented a geometric transformation to generate a key-dependent noninvertible cancellable template for fingerprint minutiae [2]. Ratha *et al.* in [42] reported an approach that sequentially applied three noninvertible transformation functions to the fingerprint data, and a case study in Ref. [41]. However, it is shown that the security of some of the schemes is degraded due to the involvement of the transformation functions [13, 46].

The main advantage of the noninvertible feature transformation approach is that the scheme provides better security even when the transformation function is compromised, since it is computationally hard to recover the original biometric data. Therefore, security can be achieved by the noninvertible nature of the transformation function. Application-level diversity can be achieved by application-specific transformation function. User-level diversity of such schemes is extremely difficult, which results in the system performance and scalability drawbacks. So if the transformation function is revised, the whole system is affected. Without storing the original biometric data, re-enrollment of all the users of the system would require user's presence and would be a huge project.

12.2.2 Biometric Salting

Savvides *et al.* proposed a biometric salting method that encrypts the training images by synthesizing a correlation filter for face recognition [44]. During the enrollment phase of this method, the training face image is convolved with a random convolution kernel, which is generated from some randomly generated numbers derived from user-provided PIN number. The convolved training image is then used to generate a single encrypted biometric filter, which can be stored on a smartcard and used to determine user's identity. Without knowing the user's PIN or the convolution kernel used, the deconvolution process is computationally hard. If the card is lost or stolen, a different convolution kernel can be regenerated to synthesize a different encrypted biometric filter. During the authentication stage, with the user's card or PIN, same convolution kernel will be generated to convolve with the query test image. The resulting convolved test image is compared to the encrypted biometric filters in the database for authentication. An enhancement of the cancellable correlation filter encryption was reported by Hirata *et al.* in [20].

Another instance of biometric salting, namely biohashing, is proposed in Refs. [27, 53]. The extracted feature vector is projected on the user-specific random matrix derived from auxiliary data, and then the acquired binary vector is stored as the template. There are other examples of biometric salting, such as multistage random projection (MRP) [54], an improved biohashing [24], biophasoring [53, 56], as well as concatenation of BioHash with random subspace technique [38], random correlator [47], multiple high-dimension random projection [28], shifted random orthonormal transformation [63], one-time face template [30], 2^N discretization [56], preserving transform with distinguishing points [15], sorted index numbers [66], augmented random projection [48], and combination of BioHashing and BioPhasor. More examples can be found in Refs. [9, 26–27, 29, 55].

The main advantage of biometric salting is the lower false acceptance rate resulted from introduction of additional information (user's password or PIN). Since the auxiliary information is user-specific, compromise of a single biometric identifier usually does not affect others. Also it is easier and efficient to generate multiple identifiers from the same biometric data (allowing diversity) and to revoke the compromised identifier and then replace it with a new one using a different user-specific information (allowing revocability). One major disadvantage of such schemes is that the transformation is usually invertible, so that the biometric identifier is not secure if the user-specific information is compromised. Moreover, sometimes this kind of a system requires a new matching mechanism that has to be designed carefully so that recognition performance is not degraded [24].

12.3 Applications

The very first biometric application is in the field of criminology and forensics, such as corpse identification, criminal investigation, parenthood determination, etc. Now, more and more government and commercial applications integrate biometrics. Government applications, like personal documents including passport, ID cards and driver licenses, border and immigration control, social security and welfare disbursement, voter registration and control during elections, as well as e-Government, have started to integrate biometric access control mechanisms [3]. An interested and challenging research area for government applications is covert surveillance. By face and body recognition technologies, it is hoped that entering or traversing security areas such as airports can be automatically identified [32]. Commercial applications include physical access control, network logins, e-Commerce, ATMs, credit cards, PDAs, e-Health, as well as biometric recognition software [3]. For example, many banks and commercial organizations are interested in the combination of customer authentication and nonrepudiation of online banking, trading, and purchasing transactions. Some developers are working on voice authentication to provide secure service over telephone [32].

12.3.1 *Electronic Passport*

Electronic passport, also referred to as ePass, ePassort, or biometric passport, is a machine-friendly travel document that contains a circuit chip within which biometric data of the passport holder and security mechanisms like a crypto infrastructure to protect the data (as shown in Fig. 12.3) are included. As we said above, even though a public key infrastructure is used to protect the biometric data in the electronic passport, the biometric data is still exposed during every authentication stage since matching cannot happen in the encrypted domain. Compromise of biometric data would cause cross-matching of the biometric information possessed by government or other organizations, which would lead to information misuse and result in security and management chaos.

Figure 12.3.   An instance of ePassport.

Figure 12.4. An instance of ATM with fingerprint authentication.

12.3.2 *Fingerprint Recognition ATMs*

Many cases of fraudulent withdrawals with fake or stolen ATM cards have been reported in these years. Fingerprint recognition can be integrated into ATM to protect from such attacks (shown in Fig. 12.4). To authorize a transaction, not only the ATM banking card and the corresponding PIN, but also the fingerprints from the legitimate customer are required. Fingerprints is one of the most acceptable and affordable biometric trait to be widely used. However, there are many weaknesses in such systems, such as the central-managed fingerprint database or fingerprint queries transmitted over the system channel.

12.3.3 *Face Recognition Vending Machines*

Another application embedding biometrics is the cigarette vending machines to ensure that buyers are age legitimate (shown in Fig. 12.5). The system operates quite similar to the face recognition access system, but uses the facial features of the buyers to estimate the age.

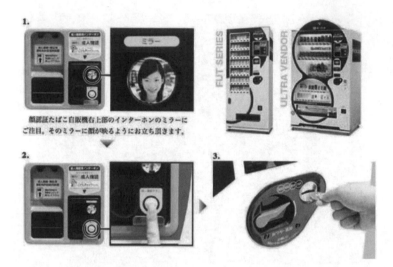

Figure 12.5. An instance of vending machines using face recognition.

The above examples show interesting applications of biometrics in real world, which are very privacy and security critical. However, we can tell that these systems either did not consider security- and privacy-related issues at all, or cannot integrate a robust protection mechanism. It is important that these biometric systems, especially some unattended remote systems, be designed robustly to be able to defeat various attacks.

12.4 Research Areas for Biometrics Security

Cancellable biometrics we introduce above is one of the existing solutions to protect biometric systems. Cancellable biometrics performs transformation or distortion on biometric features, and transformed features are directly used in matching a stage to identify or verify a user. Another category of schemes for protection of biometrics system is called biometric cryptosystem. Biometric cryptosystems were originally developed to provide biometric keys for the purpose of key management in cryptographic community; however, biometric features can further be used to derive user-dependent information in a biometric cryptosystem to directly

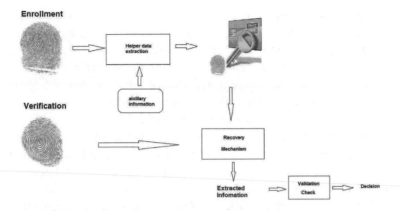

Figure 12.6. An instance of biometric cryptosystem.

verify or identify a user. According to Ref. [24], biometric cryptosystem can be categorized into key-binding and key-generation system according to how the helper data is derived. In the enrollment stage of a key-binding cryptosystem, auxiliary key information such as a cryptokey or user ID is blended with biometric features and the resultant helper data can be stored locally such as in smartcards as shown in Fig. 12.6. In the authentication stage of a key-binding cryptosystem, with the helper data and tested biometric queries whose differences from helper data are within a threshold, the key information can be derived. The key information can be used directly for crypto purposes or compared to the stored user-dependent information in the database to identify a user. Another instance of biometric cryptosystems is the key-generation system, which is designed to be tolerant with intrauser variability within biometrics so that the key information can be directly derived from biometric features. Both key-binding and key-generation cryptosystems have their advantages and limitations (refer to Ref. [24] for details). A main advantage of biometric cryptosystems over cancellable biometric system is that database cross-matching is forbidden to most extent, since a central-managed database storing biometric-related information is not needed anymore; instead users are issued smartcards that contains helper data. Another advantage of biometric cryptosystems is the user level diversity. Security compromise due to the lost of an identifier can be efficiently and straightforwardly recovered by reissuing a new identifier. One important issue in biometric cryptosystems is to determine how the security of the system and the privacy of user biometric data are compromised if the smartcards storing biometric-related information are lost. Another important issue is that the derived information is usually of lower entropy for crypto purposes sometimes. Furthermore, the performance of biometrics cryptosystems depends on how the intrauser variability is being handled; sometimes it is difficult to achieve high-recognition performance. Existing biometric cryptosystems can be found in literature Refs. [5, 7–8, 10–11, 14, 17, 31, 35–37, 51, 59, 62, 65].

We have introduced the challenges existing in cancellable biometrics as well as the design criteria of an ideal cancellable biometric system; however, it is difficult to meet all the requirements at the same time. To choose a suitable biometrics as well as the protection mechanisms and replacement features are important. The choice of biometric characteristics depends upon the requirements of the applications as well as the properties of biometric characteristics. Therefore, we can say that no biometrics is "optimal" and suitable for all applications [22, 61]. This fact leads to a very meaningful investigation of techniques that combine two or more biometric traits for authentication [52]. The fusion techniques have been investigated, e.g., Ref. [6, 16, 21]. Therefore, how to provide security and revocability for multibiometric systems is challenging.

Moreover, for providing higher level security and privacy, three basic forms of user authentication, which are knowledge-based relying on a user-known secret such as a password, token-based relying on a user possessed token such as a physical key or smartcard, and biometric-based using unique characteristics of individuals such as iris or fingerprints, can be fused and used in combination. How to combine these three forms of user authentication methods seamlessly is an interesting research area.

References

1. Adler, A. (2003) Can images be regenerated from biometric templates? *Proc. Biometrics Consortium Conf.,* 1.

2. Ang, R., Safavi-Naini, R., McAven, L. (2005) Cancelable key-based fingerprint templates, *Information Security and Privacy: 10th Australasian Conference, ACISP*, 242–252.

3. Adolph, M. (2009) Anonymous Biometrics and Standards, *ITU-T Technology Watch Report*, http://www.itu.int/en/ITU-T/techwatch/Pages/default.aspx.

4. Bolle, R., Connell, J., Ratha, N. (2002) Biometric perils and patches, *Pattern Recognition* **35**(12), 2727–2738.

5. Boult, T., Schdrer, W., Woodworth, R. (2007), Revocable fingerprint biotokens: accuracy and security analysis, *Proceedings of the IEEE Computer Scoeity Conference on Computer Vision and Pattern Recognition (CVPR' 97)*, pp. 1–8 (in Minneapolis, MN, USA).

6. Brunelli, R., Falavigna, D. (1995) Person identification using multiple cues, *IEEE Transactions on Pattern Analysis and Machine Intelligence* **17**(10), 955–966.

7. Chang, Y., Zhang, W., Chen, T. (2004), Biometrics-based cryptographic key generation, *Proceedings of the IEEE Internation Conference on Multimedia and Expo (ICME '04)*.

8. Clancy, T., Kiyavash, N., Lin, D. (2003), Secure smartcardbased fingerprint authentication, *Proceedings of the ACM SIGMM Workshop on Biometric Methods and Applications*, ACM New York, NY, USA, pp. 45–52.

9. Connie, T., Teoh, A., Goh, M., Ngo, D. (2005) PalmHashing: A novel approach for cancelable biometrics, *Information Processing Letters*, **93**(1), 1–5.

10. Dodis, Y., Reyzin, L., Smith, A. (2004) Fuzzy extractors: How to generate strong keys from biometrics and other noisy data, *Lecture notes in computer science*, 523–540.

11. Draper, S., Khisti, A., Martinian, E., Vetro, A., Yedidia, J. (2007), Using distributed source coding to secure fingerprint biometrics, *Proceedings of the IEEE International Conference on Acoustics, Speech and Signal Processing*, Citeseer **2**, 129–132.

12. Eriksson, A., Wretling, P. (1997), How Flexible Is the Human Voice?—A case study of mimicry, *Proc. of the European Conference on Speech Technology* **30**, 1043–1046.

13. Feng, Q., Su, F., Cai, A., Zhao, F. (2008), Cracking cancelable fingerprint template of Ratha, *International Symposium on Computer Science and Computational Technology (ISCSCT' 08)* **2**, 572–575.

14. Feng, Y., Yuen, P. (2006), Protecting face biometric data on smartcard with reed-solomon code, *Proceedings of the Conference on Computer Vision and Pattern Recognition Workshops*, 29–29.

15. Feng, Y., Yuen, P., Jain, A. (2008), A hybrid approach for face template protection, *SPIE Defense and Security Symposium*, Citeseer **102**, 169–177.

16. Frischholz, R., Dieckmann, U. (2000) BioID: A multimodal biometric identification system, *IEEE Computer* **33**(2), 64–68.

17. Hao, F., Anderson, R., Daugman, J. (2006) Combining crypto with biometrics effectively, *IEEE Transactions on Computers*, **55**(9), 1081–1088.

18. Harrison, W. (1981) *Suspect Documents: Their Scientific Examination*, Nelson-Hall Publishers.

19. Hill, C. (2002) Risk of masquerade arising from the storage of biometrics, *Bachelor of science thesis,* Department of Computer Science, Australian National University.

20. Hirata, S., Takahashi, K. (2009), Cancelable Biometrics with Perfect Secrecy for Correlation-Based Matching, *Lecture Notes in Computer Science*, Springer **5558**, 868–878.

21. Hong, L., Jain, A. (1998) Integrating faces and fingerprints for personal identification, *IEEE Transactions on Pattern Analysis and Machine Intelligence*, **20**(12), 1295–1306.

22. Jain, A., Ross, A., Prabhakar, S. (2004) An introduction to biometric recognition, *IEEE Trans. on Circuits and Systems for Video Technology* **14**(1), 4–20.

23. Jain, A., Ross, A., Uludag, U. (2005), Biometric template security: Challenges and solutions, *Proceedings of the European Signal Processing Conference (EUSIPO' 05)*, Citeseer (in Antalya, Turkey).

24. Jain, A., Nandakumar, K., Nagar, A. (2008) Biometric template security, *EURASIP Journal on Advances in Signal Processing*, 1–17.

25. Jain, A., Pankanti, S., Prabhakar, S., Hong, L., Ross, A., Wayman, J. (2004), Biometrics: a grand challenge, *Proceedings of the 17th International Conference on Pattern Recognition*, Citeseer **2**, 935–942.

26. Jeong, M., Lee, C., Kim, J., Choi, J., Toh, K. (2006), Changeable biometrics for appearance based face recognition, *Biometric Consortium Conference*, 1–5.

27. Jin, A., Ling, D., Goh, A. (2004) Biohashing: two factor authentication featuring fingerprint data and tokenised random number, *Pattern Recognition*, **37**(11), 2245–2255.

28. Kim, Y., Toh, K. (2007), A method to enhance face biometric security, *IEEE Conference on Biometrics: Theory, Applications and Systems*, 1–6.

29. Lee, C., Choi, J., Toh, K., Lee, S., Kim, J. (2007) Alignment-Free cancelable fingerprint templates based on local minutiae information, *IEEE Transactions on Systems Man and Cybernetics-Part B-Cybernetics*, **37**(4), 980–992.

30. Lee, Y., Chung, Y., Moon, K. (2007), One-Time Templates for Face Authentication, *International Conference on Convergence Information Technology (ICCIT 2007)*, IEEE Computer Society Washington, DC, USA, pp. 1818–1823.

31. Lee, Y., Bae, K., Lee, S., Park, K., Kim, J. (2007) Biometric key binding: Fuzzy vault based on iris images, *Lecture Notes in Computer Science* **4642**, 800–808.

32. Liu, S., Silverman, M. (2001) A practical guide to biometric security technology, *IT Professional*, **3**(1), 27–32.

33. Maltoni, D., Maio, D., Jain, A., Prabhakar, S. (2003) *Handbook of fingerprint recognition* (Springer).

34. Matsumoto, T., Matsumoto, H., Yamada, K., Hoshino, S. (2002), Impact of artificial gummy fingers on fingerprint systems, *Proc. SPIE*, Citeseer **4677**, 275–289 (in San Jose, USA).

35. Monrose, F., Reiter, M., Li, Q., Wetzel, S. (2001), Cryptographic key generation from voice, *Proceedings of IEEE Computer Society Symposium on Research in Security and Privacy*, IEEE Computer Society, 202–213 (in Oakland, Calif., USA).

36. Nagar, A., Chaudhury, S. (2006), Biometrics based asymmetric cryptosystem design using modified fuzzy vault scheme, *Proceedings of the 18th International Conference on Pattern Recognition (ICPR' 06)*, Citeseer **4**, 537–540.

37. Nandakumar, K., Nagar, A., Jain, A. (2007) Hardening fingerprint fuzzy vault using password, *Lecture notes in computer science*, 4642, 927.

38. Nanni, L., Lumini, A. (2007) Random subspace for an improved BioHashing for face authentication, *Pattern Recognition Letters* **29**(3), 295–300.

39. Ratha, N., Connell, J., Bolle, R. (2001) An analysis of minutiae matching strength, *Lecture notes in computer science*, 223–228.

40. Ratha, N., Connell, J., Bolle, R. (2001) Enhancing security and privacy in biometrics-based authentication systems, *IBM Systems Journal* **40**(3), 614–634.

41. Ratha, N., Connell, J., Bolle, R., Chikkerur, S. (2006), Cancelable biometrics: A case study in fingerprints, *In Intl. Conf. on Pattern Recognition* **4**, 370–373.

42. Ratha, N., Chikkerur, S., Connell, J., Bolle, R. (2007) Generating cancelable fingerprint templates, *IEEE Transactions on Pattern Analysis and Machine Intelligence* **29**(4), 561–572.

43. Ross, A., Shah, J., Jain, A. (2007) From template to image: Reconstructing fingerprints from minutiae points, *IEEE Transactions on Pattern Analysis and Machine Intelligence* **29**(4), 544–560.

44. Savvides, M., Kumar, B., Khosla, P. (2004), Cancelable biometric filters for face recognition, *Int. Conf. of Pattern Recognition* **3**, 922–925.

45. Schneier, B. (1999) The uses and abuses of biometrics, *Communications of the ACM* **42**(8), 136.

46. Shin, S., Lee, M., Moon, D., Moon, K. (2009) Dictionary attack on functional transform-based cancelable fingerprint templates, *ETRI Journal* **31**(5), 628–630.

47. Chin, C., Beng, Jin, A., Ling, D. (2006) High security iris verification system based on random secret integration, *Computer Vision and Image Understanding* **102**(2), 169–177.

48. Sohn, H., Ro, Y., Plataniotis, K. (2009) Biometric Authentication using Augmented Face and Random Project, *IEEE International Conference on Biometrics* (ICB 2009).

49. Stinson, D. (2006) *Cryptography: theory and practice* (CRC press).

50. Sutcu, Y., Sencar, H., Memon, N. (2005), A secure biometric authentication scheme based on robust hashing, *Proceedings of the 7 th Workshop on Multimedia and Security*, ACM, 111–116.

51. Sutcu, Y., Li, Q., Memon, N. (2007), How to protect biometric templates, *Proceedings of the SPIE*, Citeseer, 6505.

52. Sutcu, Y., Li, Q., Memon, N. (2007), Secure biometric templates from fingerprint-face features, *Proceedings of CVPR Workshop on Biometrics*, Citeseer.

53. Teoh, A., Ngo, D. (2006), Biophasor: Token Supplemented Cancellable Biometrics, *9th International Conference on Control, Automation, Robotics and Vision (ICARCV* 2006), 1–5.

54. Teoh, A., Yuang, C. (2007) Cancelable biometrics realization with multispace random projections, *IEEE Transactions on Systems Management and Cybernetics, Part B* **37**(5), 1096–1106.

55. Teoh, A., Goh, A., Ngo, D. (2006) Random multispace quantization as an analytic mechanism for biohashing of biometric and random identity inputs, *IEEE Transactions on Pattern Analysis and Machine Intelligence*, **28**(12), 1892.

56. Teoh, A., Toh, K., Yip, W. (2007) 2^N discretisation of BioPhasor in cancellable biometrics, *Lecture Notes in Computer Science* **4642**, 435–444.

57. Teoh, A., Hui, L. (2010) Cancelable biometrics, *Scholarpedia* **5**(1), 9201.

58. Tulyakov, S., Farooq, F., Govindaraju, V. (2005) Symmetric hash functions for fingerprint minutiae, *Lecture Notes in Computer Science* **3687**, 30–38.

59. Tuyls, P., Akkermans, A., Kevenaar, T., Schrijen, G., Bazen, A., Veldhuis, R. (2005) Practical biometric authentication with template protection, *Lecture Notes in Computer Science*, **3546**, 436–446.

60. Uludag, U., Jain, A. (2004), Attacks on biometric systems: a case study in fingerprints, *Proc. SPIE-EI Security, Steganography and Watermarking of Multimedia Contents VI*, Citeseer, pp. 622–633 (in San Jose, CA).

61. Uludag, U., Pankanti, S., Prabhakar, S., Jain, A. (2004) Biometric cryptosystems: issues and challenges, *Proceedings of the IEEE*, **92**(6), 948–960.

62. Vielhauer, C., Steinmetz, R., Mayerhofer, A. (2002), Biometric hash based on statistical features of online signatures, *IEEE International Conference on Pattern Recognition (ICPR)*, 1.

63. Wang, Y., Plataniotis, K. (2007), Face based biometric authentication with changeable and privacy preserving templates, *Biometrics Symposium (BSYM '07)*.

64. Westin, A. (2002) The American Public and Biometrics, presented at a conference organized by the National Consortium of Justice and Information Statistics, (in New York City 5 November 2002)

65. Yang, S., Verbauwhede, I. (2005), Automatic secure fingerprint verification system based on fuzzy vault scheme, *Proceedings of the IEEE International Conference on Acoustics, Speech and Signal Processing (ICASSP '05)*, Citeseer, 5, 609–612 (in Philadelphia, PA., USA).

66. Yongjin, W., Dimitrios, H. (2009) Sorted Index Numbers for Privacy Preserving Face Recognition, *EURASIP Journal on Advances in Signal Processing*, 2009.

Chapter 13

Continuous Biometric Verification

Qinghan Xiao[a] and Xue Dong Yang[b]

[a] *Defence Research and Development Canada – Ottawa,*
3701 Carling Avenue, Ottawa, Ontario K1A 0Z4, Canada
[b] *Department of Computer Science, University of Regina,*
3737 Wascana Parkway, Regina, Saskatchewan S4S 0A2, Canada
Qinghan.xiao@drdc-rddc.gc.ca

13.1 Introduction

Nowadays, people are becoming increasingly dependent on computers and the internet for matters ranging from communication, entertainment, and financial transactions, to education and government services. Cyberspace brings people together and creates new opportunities as well as challenges for our society [1]. Cyber security is a very serious concern for individuals, businesses, and governments, as it focuses on protecting and defending both information and information systems.

A variety of multilayered security products have been developed to increase system security (Fig. 13.1). Firewalls are used to control incoming and outgoing network traffic, thereby blocking unwanted traffic and suspicious connections. Authentication, also referred to as verification, validates the identity of a user or a device. Access

Biometrics: From Fiction to Practice
Edited by Eliza Yingzi Du
Copyright © 2013 Pan Stanford Publishing Pte. Ltd.
ISBN 978-981-4310-88-8 (Hardcover), 978-981-4364-13-3 (eBook)
www.panstanford.com

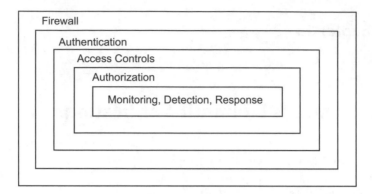

Figure 13.1. Multi-layered security [1].

control is mediated by a set of policies that can restrict access based on a wide variety of criteria other than the identity of the user, such as the network address of the client, the time of the day, and the actions that a user is performing. Authorization is a process that grants permission to access and utilize network and computer resources based on the user's credentials. Various intrusion detection systems have been implemented in software or hardware to detect known types of attacks and to monitor user activity and behavior in a computer network.

Authentication is one of the most important security concepts because it acts as the first defense against attackers. However, authentication is also a weak link in the security infrastructure as identity theft becomes more and more prevalent. As a solution to resolve this problem, multifactor authentication scenarios have been proposed in which several authentication methods are combined. This combination often includes biometric authentication.

Even when performing multifactor authentication, there is still a security hole since the authentication only happens at user login. Once the user is successfully authenticated, there is no security mechanism in place to monitor whether the system remains under the control of that same legitimate user. If a user leaves a terminal without logging out or locking the system, an intruder would be able to use this authenticated session to access the resources of the organization. To fill this security gap, the concept of continuous verification has been proposed in which biometric technologies are adopted to verify the user's identity throughout the entire session.

Various biometric technologies have been developed that use measurable physiological or behavioral characteristics to distinguish one person from another. Common physiological biometric traits include fingerprints, hand geometry, retina, iris, and facial images; common behavioral biometric traits include signature, voice recordings, and keystroke rhythms; and new types of biometric modalities include electrocardiography (ECG), electroencephalography (EEG), vascular patterns, and gait. Biometric technologies can be further defined as either active or passive based on the level of user involvement when capturing the biometric traits. The difference is that passive biometrics can be captured without user cooperation or knowledge, while active biometrics requires the cooperation of the user [2, 3]. Therefore, passive biometric modalities are more suitable for use in continuous verification because user identity can be verified without interruption of the user's activities. In the literature [4–10], different biometric technologies have been proposed to perform continuous user verification, such as keystroke analysis [11, 12], ECG and EEG analysis [13–15], facial recognition [16–21], and multimodal biometrics [22–26].

After comparing the advantages and disadvantages of different biometric continuous verification strategies, we selected video-based facial recognition in our present study. A novel system architecture has been developed and implemented, which consists of input/output interfaces and face detection, face segmentation, lighting normalization, and facial feature matching modules. The system verifies the user's identity continuously in near real time on desktop or laptop computers. If the face of the authenticated user disappears for a preset time interval or changes to another face, the system will automatically execute a log-off or screen-lock operation. The objective is to provide secured transactions continuously by ensuring that the current user is the same person that logged on to the system.

The remainder of this chapter is organized as follows. Section 13.2 presents a general overview of user authentication. Section 13.3 analyzes different continuous biometric verification approaches and illustrates the related state-of-the-art technologies.

Section 13.4 describes video-based facial recognition technologies. Section 13.5 presents our continuous user verification system and Section 13.6 presents the experimental results. Finally, Section 13.7 concludes the chapter with directions for future work.

13.2 User Authentication

User authentication is a process that verifies the identity of a particular individual. The goal of user authentication is to allow valid parties' access to a system or database while preventing impersonation. This can be accomplished by using one or more of the following validation approaches: the knowledge factor (something users know), the possession factor (something users have), or the biometrics factor (something users are) [27]. Strong authentication is defined not only by the concept of using more than one authentication factor, but also by the need to prevent attackers from impersonating other users' identities. Biometrics, which uses a unique physical or behavioral trait as a method to confirm user identity, satisfies this requirement better than traditional methods that check user identities by personal knowledge or belongings [2].

13.2.1 *Authentication Systems*

An authentication system verifies that the identity of the user is as claimed during login, and as such is a critical component in IT security infrastructure. Several elements are usually present in an authentication system. There is a user to be authenticated, an administrator to enforce certain system settings, the characteristics used to help distinguish this particular user from others, and an authentication server to verify and manage these distinguishing characteristics (Fig. 13.2). Depending on the success or failure of the authentication process, the user can be granted or denied access to the system.

A common method of authentication is the use of user-name/password pairs. A user who applies for an account will be assigned a username and password by the system administrator. The authentication procedure is as follows: the system asks the

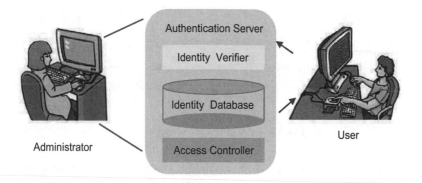

Figure 13.2. Authentication elements.

user to input a username and password, then it matches the typed-in password (in plaintext or after the application of a one-way function) to the corresponding credentials in the system's password database, and finally it allows the user to access system resources if the match succeeds.

13.2.2 *Biometrics and Multifactor Authentication*

Password-based authentication is the most commonly used authentication mechanism because of its simplicity, although it is not very secure. For example, passwords can be recovered using brute-force and dictionary attacks, the contents of weakly protected password files can be stolen, and the interception and replay of a one-time password can block legitimate users. Stronger authentication can be achieved using biometric techniques and by incorporating multiple authentication factors so that the benefits of one factor can compensate for the shortcomings of another.

Biometrics is the science of measurement that uses physiological or behavioural characteristics to reliably distinguish one person from another. In general, a biometric authentication system consists of a sensor to capture biometric data, a preprocessing step to extract features from the captured data, an algorithm to convert the information into a template, and a verifier to calculate the similarity between templates. When a user needs to be authenticated, the system will capture the biometric trait, translate the data into

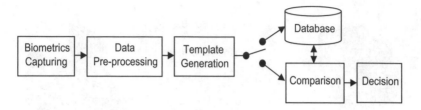

Figure 13.3. A general biometric system.

a template using the same algorithm with which the original templates were computed, and then compare the newly generated template against a previously stored template of the same user to determine if there exists a match (Fig. 13.3).

Since each authentication method has its own advantages and limitations, several authentication factors can be combined to provide additional layers of protection. The U.S. Department of Defense (DoD) has been a leader in using the Common Access Card (CAC) to achieve multifactor authentication (Fig. 13.4). The CAC is designed as a simple and effective authentication solution to control physical access to facilities and logical access to the department's computers and military's network [28]. Various technologies and multiple authentication factors, such as magnetic

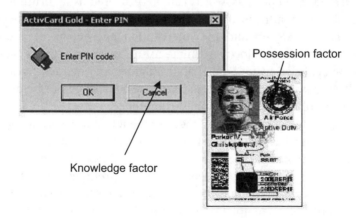

Figure 13.4. Common access card log in.

strips, radio frequency transmitters, encryption measures, photo identification, and fingerprints, have been implemented to comply with a presidential mandate to issue secure and interoperable federal credentials (HSPD-12). The credentials embedded on the card are compared against DoD's database of authorized users. Access to resources is granted or denied based on the validation results for the multiple factors employed. Since the card could be lost or stolen and biometrics could be forged, it is necessary to verify the identity of the user continuously in some high-security applications.

13.3 Overview and Analysis of Existing Continuous Verification Approaches

For any security system, reliability and accuracy are critically important. Reliability requires that the false reject rate (FRR) is sufficiently small such that legitimate users can comfortably perform their normal operations without interruptions. Frequent false rejections may frustrate legitimate users and prevent them from adopting the technology. On the other hand, accuracy must be enforced to prevent illegal access. Therefore, it is beneficial to review common user authentication techniques at a more detailed level and to examine their suitability for continuous user verification in particular.

13.3.1 *Passwords*

As mentioned above, password protection is the simplest and the most commonly used mechanism for user authentication at the login stage. Most operating systems also have a function that locks the screen if the system has been idle for a prespecified length of time, for example when a user is away from his/her desk without logging out of the session. To resume the session, a password must be re-entered. If the preset time length is too short, a user may become annoyed when the screen locks too frequently during normal operation. In this case, the user will often tend to increase the time length. This creates a potential window of time in which unauthorized persons may gain access to the system if the user leaves without locking the computer. This is a typical situation in which continuous user verification is required.

Periodic password verification during a normal session is a simple, low-cost solution to this problem. Operating systems do not typically provide this functionality; it is usually the responsibility of application software to provide this capability. Furthermore, since it is well known that passwords are vulnerable to intruders, a more sophisticated authentication technology is needed to provide continuous user verification. In the following sections, we review several technologies that can potentially address this problem.

13.3.2 *Keystrokes*

Monrose and Rubin [12] argued that keystroke rhythm is a natural choice for computer security based on the observation that a user's typing pattern exhibits neuro-physiological factors similar to what makes written signatures unique [29]. In addition, a recognition technique based on typing rhythm will be nonintrusive and has a very low cost.

Research in this area conducted by Gaines *et al.* [11] investigated the possibility of using keystroke timings for authentication. Statistical independence of user profiles was analyzed using the T-Test. The authors reported that they could achieve an FRR of about 5.5% and a false accept rate (FAR) of approximately 5.0%. A single low-pass temporal filter can be used for the removal of outliers [30]. However, applying one filter value for all typists does not yield optimal performance. A study [31] showed that instead of using one low-pass filter, a measurable improvement in verification accuracy can be achieved by using diagraph-specific measures of variability. The measurement of key down-to-down time can be separated into two components – the keystroke duration (the total time for which the first key is depressed) and the keystroke latency (the time between when a key is released and the next key is depressed) [30]. The authors of Ref. [31] have found a substantially improved accuracy in their results due to the use of this bivariate measure of latency.

Monrose and Rubin [12] conducted an experiment with a relatively large group of 63 unsupervised users over a period of 11 months. A data extraction toolkit was developed to partition users, based on a heuristic clustering approach, into distinct groups of possibly disjoint feature sets. For example, members of group i may exhibit strong individualistic typing pattern for features in the set $S = \{th, ate, st, ion\}$, whereas members of group j may be more distinctive over the features $S = \{ere, on, wy\}$. By applying the classifiers proposed by Joyce and Gupta [29], they have achieved the recognition accuracy ranging from 83.22% to 92.14%, depending on the approach being used.

The use of Neural Networks to identify keystroke patterns has also been attempted by a number of researchers (for example Ref. [32]). A main limitation of this approach is that the training requirements are expensive and time consuming, particularly in the situation where there is a high turnover of users.

A major drawback of keystroke systems is that almost all operating systems today have a graphical user interface (GUI), and many operations are performed with a mouse. It is possible to access documents from a system without a single keystroke. Even if a user is forced to enter text for authentication or verification purposes, the cut and paste functions available in every GUI may allow a user to avoid typing anything at all. Therefore, the use of keystroke rhythm recognition for continuous verification will be very limited.

13.3.3 *Fingerprints*

Fingerprint verification has become an increasingly popular mechanism for user authentication. The performance of fingerprint matching algorithms has improved significantly in terms of accuracy and computational speed. It is well-known that fingerprints are static physical characteristics and thus can be forged. However, assuming that a user has been initially authenticated, fingerprints could be used as a relatively reliable, low-cost, and unobtrusive method for continuous user verification. We will not review the technical details of the state-of-the-art fingerprint algorithms herein (interested readers may refer to Ref. [33] for a comprehensive overview). Rather, we will examine commercially available technologies with respect to the problem of continuous user verification.

Current very-large-scale integration (VLSI) technology allows a fingerprint reader to be integrated, at an affordable price, into a laptop computer (e.g., IBM ThinkPad), a mouse (e.g., Microsoft Wireless IntelliMouse Explorer with Fingerprint Reader), a keyboard (e.g., Microsoft Optical Desktop with Fingerprint Reader Keyboard), or as a separate device with a convenient USB connection (e.g., Microsoft Fingerprint Reader Win and Silex USB Fingerprint Reader). Although manufacturers of these devices often promote the fingerprint reader as a convenient replacement for a username and password, it certainly provides a tool to those users who are more interested in access control and security.

We consider two situations in which fingerprints might be useful for continuous user verification. In the first situation, the security concern is mainly with locally stored data on a PC or workstation. This is the most common situation in an office environment. Each desktop or laptop computer in an office typically has one or two main users, in addition to any authorized access by managers and system administrators. Since each computer only has a very small number of authorized users, fingerprints could provide a suitable mechanism for user authentication: the size of the fingerprint database will be very small, as will the computational cost for fingerprint matching. Because of these two factors, it is possible to adjust the threshold to such a level that both reliability and accuracy can be satisfactorily achieved. If a fingerprint reader is built into a mouse or keyboard, continuous verification can be implemented in a relatively unobtrusive manner. When the fingerprint reader has no valid input for a prespecified period, the system can prompt the user to touch the reader until a valid input is received; otherwise the access will be terminated.

The second situation involves PCs or workstations in public places, such as libraries, which allow access by a very large number of users with preregistered accounts. In this case, the PC or workstation serves mainly as a terminal to access information stored on the servers located elsewhere on the network. This also includes the situation in which users of personal desktop or laptop computers in offices must access secure data stored remotely on the organization's servers. Due to the large size of the resulting fingerprint database, it can only be stored on the server. The performance of fingerprint verification will drop in terms of accuracy as the size of the database is significantly increased. Deployment of fingerprint readers on public computers is not only expensive, but also difficult to maintain. Furthermore, the transmission of fingerprint data creates a potentially vulnerable link in the security system, even if an encryption mechanism is employed.

13.3.4 *EEG/ECG*

EEG [34, 35] and ECG [13, 14] were also proposed by researchers as means of authentication and verification in recent years. These techniques offer one unique advantage over other biometric techniques: since EEG and ECG are biodynamic signals, they ensure the aliveness of the individual. This feature is very important and useful because most other biometric techniques use static physical characteristics that can be digitally duplicated. For example, a face could be replaced by a photograph in front of a security camera, and fingerprints could be collected from the surfaces that a person just touched and could then be forged with artificial fingerprints. Spoofing is relatively difficult with EEG/ECG signals, but it is not impossible. If a voice print used for a biometric purpose could be replaced by a recording (as argued in [10]), we would also argue that EEG/ECG signals could similarly be replaced by duplicated signals.

Human Monitoring and Authentication using Biodynamic Indicators and Behavioural Analysis (HUMABIO) [10] is a large European initiative to develop an unobtrusive multimodal biometric authentication system. This project focuses on EEG and ECG because these emerging technologies have a potential to act as biological signatures suitable for continuous monitoring. Because every individual has a different brain configuration, spontaneous EEG signals should differ from person to person. However, to catch such differences, a number of sensors have to be placed in the different areas on the scalp of a human head to detect the signals. One of the research efforts in this area seeks to reduce the number of channels that are required for differentiating between individuals.

Riera *et al.* [34] presented a "ready-to-use" system that employs as few as three EEG channels. The recorded signals are segmented into 4-s epochs in the preprocessing stage. A set of initial features is extracted, and six features with higher discriminative power, namely Higuchi fractal dimension, entropy, skewness, kurtosis, mean, and standard deviation, are selected through the preliminary analysis. EEG authentication in Ref. [34] employed the classical Fisher's Discriminant Analysis and achieved a 79.2% true acceptance rate (TAR) and a 21.8% FAR. An ECG authentication method was also studied in Ref. [34]. Among many different features, the heartbeat waveform recorded the best performance, with 97.9% TAR and 2.1% FAR.

The medical EEG and ECG equipment used in hospitals is not only expensive but also so intrusive that it is not suitable for continuous user verification applications. However, this intrusiveness can be significantly reduced when wireless sensors become available, e.g., the ENOBIO device developed by STARLAB [36] and the wireless heart monitor from Alive Technologies [37]. It should also be noted that normal electrodes used in medical exams require the application of conductive gel to ensure the quality of the signals. If dry electrodes are used, they can only be used in hairless areas. The recordings in Ref. [34] were also carried out under ideal conditions. For example, the subjects were asked to sit in a comfortable armchair, and be quiet and relaxed with eyes closed. This is because both EEG and ECG signals vary with the physical and emotional conditions of a person. As compared with other biometric technologies, EEG and ECG are at a relatively early stage and are thus too immature for general applications.

13.3.5 *Facial Recognition*

Facial recognition is another biometric technique that has been used for the identification and verification of individuals in many applications. Starting in the 1960s, scientists began researching methods for recognizing human faces using computers [16]. Since then, various facial recognition algorithms have been developed, such as eigenfaces, neural networks, and elastic graph matching. A comprehensive survey of state-of-the-art face recognition algorithms can be found in Ref. [17].

The main factors that affect the performance of facial recognition algorithms include, but are not limited to, the variation in illumination conditions and the change in head orientation. A majority of the research effort in the past two decades has focused on handling these two issues. In the case of continuous computer user verification, we can reasonably expect that the illumination conditions in indoor office environments will be relatively stable during normal operation. The main challenge lies with changes in head orientation, since a user should be allowed to move freely and comfortably within his/her normal working space.

Facial recognition algorithms can be categorized into image-based and video-based approaches. Although video-based methods may be hindered by poor image quality [18], such techniques still hold significant advantages over image-based methods in that recognition is facilitated by the availability of multiple frames, temporal continuity, and motion information [19–21]. Video-based techniques do not require the user to interact with any devices [5], making them ideal passive methods for continuous user verification. Most modern laptop computers come with a built-in webcam, and a portable webcam can be easily attached to a desktop PC at a very affordable price. For all of these reasons, a video-based approach was chosen for this continuous verification project. Before the design of our system is introduced in Section 13.5, it is beneficial to review the existing video-based facial recognition techniques in more detail in the upcoming section.

13.4 Video-Based Facial Recognition

As it has been mentioned in the previous section, the facial recognition approaches can be categorized into image-based (a still image) and video-based (a sequence of images) according to the type of input. Most research has been focused on the development of image-based facial recognition technologies. To achieve more robust performance, video-based approaches have emerged to deal with variations due to illumination, pose, and facial expression. There are some differences between performing image-based and video-based facial recognition. On one hand, video-based facial recognition needs to deal with low spatial resolution images and pose, and illumination variations from frame to frame. On the other hand, video sequence contains temporal information that can be utilized to facilitate the facial recognition task [19]. In addition, video-based technology makes it possible to track a face over a period to obtain rich dynamic information through the capture of the same face at different orientations, scales, and facial expressions. Since video can be segmented into groups of sequential frames, this feature allows for the application of many image-based techniques.

Facial recognition approaches can be roughly categorized as feature-based, holistic, and hybrid. A number of studies focus on feature-based methods that detect a set of geometrical feature points on the face, such as the eyes, nose, and mouth. Properties and relations such as areas, distances, and angles between the feature points are measured as descriptors for face recognition [38]. Holistic or appearance-based approaches consider the whole facial region, rather than only specific features, in the recognition process. The eigenface method is a well-known and widely used approach that is based on principal component analysis (PCA) [39]. Hybrid approaches combine both holistic and local features to obtain a more complete representation of facial images [40].

Chen *et al.* [41] proposed an algorithm based on computing the optical flow extracted from the motion of the face. First, they collected a set of face image sequences, calculated the motion flow fields from the sequences using wavelet transforms, and concatenated these flow fields to form a high-dimensional vector. Then, the high-dimensional motion vectors were reduced in size by applying PCA followed by a linear discriminant analysis (LDA). The resulting feature vector contains spatial and temporal information for a face. Finally, a nearest neighbor classifier was implemented to perform an identity check. A training database with face image sequences for 28 subjects was created. For each subject, nine sequences of face images were captured with pose variations. A synthetic face database with illumination variations was generated to evaluate the robustness of the proposed approach. Comparing with an intensity-based approach [42], this method was more robust to illumination changes.

Liu and Cheng [19] proposed a video-based face recognition algorithm based on adaptive Hidden Markov Models (HMM). The face images were reduced to low-dimensional feature vectors by applying PCA. In the training process, an HMM was generated to learn both the statistics of the video sequences and the temporal dynamics of each subject. In the recognition stage, the temporal characteristics of the probe face sequence were analyzed over time by the HMM corresponding to each subject. The identity of a face was recognized based on maximum likelihood scores. The test database included 21 subjects, and 2 sequences were collected for each subject: one sequence contained 322 frames for training and the other had around 400 frames for testing. Compared with a PCA method, the HMM algorithm demonstrated improved accuracy. In the experiments, face regions were manually extracted from the images.

Zhou and Chellapa [43] proposed a method that uses the sequential importance sampling (SIS) algorithm to propagate a joint posterior probability distribution of identity and motion over time. A time series state space model was applied in conjunction with the identity variable to simultaneously characterize the kinematics and identity. For identity n at each time instant t, the posterior recognition probability $p(nt, \theta t | y0 : t)$ is calculated, where nt is the identity variable, θt is the tracking state parameter (e.g., affine transform parameter), and $y0 : t = \{y0, y1, \ldots, yt\}$ is the video observation. A database with 30 subjects, each having one face template and one upper body template, was generated to test the proposed approach. The probe set contained 30 video sequences with the subjects walking straight toward the camera. Based on the SIS technique, two algorithms were developed to compare the computational efficiency.

Aggarwal *et al.* [44] presented a video-based face recognition method that modeled the moving face as a linear dynamical system. The face sequence was treated as a first-order auto-regressive and moving averaging (ARMA) random process. At each time instant t, a state vector θt can be used to characterize the pose of the face, such that $\theta_t + 1 = A\theta_t + v_t, y_t = C\theta_t + w_t$, where $v_t \sim N(0, Q)$ and $w_t \sim N(0, R)$. To model the face in the video, it is necessary to estimate the parameters A, C, Q, and R from the observations $\{y_0, y_1, \ldots, y_t\}$. Two data sets were used to evaluate the algorithm. One contained face videos for 16 subjects with 2 sequences per subject, and the other consisted of 15 gallery and 30 probe video sequences. The experiments showed promising results of better than 90% recognition rates on both data sets given the extent of pose and expression variations in the video sequences.

13.5 System Implementation

As mentioned above, the traditional authentication process verifies the identity of a user only once at login or sign-on. Afterward, it is assumed that the system operates under the control of the same authenticated user. This authentication mechanism is fairly secure for one-time applications, such as accessing a particular file or withdrawing money from an automatic banking machine. However, there is a security risk if an attacker is able to take over the session after a valid user successfully logs in. To fix this security hole, we developed a facial presence monitoring system to verify the user's identity throughout the entire session. A key challenge in developing such an application is that the system must be able to perform multiple tasks and recognize the user's face in near real time. As shown in Fig. 13.5, the system periodically performs the facial verification while a user is working with Microsoft Word.

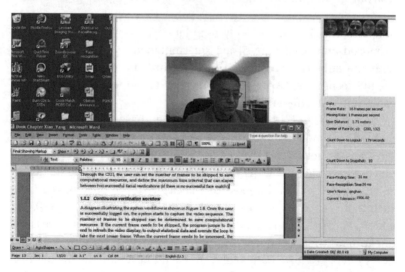

Figure 13.5. An identity check is performed in parallel with the other tasks.

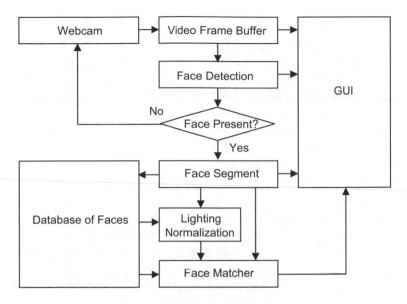

Figure 13.6. System architecture.

13.5.1 *System Architecture*

To make the verification system cost efficient, a low-resolution webcam is used to acquire a video stream targeting the user in front of the PC monitor. A set of still frontal images is collected to create a database containing the identities of legitimate users. Facial recognition is performed in near real time by comparing a face detected in the video sequence with a stored facial template. Figure 13.6 shows the architecture of the prototype system that includes the input module, face detection module, face segmentation module, lighting normalization module, and facial feature matching module.

13.5.1.1 Input module

A webcam is used to capture a video sequence at a resolution of 640×480 pixels. The software processes images in either 24-bit or 32-bit color. The captured images are displayed on the computer screen in real time via Microsoft DirectX.

13.5.1.2 Face detection module

Given a frame from a video sequence, the first task of the system is to detect the faces in the captured images. The objective of the face detection module is to automatically and reliably locate the position of all regions that contain a face regardless of pose and lighting conditions. However, to meet the near-real-time requirement, this module cannot be expected to perform perfectly. It is anticipated that some detected objects may not be human faces. To increase the detection accuracy, the module examines more than one image frame to determine if an object is likely to be a human face or not. This capability is one of the advantages of using video sequences. When a potential face is detected in one frame, the corresponding region in the previous frame is compared for confirmation. If a face is also present within the same region of the previous frame, this increases the likelihood that the current object represents an actual face. The output of the face detection process identifies both the location and size of each potential face in the captured images.

13.5.1.3 Face segmentation module

The performance of a facial recognition system largely depends on the accuracy with which it can locate the face in the image To address this challenge a face segmentation module has been developed to isolate the facial region from its (simple or complex) background. Since the size of a user's face appearing in a video frame also varies depending on the distance between the user and the web camera, the facial area must be normalized to a standard size. Moreover, there are features in facial images that may change from time to time. For example, hairstyle can change significantly from one day to another. In order to reduce the effects of such dynamic features, a standard elliptical region with a fixed aspect ratio is used to extract the face region. The output of our segmentation module uses a rectangle to determine the face bounding box and an ellipse to indicate a more precisely detected face region.

13.5.1.4 Lighting normalization module

Another factor that has a significant effect on the result of facial recognition is lighting. A lighting normalization module has been

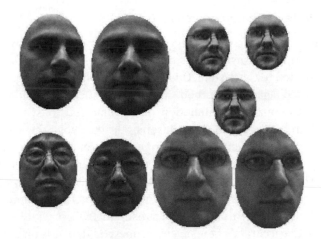

Figure 13.7. Well-lit face.

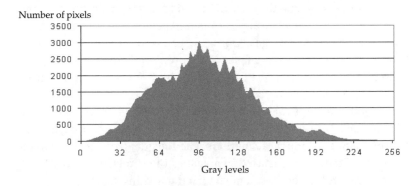

Figure 13.8. Well-lit face intensity histogram.

developed that uses a histogram-based intensity mapping function to normalize the intensity distribution of the segmented face image. A composite of several properly lit faces was built using a combination of front and side lighting (Fig. 13.7) and its intensity histogram was calculated (Fig. 13.8). A histogram of the facial ellipse region is computed for each frame being processed. Then, a simple algorithm constructs a mapping function to normalize the lighting condition to best match the frame's intensity histogram with the ideal histogram.

13.5.1.5 Facial feature matching module

The goal of the face-matching module is to determine whether the person who is using the computer is the same person who is authenticated to the system. One of the most popular approaches is a PCA-based eigenface method that uses holistic information about the face to create a combination of eigenfaces to best represent the captured image [45]. The reasons that we chose the eigenface method are as follows: (1) it does not require significant low-level or mid-level processing before raw intensity data are used for learning and recognition; (2) there are no requirements on knowing the geometry and reflectance of faces; and (3) the method is simple and efficient, although learning is time consuming.

Since the accuracy of the eigenface method depends on the scale of a face, it is important to obtain a close alignment between the live and stored face images. We devoted significant effort to addressing issues such as placing the nose in the middle of the face, maintaining the eyes at a stable vertical position, and generating the normalized face images. When a range of poses are captured in a video sequence, the similarity between the faces of different individuals with similar poses may be greater than the similarity among multiview faces taken from the same person [46].

Finally, an elliptical facial region is extracted and each face image is converted to a vector. This vector is projected onto eigenfaces through inner product calculations. The Euclidean distance between two weighted vectors is used to measure the similarity between the two faces, and to generate a normalized matching score.

13.5.1.6 Graphical user interface

A GUI has been developed to not only display face detection and facial recognition results, but also enable the user to adjust system settings. The system provides the following outputs:

- Live video is displayed on the monitor while the detected face is indicated by a red rectangle.
- Matching results are displayed in the upper right-hand window along with up to five candidate faces from the

database, listed according to the degree of similarity in descending order.

- Performance data are displayed in real time, such as the overall frame rate, the face detection time, the face recognition time, and the best matching score.
- Through the GUI, the user can set the number of frames to be skipped in order to save computational resources, and can define the maximum time interval that can elapse with no successful face match.

13.5.2 *Continuous Verification Workflow*

A diagram illustrating the system workflow is shown in Fig. 13.9. Once the user has successfully logged on, the system starts to capture the video sequence. If the current frame needs to be skipped, the program jumps to the end to refresh the video display, output the statistical data, and execute the loop to take the next image frame. When the current frame needs to be processed, the first step is to use the face detection module to locate objects suspected to be human faces. If no face is detected in the scene, the program jumps to the end and performs the same operations as those for skipped frames. Otherwise, the face segmentation module is executed to obtain more precise locations of the faces. The module contains a number of subcomponents: skin tone profile, face ellipse computation, eye detection, and the continuously adaptive mean shift (CAMSHIFT) algorithm to recognize and track the X, Y coordinates and the area of the flesh color probability distribution representing a face [47]. However, it may lose the target when the shape and orientation of the face are changing [48].

Next, lighting normalization is performed to reduce the variability due to illumination differences. The resulting faces are evaluated to determine if their qualities meet the requirements of facial verification. If none of them is good enough, the program jumps to the end and performs the same operations as those for skipped frames. Otherwise, either facial enrollment or verification will be performed. In the verification mode, if none of the detected faces comes from the legitimate user, the program will lock the screen or log the user out immediately. If the legitimate user is detected, the

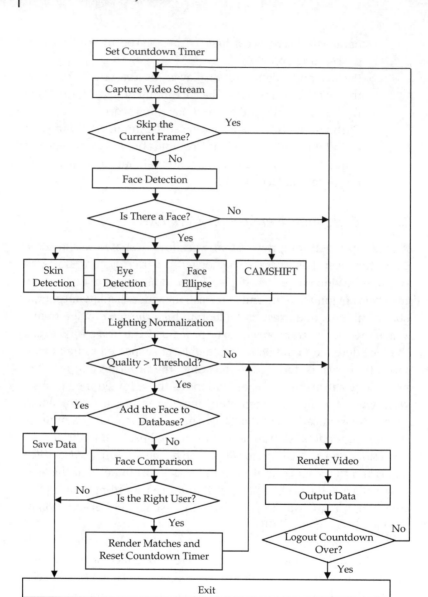

Figure 13.9. Block diagram of video-based continuous verification system.

program resets the countdown timer, performs the same operations as those for skipped frames, and loops back to perform continuous verification.

13.6 Experiments

Experiments have been carried out with real users on webcam-equipped PC computers to study the feasibility of continuous facial verification in an office environment. The user sits in front of the computer within a reasonable distance and angle from the webcam (at least 9 pixels between eyes). Once the user is authenticated successfully, the system starts to capture the video images and perform continuous facial verification. The processing speed varies from as low as 13 frames per second on a 1.4 GHz Pentium M processor with 2 GB of RAM to as high as 17 frames per second when

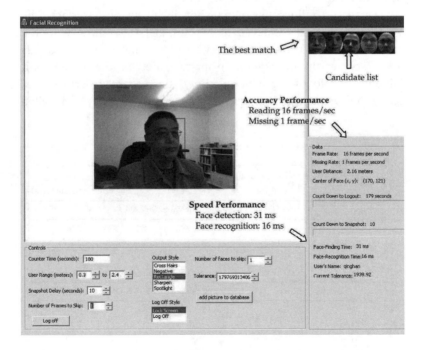

Figure 13.10. Snapshot of system interface. See also Color Insert.

using a dual-processor computer with a processing speed of 1.66 GHz and 1 GB of RAM. The face detection is the most time-consuming procedure because we allow the user to sit either close to or far from the webcam and to change body positions.

Since each computer may be used by several users, five people were enrolled as legitimate users. Testing under consistent lighting conditions, the verification rate reached about 99.6% in two consecutive seconds. There is a decrease in the verification accuracy when lighting conditions changed, despite the lighting normalization step. To examine this effect, the facial templates were enrolled in one office and continuous verification was tested in another location. When lighting conditions were similar in both rooms, the system performed well. However, when the lighting conditions were dramatically different from the one used for the training image, the verification rate was lower. Therefore, if this situation occurs during real operation, the user needs to be enrolled again in the new working environment.

Figure 13.10 illustrates a snapshot of the system interface. The video sequence is displayed at the upper-left window with the currently detected face enclosed by a red rectangle. Five candidates are displayed in descending priority order in the upper-right window. The following window shows the accuracy performance using the rate at which a legitimate user is not recognized, called

Table 13.1.   Summary of experimental results

User	Face detection time (ms)	Face recognition time (ms)	Frame rate	Missing rate	Distance (m)
	1.4GHz Pentium M processor with 2GB RAM				
1	40	20	13/s	5/s	1.52
1	100	10	13/s	2/s	1.58
2	50	10	15/s	2/s	1.42
2	40	10	14/s	1/s	1.52
	1.66GHz Intel core 2 Duo processor with 1GB RAM				
1	31	15	16/s	2/s	1.70
1	31	15	16/s	1/s	2.16
2	31	16	16/s	1/s	1.51
2	62	16	17/s	1/s	1.82

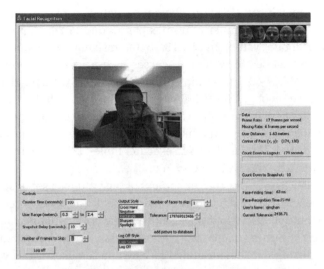

(a) Answering a phone call

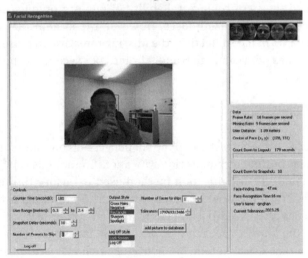

(b) Drinking a soda

Figure 13.11. Recognition of partially occluded faces.

false nonmatch rate (FNMR), which is related to the missing rate that indicates the number of frames per second in which no face is detected in our system. In Fig. 13.10, the missing rate is one frame per second, while the system processes 16 frames per second. That is, the FNMR is 6.25% within a single second. If we consider two consecutive seconds, the FNMR in a row reduces to $0.0625 \times 0.0625 = 0.0039$. The bottom-right window shows the speed performance, e.g., the face detection module takes 31 ms and the facial feature matching module takes 16 ms to execute. Table 13.1 summarizes the performance of the proposed system.

In order to evaluate the robustness of the system, a set of scenarios representative of a real office environment was tested, including having multiple users in a scene, a user answering a phone call, and taking off or putting on glasses. Figures 13.11a and b show examples of recognizing partially occluded faces while the user is answering a phone call and drinking a soda, respectively. The experiments confirmed the performance reliability of our prototype system in detecting and recognizing faces. However, the system takes more time to perform face detection: the missing rates are increased from 1 or 2 frames per second to 6 and 9 frames per second, respectively.

13.7 Conclusion

In this chapter, we investigated the challenges and possible solutions regarding continuous biometric verification. Continuous verification is an enhanced authentication method used to ensure the security and integrity of information resources. In the literature, most of the approaches are based on biometric authentication factors, rather than on the knowledge factor or possession factor. Several existing methods that use different biometric technologies are introduced and analyzed, including keystroke analysis, ECG/EEG analysis, facial recognition, and multimodal biometrics. After comparing the advantages and limitations of different biometric technologies that could be used to verify the user's identity continuously, we selected video-based facial recognition because it can be used to passively observe the user without interrupting or interfering with user activities.

A novel system architecture has been developed and implemented that consists of input/output interfaces and face detection, face segmentation, lighting normalization, and facial feature matching modules. The system can automatically lock the screen or log the user out, either when the legitimate user's face disappears from the vicinity of the webcam for a preset and adjustable time interval, or when the current face is not that of the user who originally logged on. The objective is to prevent unauthorized entities from slipping in and using the computer system

A lowcost webcam was used to capture video sequences in an office environment without any extra light source Facial detection and recognition are achieved in near real time on PC platforms Several experiments have been conducted with a set of scenarios representative of real situations when a user works with a computer. The resulting prototype demonstrates the feasibility of our design with lowcost webcams to perform continuous biometric verification in near real time.

Further research is concentrating on video-image fusion technology to achieve greater robustness. One major improvement could be in the area of antispoofing. For example it is possible to distinguish between a real 3D face and a false 2D printed face either through dynamic analysis of the video frame sequence or by combining the images captured by two webcams Another possibility is that by fusing the front and angled facial images, we may extract some nose features, such as nose slope and depth, which should improve the recognition accuracy. It is expected that the proposed continuous verification method will be put into operation within the upcoming development phases of the project.

References

1. Dasgupta, D. (2009) Computational intelligence in cyber security, *2009 IEEE Symposium on Computational Intelligence in Cyber Security*, Nashville, TN, USA.
2. Reid, P. (2004) *Biometrics for Network Security*, Prentice Hall, Upper Saddle River, NJ.

3. Ives, R. W., Etter, D. M. (2006) An introduction of biometrics (Chapter 24), in *Electrical Engineering Handboook: Circuits, Signals, and Speech and Image Processing*, 3rd edn. (Dorf, R. C., ed.), CRC, Boca Raton.

4. Rao, B. (2005) Continuous keystroke biometric system, M.S. Thesis, *Media Arts and Technology*, Univ. of California, Santa Barbara, CA.

5. Janakiraman, R., Kumar, S., Zhang, S., Sim, T. (2005) Using continuous face verification to improve desktop security, *Proc. IEEE Workshop on Applications of Computer Vision*, pp. 501–507.

6. Xiao, Q., Yang, X. D. (2009) A facial presence monitoring system for information security, *Proc. 2009 IEEE Workshop on Computational Intelligence in Biometrics: Theory, Algorithms, and Applications*, (CIB), pp. 69–76.

7. Altinok, A., Turk, M. (2003) Temporal integration for continuous multimodal biometrics, *Proc. Workshop Multimodal User Authentication*, pp. 131–137.

8. Yap, R. H. C., Sim, T., Kwang, G. X. Y., Ramnath, R. (2008) Physical access protection using continuous authentication, *Proc. 2008 IEEE Conference on Technologies for Homeland Security*, Waltham, MA, pp. 510–512.

9. Gamboa, H. F. S. (2008) Multi-modal behavioral biometrics based on HCI and electrophysiology, Ph.D. Thesis, Instituto Superior Técnico, Technical University of Lisbon, Portugal.

10. Damousis, I. G., Tzovaras, D., Bekiaris, E. (2008) Unobtrusive multimodal biometric authentication: The HUMABIO project concept, *EURASIP Journal on Advances in Signal Processing* 2008.

11. Gaines, R., Lisowski, W., Press, S., Shapiro, N. (1980) Authentication by keystroke timing, some preliminary results, *Rand Report R-256-NSF*, Rand Corporation.

12. Monrose, F., Rubin, A. D. (2000) Keystroke dynamics as biometrics for authentication, *Future Generation Computer Systems* **16**(4), 351–359.

13. Israel, S. A., Irvine, J. M., Cheng, A., Wiederhold, M. D., Wiederhold, B.K. (2005) ECG to identify individuals, *Pattern Recognition* **38**(1), 133–142.

14. Biel, L., Pettersson, O., Philipson, L., Wide, P. (2001) ECG analysis: A new approach in human identification, *IEEE Trans. on Instrumentation and Measurement* **50**(3), 808–812.

15. Riera, A., Dunne, S., Cester, I., Ruffini, G. (2008) STARFAST: A wireless wearable EEG/ECG biometric system based on the ENOBIO sensor, *Proc. 5th pHealth Workshop on Wearable Micro and Nanosystems for Personalised Health* (pHealth'08), Valencia, Spain.

16. Li, S. Z., Jain, A. K., eds. (2004) *Handbook of Face Recognition*, Springer, New York, NY, USA.

17. Zhao, W., Chellappa, R., Phillips, P. J., Rosenfeld, A. (2003) Face recognition: A literature survey, *ACM Computing Survey* **35**(4), 399–458.

18. Tang, X., Li, Z. (2004) Video based face recognition using multiple classifiers, *Proc. 6th IEEE Int. Conf. on Automatic Face and Gesture Recognition*, pp. 345–349.

19. Liu, X., Chen, T. (2003) Video-based face recognition using adaptive hidden Markov models, *Proc. of IEEE Conference on Computer Vision and Pattern Recognition* **1**, 340–345.

20. Li, J., Wang, Y., Tan, T. (2004) Video-based face recognition using a metric of average Euclidean distance, *Lecture Notes in Artificial Intelligence* (Springer, Berlin) **3338**, 224–232.

21. Li, J., Wang, Y. (2007) Video-based face tracking and recognition on updating twin GMMs, *Lecture Notes in Artificial Intelligence* (Springer, Berlin) **4642**, 848–857.

22. Rodrigues, R. N., Ling, L. L., Govindaraju, V. (2009) Robustness of multimodal biometric fusion methods against spoof attacks, *Journal of Visual Languages and Computing Archive* **20**(3), 169–179.

23. Ross, A., Jain, A. K. (2004) Multimodal biometrics: An overview, *Proc. 12th European Signal Processing Conference* (EUSIPCO), pp. 1221–1224, September.

24. Hong, L., Jain, A. K. (1998) Integrating faces and fingerprints for personal identification, *IEEE Transactions on Pattern Analysis and Machine Intelligence* **20**(12), 1295–1307.

25. Sim, T., Zhang, S., Janafiraman, R., Kumar, S. (2007) Continuous verification using multimodal biometrics, *IEEE Transactions on Pattern Analysis and Machine Intelligence* **29**(4), 687–700.

26. Azzini, A., Marrara, S. (2008) Impostor users discovery using a multimodal biometric continuous authentication fuzzy system, *Lecture Notes in Artificial Intelligence* (Springer Berlin) **5178**, 317–378.

27. Smith, R. E. (2001) *Authentication: From Passwords to Public Keys*, Addison-Wesley, Upper Saddle River, NJ.

28. Chong, M. (2003) Department of Defense (DoD) Common Access Card (CAC) and Biometrics Program Overview, *2003 Biometric Consortium*, Arlington, Virginia.

29. Joyce, R., Gupta, G. (1990) Identity authorization based on keystroke latencies, *Communications of the ACM* **33**(2), 168–176.

30. Leggett, J., Williams, G., Umphress, D. (1989) Verification of user identity via keystroke characteristics, *Human Factors in Management Information Systems*.

31. Mahar, D., Napier R., Wagner, M., Laverty W., Henderson, R. D., Hiron, M. (1995) Optimizing digraph-latency based biometric typist verification systems: Inter and intra typist differences in digraph latency distributions. *International Journal of Human-Computer Studies* **43**(4), 579–592.

32. Brown, M., Rogers, S. J. (1993) User identification via keystroke characteristics of typed names using neural networks, *International Journal of Man-Machine Studies* **39**(6), 999–1014.

33. Maltoni, D., (2005) A tutorial on fingerprint recognition. *Lecture Notes in Computer Science* (Springer Berlin) **3161**, 43–68.

34. Riera, A., Soria-frisch, A., Caparrini, M., Cester, I., Ruffini, G. (2009) Multimodal physiological biometrics authentication (Chapter 18), in *Biometrics: Theory, Methods, and Applications* (Boulgouris, N. V., Konstantinos N., Plataniotis, K. N., Micheli-Tzanakou, E., eds.), IEEE Press, Piscataway, NJ, pp. 461–482.

35. Poulos, M., Rangoussi, M., Alexandris, N., Evangelou, A. (2001) On the use of EEG features towards person identification via neural networks, *Medical Informatics and the Internet in Medicine* **26**(1), 35–48.

36. Ruffini, G., Dunne, S., Farres, E., Cester, I., Watts, P.C.P., Ravi, S., Silva, P., Grau, C., Fuentemilla, L., Marco-Pallares, J., Vandecasteele, B. (2007) ENOBIO dry electrophysiology electrode; first human trial plus wireless electrode system, *Proc. of the 29th IEEE EMBS Annual International Conference*, vol. 22–26, pp. 6689–6693.

37. Alive Heart and Activity Monitor Brochure, *Alive Technologies*, online available: http://www.alivetec.com/products.htm

38. Kong, S., Heo, J., Abidi, B., Paik, J., Abidi, M. (2005) Recent advances in visual and infrared face recognition: A review, *Journal of Computer Vision and Image Understanding* **97**(1), 103–135.

39. Gandhe, S. T., Talele, K. T., Keskar, A. G. (2007) Intelligent face recognition techniques: A comparative study, *International Journal on Graphics, Vision and Image Processing* **7**(2), 53–60.

40. Saeed, U., Dugelay, J. (2007) Person recognition form video using facial mimics, *Proc. IEEE International Conference on Acoustic, Speech and Signal Processing* **1**, 493–496.

41. Chen, L., Liao, H., Lin, J. (2001) Person identification using facial motion, *Proc. International Conference on Image Processing*, pp. 677–680.

42. Belhumeur, P. N., Hespanha, J. P., Kriegman, D. J. (1997) Eigenfaces vs. fisherfaces: Recognition using class specific linear projection. *IEEE Transactions on Pattern Analysis and Machine Intelligence* **19**(7), 711–720.

43. Zhou, S., Chellappa, R. (2002) Probabilistic human recognition from video, *European Conference on Computer Vision* **3**, 681–697.

44. Aggarwal, G., Chowdhury, A. K. R., Chellappa, R. (2004) A system identification approach for video-based face recognition, *Proc. International Conference on Pattern Recognition* **4**, 175–178.

45. Turk, M. A., Pentland, A. P. (1991) Eigenfaces for recognition, *Cognitive Neurosci.*, **3**(1), 71–86.

46. Huang, P., Wang, Y., Shao, M. (2008) A new method for multi-view face clustering in video sequence, *Proc. IEEE International Conference on Data Mining Workshop*, pp. 869–873.

47. Bradski, G.R. (1998) Computer vision face tracking as a component of a perceptual user interface, *Workshop on Applications of Computer Vision*, Princeton, NJ, pp. 214–219.

48. Zhang, C., Qiao, Y., Fallon, E., Xu, C. (2009) An improved CamShift algorithm for target tracking in video surveillance, *9th. IT & T Conference*, Paper 12.

Chapter 14

Trends in Biometrics

Kai Yang and Eliza Yingzi Du

Department of Electrical and Computer Engineering, Indiana University–Purdue University Indianapolis, 723 W. Michigan St., Indianapolis, IN 46202, USA
kaiyang@iupui.edu

14.1 Introduction: Current Situation of Biometric Technology

Although more and more biometric applications have emerged in the market, many people are still skeptical about this technology. This lack of trust mainly springs from security and privacy concern. It is true that current biometric technologies are far from perfect, although some of them can already achieve 99.99% accuracy. First of all, people are worried that their biometric information could be stolen by some bad guys and be used to invade into their personal accounts. For example, fingerprint can be obtained from the things we touch every day; face and iris information can be directly obtained by taking a photo of one's face or eyes. Once the information is lost, there is no easy way to recover it as reissuing a password. Moreover, there are still no complete laws or regulations to protect the privacy of biometric data, which makes people feel

Biometrics: From Fiction to Practice
Edited by Eliza Yingzi Du

uncomfortable and intrusive while furnishing these data. Also, standards for some biometric modalities are still missing, such as the iris, which prevents their relevant technologies from spreading widely. Last but not least, the prices of some biometric devices are still very high, which makes them difficult to be acquired in the market. In this chapter, we discuss the possible solutions to these problems.

14.2 Trends in Biometric Technology

In this section, we discuss and analyze the needs of the market and the user for biometric technologies. We talk about 12 trends in biometric technology in the future.

14.2.1 *Less Vulnerable*

No system is perfect. The designers and operators of biometric systems should consider possible attacks and reduce the vulnerability of the systems. These vulnerabilities include (but are not limited to) the following.

14.2.1.1 Spoofs

People who want to fool a biometric system usually use artificially created biometric traits or recorded biometric data. A liveness test [11, 12] is a way to identify whether the biometric traits are from a living person rather than from artificial material or a lifeless person. For example, the natural pupillary response (changing pupil size in response to illumination) can be used to confirm the liveness of an iris. The response of a finger to a low electronic current or temperature could be used to test the liveness of a finger.

14.2.1.2 Hacking and privacy attacking

Hacking is a big problem for any networked system. Criminals may hack a biometric system and alter the biometric data in the database. Jain *et al.* [5] divided all types of attack into two categories: zero-effort attacks, which are due to the probability of having similar

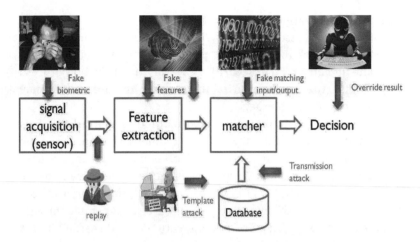

Figure 14.1. Eight types of possible attacks on a traditional biometric system.

templates from different sources by chance, and adversary attacks, wherein an imposter uses an artificially similar biometric template to deceive the recognition system.

Ratha *et al.* [13] analyzed these attacks and grouped them into eight classes. The attacks and vulnerable components of a common biometric system [18] are shown in Fig. 14.1. Each part of the system, including sensor, extractor, matcher, database, and the channel between them, is vulnerable to the danger of Trojan horse, phishing, and overriding templates and results.

Methods to protect true patterns and templates are required to be adopted in practical biometric applications in the future. In particular, it is desirable to have a system that can generate a new unique pattern if the one being used is lost, or generate unique patterns for different applications to prevent cross-matching.

Several methods have been proposed to tackle these problems. Some researchers proposed applying traditional cryptographic methods to biometrics [6, 7, 9, 10, 15–17, 19]. Three types of methods have been proposed by the crypto community.

The most popular method used is biometric hardening. The feature template is combined with user-specific random information in order to be projected to a new representation. An error-tolerant discretization method is then used to quantize the feature description to reduce uncertainty. The projection acts like a linear transformation of the biometric pattern. It can protect the true template and ensure high security. However, the projection process may change the information of the original feature, which may reduce recognition accuracy.

The second most commonly used method is bioHashing. This method directly extracts a key from the biometric features and then uses a Hash function to encrypt it. BioHashing is actually a one-way transformation like a cryptographic cipher which can ensure a high-degree protection of biometric patterns. However, it is very hard to ensure that the extracted patterns are always stable through all access processes. The inconsistent features are discarded in this method, and therefore entropy is reduced.

A third method incorporates error correction with local iris features to tolerate the within-class variance, which is referred as "fuzzy vault." This method makes use of the effectiveness of fuzzy logic in reducing uncertainty; however, it is not easy to revoke and reissue the templates.

Aside from the methods presented by the cryptography community, the idea of "cancelable biometrics" [14] proposed by IBM is a preferable choice in the biometric community. This type of system implements "cancelability" by designing methods to hide the true signal and create alternatives for matching. These methods can be divided into two categories: one tries to mask the original patterns by mixing artificial texture or noise – this is called "salting" – whereas the other uses some noninvertible transformations to distort the original biometric patterns. Table 14.1 compares the above methods.

All these methods try to make a biometric system more secure and less vulnerable, which is the most important trend in biometric technology in the future. People will be willing to accept biometric technology only if it is proved to be secure and trustable.

14.2.2 *Legal*

Any technology is a two-edge sword. Proper use of biometric data can be helpful in protecting privacy, while misuse can do great harm.

Table 14.1. Comparison of different types of method to enhance security

	Biometric modality applicability	Stableness	Preserve representation	Revocable	Information loss
Biometric Hardening	Low	Low	No	Yes	Medium
BioHashing	Low	Low	No	Yes	Medium
Fuzzy Vault	Medium	High	No	No	Low
Cancelable Salting	High	Medium	Yes	yes	Low
Cancelable Transform	High	Medium	Yes	Yes	Low

Legislation to address this issue is urgently needed to protect public privacy. On the other hand, ethics education should be enforced. Companies and government agencies should be very careful about people who have the privilege to access the database/important information in biometric systems. Stringent laws should be made to deal with violation of privacy to eliminate peoples' scruple.

14.2.3 *Standard*

The Biometric Consortium website defines standards as "a general set of rules to which all complying procedures, products or research must adhere." Currently, there are hundreds of kinds of biometric systems using different interfaces, data formats, measurements, and outputs. This creates a tremendous problem for integrators and end users.

Standards enable development of integrated, robust, and scalable solutions to reduce costing for both research and manufacture. Biometric standards have been developed both on national and on international levels. The National Institute of Standards and Technology (NIST) has played a great role in standardizing biometric systems/technologies. Seventeen American national standards developed by INCITS M1 were published as ANSI INCITS standards, and 16 international standards developed by JTC 1/SC 37 were published as international standards (ISO/IEC) in 2007. Further progress should be made to standardize the interoperability and compatibility of future biometric products and research procedures.

14.2.4 *Lower Cost*

Cost is always the key factor for people to make decisions. After all, any technology is driven by the market. The high price of some biometric devices, especially the intellectual property inside them (e.g., license, software) is becoming the bottleneck of the biometric market. Once biometric systems prove to be effective and economical within companies, the future of reliable biometric identification will be brighter.

14.2.5 *More Intelligent*

Another problem for currently used biometric systems is that they can be easily cheated. Even if the liveness test is applied to prevent spoof, guarded biometric systems can be accessed when users are under threat, reluctant, or even unconscious. For future consumer biometric applications (such as biometric ATM machines or biometric credit cards), the biggest concern is user safety: criminals may intimidate or even hurt users to get into their accounts. Future biometric systems should be able to deal with this kind of situations to prevent serious consequences.

A novel concept, named consent biometrics, is presented in Ref. [8] to tackle this problem. A consent signature can be used to confirm the willingness of a user, and it can be extracted from the user's physiological or behavior features to enhance security and thereby protect the user. Consent biometric systems can distinguish whether the user is truly willing to do the transaction by checking the extracted consent signature. The consent signature is also intrinsic and unique to each user, so it can provide additional information for biometrics.

Two consent biometric schemes (Fig. 14.2) are introduced next: combinational consent biometrics and incorporating consent biometrics.

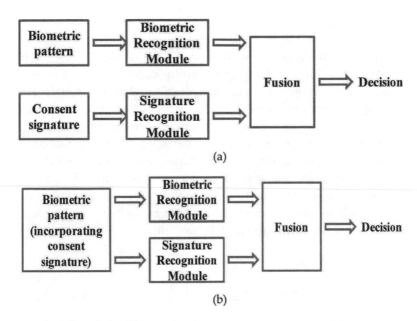

Figure 14.2. The two proposed consent biometrics schemes: (a) combinational consent biometrics and (b) incorporating consent biometrics.

14.2.5.1 Combinational consent biometric scheme

The biometric pattern and the consent signature are acquired separately (Fig. 14.2a). The consent signature is transmitted into the signature recognition module for processing, feature extraction, and signature matching. Finally, the two outputs are combined to give the final identification result. This scheme may need two kinds of sensors to acquire data. But traditional biometric systems can be used to obtain, process, extract, and match biometric features.

14.2.5.2 Incorporating consent biometric scheme

The consent signature is acquired simultaneously with the biometrics data (Fig. 14.2b). In other words, the biometric data incorporates the consent signature. It consists of a set of uniquely preassigned behavioral passwords for each user. This requires the biometric sensor to have the capability of acquiring sequential data (such as videos).

Some researchers recently presented the idea of cognitive-based biometrics. This approach uses the cognitive aspects of human behavior as biometric modalities. It typically utilizes bio-signals (such as the EEG and ECG) produced by cognitive and emotional brain states as the authentication medium. The bio-signals can be acquired via human-machine interaction. Cognitive biometrics fills the gap between physiological and behavioral biometrics. The commonly used interaction environment includes textual-based password systems, graphics- and virtual-reality-based mechanism, game-playing-based mechanisms, etc. For example, Hamdy *et al.* [2] proposed the idea of using two new cognitive factors, namely, visual scan and detection, and short-term memory, which are collected in a keyboard-typing situation, for static user identification.

14.2.6 *Remote Biometrics*

Most biometric technologies can be categorized into three types: contact, contactless, and at a distance. Biometrics at a distance or remote biometrics is an important developing direction in the future. Remote biometrics can identify a person at a distance and requires least user cooperation. This technology will be extremely helpful in access control of large populations and watch-list surveillance. This kind of system will be very well suited to integrate identity recognition and surveillance tasks.

14.2.7 *Biometrics Surveillance*

Surveillance using biometrics (Fig. 14.3) cannot be dismissed in the future, even if there are strong objections from privacy advocates. For example, scanning of crowds for facial characteristics of criminals will be substantially helpful to public security. Biometric surveillance is a strong deterrent to crime. However, one thing we cannot forget is that law enforcement should be required to protect the privacy of innocents.

Figure 14.3.   Biometric surveillance cameras.

14.2.8 *Smaller*

Size is a crucial factor for real-time applications. Compact biometric devices which are portable and easy to use should be developed in the future, especially in e-commerce applications. Figure 14.4 shows some example of compact biometric devices. Some of these have already been integrated into cell phones and USB drives. More compact and integrated devices will appear in the future.

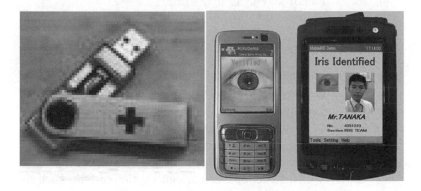

Figure 14 4   Some compact biometric devices.

14.2.9 *More Accurate and Robust*

There is no doubt that accuracy and robustness are the most important factors in practical biometric systems. They are the most direct way to measure a system. No matter how fancy a device looks, high reliability is always the key point people care most about. Many biometric system vendors claim that they have an accuracy rate of over 99%. But some of their test results are based on very small number of data in well-controlled laboratory situations. For these kind of biometric systems, the accuracy rate is much lower in real-life situations. These issues should be addressed in future biometric systems.

14.2.10 *More Efficient*

Processing speed is also an inevitable factor to consider while designing a real-life system, especially in real-time applications. A biometric system for monitoring and access control in large population areas has a higher requirement for efficiency. With the collection of biometric data from large populations, the size of the database could increase dramatically. The biometric system should be able to deal with large databases and have sufficient accuracy to identify large populations, even the total 6 billion people in the world. This would be especially important for biometric ID card applications and border checks in the future.

14.2.11 *More User-Friendly*

User experience is the most direct way to gain customers in the first stage. A well-designed user interface which is easy to use has higher chances of acceptance. Moreover, the repeating trials demanded by some biometric systems may annoy the user. For example, most commercialized iris recognition systems can only do cooperative identification, which means the user has to be very cooperative under a series of instructions demanded by the system, such as move close, move left, etc. Noncooperative iris recognition methods have been proposed for years [1, 3], but such systems are not yet available in the market.

User safety is also another issue related to user-friendliness. Some biometric systems in the market now may do harm to people or make them very uncomfortable. For example, the fingerprint acquisition device may transmit virus and disease. Iris scans use near-infrared (NIR) light, which is a concern for many users. Is NIR light safe for a user? Is it safe for a frequent user? Retina scan is very intrusive and uncomfortable for users. Further research should be done in these aspects to ensure user safety. Future biometric systems should be less intrusive and have less contact.

14.2.12 *More Choices*

More and more kinds of biometric systems will be on the market in the near future. People will have more choices. In addition, multimodal biometric systems may enable more choices for users in presenting biometric data.

In addition to all the popularly used biometric modalities, some researchers proposed some more intrinsic features of the human body for identification, such as bone structure, body resistance, vein pattern, and sclera pattern. These new biometrics may become popular in the future.

Soft biometrics is another hotspot for the future. It involves characteristics that can be used to describe, but not uniquely identify, an individual. These include traits such as ethnicity, height, weight, gender, hair, skin, eye color, and clothing. Soft biometrics can be easily captured from far away by using a surveillance camera without any user cooperation. It can work as an auxiliary feature for traditional unique biometrics to increase accuracy.

14.3 Trends in the Biometric Market

According to the statistics of the International Biometric Group (IBG) [4], the world market size of biometric systems in 2009 was US$3422 million. Among them, fingerprint recognition applications along with live scanners form the dominant part, which is more than two-thirds. (See the pie chart in Fig. 14.5).

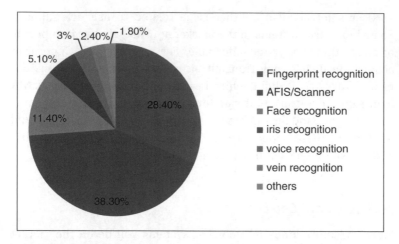

Figure 14.5. World biometrics market share by technology in 2009. See also Color Insert.

IBG also made a prediction of the biometric market for the next five years. The total market in 2010 will exceed $4300 million. A 22.3% compound average growth rate is expected for the next four years (Fig. 14.5).

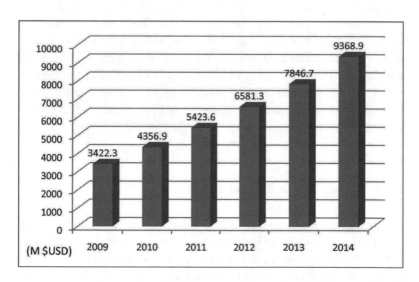

Figure 14.6. World biometrics market trend (2009–2014).

Table 14.2. World biometric market trend by technology (2009–2014) (in $US million)

	2009	2010	2011	2012	2013	2014
Fingerprint	971.0	1380.9	1740.1	2064.1	2422.9	2827.2
AFIS	1309.1	1489.9	1816.5	2154.4	2525.9	2965.8
Iris	174.4	287.8	360.8	480.5	578.3	730.3
Hand geometry	62.0	62.8	63.7	68.2	76.0	85.0
Middleware	275.0	327.7	413.8	525.2	625.2	732.6
Face	390.0	510.8	675.4	848.5	1097.3	1417.8
Voice	103.8	109.3	113.5	136.3	167.5	189.7
Vascular	83.0	102.1	132.2	172.2	199.5	235.7
Others	54.0	85.6	107.5	131.8	154.2	184.9
Total	**3422.3**	**4356.9**	**5423.6**	**6581.2**	**7846.7**	**9368.9**

Table 14.2 shows the predictions for the world biometric market volume in the next several years. From this table, we can see that fingerprint recognition, face recognition, and iris recognition will undergo a sustainable increment in the near future.

14.4 Conclusions

In this chapter, we presented some expected trends for the future of biometrics. We believe that, with the endeavors of the government, research institutes, and companies, biometric technologies will be accepted and adopted by more and more people. The future of biometrics is bright.

References

1. Belcher, C., Du, Y. (2009) Region-based SIFT approach to iris recognition, *Optics and Lasers in Engineering*, **47**(1), 139–147.
2. Denman, S, Fookes, C., Bialkowski, A., Sridharan, S. (2010), Soft-biometrics: Unconstrained authentication in a surveillance environment, *IEEE*, 196–203 (in).

3. Du, Y., Arslanturk, E., Zhou, Z., Belcher, C. (2010) Video-based non-cooperative iris image segmentation, *IEEE Transaction on System, Man, and Cybertics, Part B.*

4. Group, I. B. (2009) Biometrics Market and Industry Report 2009–2014.

5. Jain, A. K., Ross, A., Pankanti, S. (2006) Biometrics: A tool for information security, *IEEE Transactions on Information Forensics and Security*, **1**(2), 125–143.

6. Jin, A., Ling, D., Goh, A. (2004) Biohashing: Two factor authentication featuring fingerprint data and tokenised random number, *Pattern Recognition*, **37**(11), 2245–2255.

7. Juels, A., Wattenberg, M. (1999), A fuzzy commitment scheme, *6th ACM Conf. Comput. Commun. Security*, ACM, 28–36 (in).

8. Kai Yang, E. D. (2011) Consent biometrics, *IEEE Symposium Series on Computational Intelligence* (submitted).

9. Kanade, S., Petrovska-Delacretaz, D., Dorizzi, B. (2009) Cancelable iris biometrics and using error correcting codes to reduce variability in biometric data, 120–127 (in).

10. Lee, Y., Park, K., Lee, S., Bae, K., Kim, J. (2008) A new method for generating an invariant iris private key based on the fuzzy vault system, *IEEE Transactions on Systems, Man, and Cybernetics, Part B*, **38**(5), 1302–1313.

11. Nikam, S. B., Agarwal, S. (2008) Fingerprint liveness detection using curvelet energy and co-occurrence signatures, *Fifth International Conference on Computer Graphics, Imaging and Visualisation, 2008. CGIV '08.* 217–222 (in).

12. Nikam, S. B., Agarwal, S. (2008) Fingerprint anti-spoofing using ridgelet transform, *Biometrics: Theory, Applications and Systems, 2008. BTAS 2008. 2nd IEEE International Conference on*, 1–6 (in).

13. Ratha, N., Connell, J., Bolle, R. An analysis of minutiae matching strength, Springer, 223–228 (in).

14. Ratha, N., Connell, J., Bolle, R. (2001) Enhancing security and privacy in biometrics-based authentication systems, *IBM Systems Journal*, **40**(3), 614–634.

15. Takahashi, K., S. H. Hitachi (2009), Generating provably secure cancelable fingerprint templates based on correlation-invariant random filtering, *Biometrics: Theory, Applications, and Systems, 2009. BTAS '09. IEEE 3rd International Conference on*, 1–6 (in).

16. Teoh, A., Goh, A., Ngo, D. (2006) Random multispace quantization as an analytic mechanism for biohashing of biometric and random identity

inputs, *IEEE Transactions on Pattern Analysis and Machine Intelligence*, **28**(12), 1892–1901.

17. Tulyakov, S., Farooq, F., Govindaraju, V. Symmetric hash functions for fingerprint minutiae, *Pattern Recognition and Image Analysis*, pp. 30–38.

18. Uludag, U., Jain, A. (2004) Attacks on biometric systems: a case study in fingerprints, Citeseer, 622–633.

19. Youn Joo, L., Kang Ryoung, P., Sung Joo, L., Kwanghyuk, B., Jaihie, K. (2008) A new method for generating an invariant iris private key based on the fuzzy vault system, *Systems, Man, and Cybernetics, Part B: Cybernetics, IEEE Transactions on*, **38**(5), 1302–1313.

Index

Color Insert

ridge
(black line)

valley
(white line)

ridge ending

bifurcation

Figure 2.1

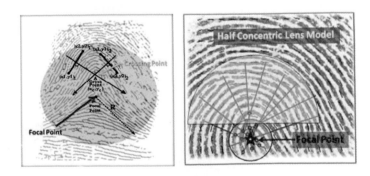

Figure 2.5

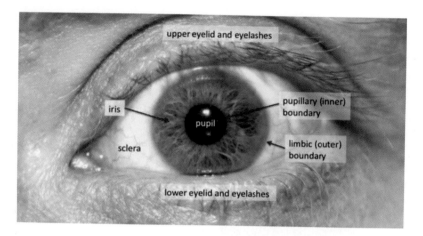

Figure 4.1

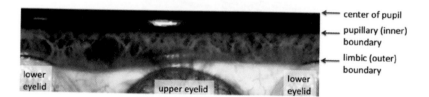

Figure 4.4

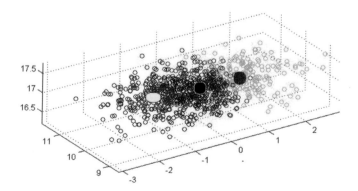

Figure 5.14

Figure 12.1

Figure 12.2

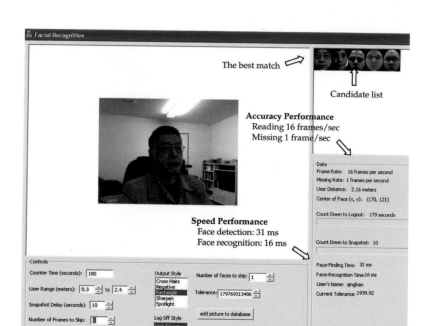

Figure 13.10

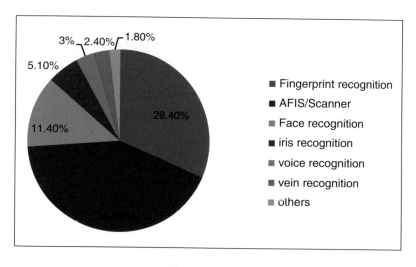

Figure 14.5